Anxiety in College Students

ANXIETY IN COLLEGE STUDENTS

BENJAMIN AYRES
AND
MICHELLE BRISTOW
EDITORS

Nova Biomedical Books
New York

For permission to use material from this book please contact us:
Telephone 631-231-7269; Fax 631-231-8175
Web Site: http://www.novapublishers.com

Library of Congress Cataloging-in-Publication Data

Ayres,Benjamin.
Anxiety in college students / Benjamin Ayres and Michelle Bristow.
p. cm.
Includes index.
ISBN 978-1-60692-282-8 (hardcover)
1. College students--Psychology. 2. Anxiety. I. Bristow, Michelle. II. Title.
LB3609.A96 2009
378.1'98--dc22

2009001694

Published by Nova Science Publishers, Inc. ✢ New York

Contents

Preface

This book describes the etiology, prevalence and frequency of anxiety disorders among college students. An overview of stress among students in developing countries is given, and how it may affect the emergence of certain diseases, such as cancer and diabetes. The effects of disclosure of past stressful events in students is also examined as well as the variables that point to the emotional processing of certain events. This book reviews the coping, mental health status, and current life regret in college women who differ in their lifetime pregnancy status. In addition, the association between gender differences and proneness to depression among college students is examined, including the risk factors (such as anxiety) in the development of depression. Furthermore, the factors that lie behind students' motivated behavior and academic goals are addressed. Finally, the current alcohol and tobacco use in pharmacy studies is reviewed as well as the ways in which to prevent further alcohol and drug abuse among these students.

Short Communication - Self-concept disturbances have been considered to play a determining role in the development of eating disorders. However, questions remain unanswered about the aspects of self-concept that distinguish eating-disordered women from other populations, and about the mechanisms that link the self-concept to the disordered behaviors. Referring to Markus' self-schema model (1977), a limited collection of positive self-schema available in memory, in combination with a chronically and inflexibly accessible schema about body weight, may contribute to the development of an eating disorder. To test this model, two multidimensional self-concept questionnaires, the Self Description Questionnaire III and the Physical Self Description Questionnaire, were administered to two groups of female high school students: 125 eating-disordered (both anorexic-like and bulimic-like) students and 103 normal controls. No significant differences emerged in the academic-related aspects of the self-concept. However, nonacademic-related dimensions, particularly body-weight/appearance aspects, revealed significantly differences between the eating-disordered students and their normal peers. Less differences appeared between the anorexic-like and bulimic-like subgroups. Disturbances in body-weight/appearance aspects of the self-concept may be useful as early signals in the detection of students at risk for developing an eating disorder.

Chapter 1 - This chapter describes how the Rasch model was applied to construct an interval-level scale measuring student use and disposition towards information and communication technology (ICT). Scale development was based upon an hypothesised model of classroom ICT learning culture comprising self and collective values, attitudes and behaviours. Specifically, the study aimed to produce a scale that: Measured student self-reported learning behaviours and attitudes towards use of ICT; had calibrated item difficulties and self-reported learning behaviours and attitudes towards ICT measures on the same scale; and elicited data to fit the theoretical model. A 126 item Likert scale type instrument was developed, administered to 439 primary and secondary school students, and then refined and validated by Rasch analysis. The validated data comprised 62 items on five aspects of ICT learning culture. These five aspects were: Student reported learning attitudes and behaviours; student reported teacher attitudes and behaviours; student reported attitudes and behaviours towards ICT networks; student reported home ICT attitudes and behaviours; and student reported values towards ICT use at school. Examination of the psychometric properties of the data identified common and uncommon attitudes and behaviours. This illustrated how students viewed their classroom ICT learning culture.

Chapter 2 - Most college students experience some degree of social anxiety on occasion. However, many suffer chronic anxiety across social situations coupled with a strong fear of negative evaluation. In addition to impaired occupational and social functioning, severe social anxiety or social phobia can carry profound consequences for college students. Social anxiety is a prominent motivation for college student drinking (Burke and Stephens, 1999). In addition to social isolation, social anxiety is associated with depressogenic cognitions, both of which leave socially anxious students at an increased risk for depression (Johnson et al., 1992). Anxiety sensitivity – fear of anxiety-related sensations due to perceived consequences of physical, mental, or social harm – might play an important role in the development of social anxiety (Hazen et al., 1995). Unlike panic disorder, in which individuals typically fear anxiety symptoms out of fear of physical harm or loss of mental control, socially anxious individuals fear perceived social consequences of others noticing their anxiety. Socially anxious college students also judge others who appear anxious more negatively than do college students without social anxiety (Purdon et al., 2001). Although panic disorder treatments target anxiety sensitivity directly with interoceptive exposure strategies, this approach is just beginning to receive attention for the treatment of social anxiety. After a brief review of the literature describing the nature of social anxiety among college students, this chapter will examine the specific role of anxiety sensitivity in its development and maintenance. Finally, results from a preliminary investigation comparing the effects of interoceptive exposure delivered in a social context to social context exposure without the interoceptive component will be presented and discussed.

Chapter 3 - Some educators have failed to acknowledge the prevalence of test anxiety and its effect on academic performance among university students. This study addresses this issue at the university level using data collected through the Revised Test Anxiety (RTA) instrument and Sarason's four-factor model as a basis for measuring test anxiety. The study also investigates the effect of demographic factors on test anxiety. Findings reveal that test anxiety is significantly and negatively related to academic performance. Reasons for these findings are addressed.

Chapter 4 - In 1986 Pennebaker and Beall published their renowned study on the long-term beneficial health effects of disclosing traumatic events in 4 brief sequential writing sessions. Their results have been confirmed in various studies, but conflicting results have also been reported. The intent of our study was to replicate the experiments from Pennebaker and Beall (1986), Pennebaker et al. (1988), and Greenberg and Stone (1992) using a German student sample. Additionally, essay variables that point to the emotional processing of events (e.g., depth of self-exploration, number of negative/positive emotions, intensity of emotional expression) were examined as potential mechanisms of action. Trait measures of personality which could moderate the personal consequences of disclosure (alexithymia, self-concealment, worrying, social support) were also assessed. In a second study the experimental condition (disclosure) was varied by implementing "coping" vs. "helping" instructions as variations of the original condition. Under the coping condition participants were asked to elaborate on what they used to do, continue to do, or could do in the future to better cope with the event. Under the helping condition participants were asked to imagine themselves in the role of a adviser and elaborate on what they would recommend to persons also dealing with the trauma in order to better cope with the event. The expected beneficial effects of disclosure on long-term health (e.g., physician visits, physical symptoms, affectivity) could not be corroborated in either the first or the second study. None of the examined essay variables of emotional processing and only a single personality variable was able to explain significant variance in the health-related outcome variables influence. Nevertheless, substantial reductions in posttraumatic stress symptoms (e.g., intrusions, avoidance, arousal), were found in both experiments. These improvements were significantly related to essay variables of emotional expression and self-exploration and were particularly pronounced under the activation of a prosocial motivation (helping condition).

Repeated, albeit brief, expressive writing about personally upsetting or traumatic events resulted in an immediate increase in negative mood but did not lead to long-term positive health consequences in a German student sample. It did, however, promote better processing of stressful or traumatic events, as evidenced by reductions in posttraumatic stress symptoms. The instruction to formulate recommendations for persons dealing with the same trauma seems more helpful than standard disclosure or focusing on one's own past, present, and future coping endeavours. Overall, expressive writing seems to be a successful method of improving trauma processing. Determining the appropriate setting (e.g., self-help vs. therapeutic context) for disclore can be seen as an objective of future research.

Chapter 5 - Mankind since the dawn of history has been afflicted with various forms of diseases. Communicable diseases that took a heavy toll of human life in medieval and prehistoric times, have been replaced by non- communicable diseases and conditions in the recent times. Among the six factors which are responsible for the major share of these diseases, Stress occupies an important place (Rose, G.A. and Blackburn H. 1968). The Oxford English dictionary defines stress as pressure, tension or worry resulting from the problems in one's life. It is thus a condition of the mind, in which a person loses his calm tranquility and equanimity and experiences extreme discomfiture.

Chapter 6 - This study examined the current mental health status, coping strategies, and perceived life regret of three types of female college students (n = 277): those who had never been pregnant (67.9%, n= 188); those who became pregnant at or before age 18 who were a priori considered to be resilient (14.8%, n = 41); and those who had experienced a pregnancy after age 18 (17.3%, n = 48). Data were collected at a diverse urban public university in the

Southeast. This university has a significant number of commuter and non-traditional students. Results indicated that college women who had experienced an adult pregnancy reported significantly fewer maladaptive coping strategies than never-pregnant college women and those who had experienced a teenage pregnancy. Surprisingly, both groups of ever pregnant college women expressed significantly more life regret than never pregnant college women. Among the college women who had experienced a teenage pregnancy, two groups were delineated: those who were "thriving" versus those who were "at-risk" with regards to their current symptoms of depression, hostility, and hopelessness. Women in the "at-risk" group were significantly *less* likely to be simultaneously parenting and attending college than those in the "thriving" group. One potential implication is that identifying and intervening with these potentially at-risk college women may help improve retention rates and student morale at universities with a diverse student body.

Chapter 7 - *Aims:* The authors' research aimed to find out what role the risk mechanisms, as described in Goodman and Gotlib's (1999) model (genetic-biological, interpersonal, social learning related cognitive and stress related factors), play in the development of increased risk for depression in the case of men and women.

Methods: The genetic-biological factors were examined with certain temperament characteristics, the interpersonal factors with parental educational purpose, educational attitudes, educational style and parental treatment. In the case of factors related to social learning we looked at the dysfunctional attitudes and the attributional style. As far as the stressors are concerned, we observed the quality of family atmosphere, and the number of the positive and negative life events of the preceding six months and their subjective evaluation. Six hundred and eighty-one students took part in the research (465 female and 216 male).

Results: The authors' research results show that all of the increased risk mechanisms, namely the genetic-biological, interpersonal, social learning related cognitive, and stress related factors are connected with the development of vulnerability to depression, explaining 41.4% of the depression symptoms' variance in the case of women, and 36.5% in the case of men. Harm avoidance, a genetic-biological factor, proved to be the most significant risk mechanism, irrespective of the sexes. From among the environmental factors – irrespective of the sexes – one stress-related factor, the subjective evaluation of negative life experiences, which implies an increased sensitivity to stress, proved to be the strongest risk mechanism. While the above factors played an important role in the development of vulnerability to depression in both sexes, the social learning related cognitive and interpersonal risk mechanisms differed in their degree in women and men. In the case of women, the social learning-related mechanisms proved to be stronger and higher impact risk factors than in the case of men. The effect of interpersonal factors seemed to be relatively the weakest in the development of increased risk for depression.

Limitations: The results of the authors' research cannot be generalised to represent present day 18- to 23-year-old Hungarian youth due to the limitations of our sample.

Conclusion: The mental hygienic interpretation of our research findings is that in the future there should be more emphasis put on the personality development of college and university students, especially on the development of such competencies which aid them in effectively coping in their struggle with the depressive mood.

Chapter 8 - The question of what lies behind students' motivated behaviour has given rise to a complex network of models and constructs in an attempt to clarify this important issue. A fundamental component of motivation, regardless of the theoretical perspective adopted, is that of value, which includes the goals adopted by students in order to ensure involvement in their tasks, as well as their beliefs regarding the importance, usefulness or interest of the latter (Pintrich, 2003; Pintrich and DeGroot, 1990).

Essentially, the value component of motivation responds to the following question: *"Why am I doing this task?"*, alluding, therefore, to the motives, purposes or reasons for becoming involved in the performance of an activity, these all being aspects closely related to both cognitive and self-regulating activities and choice, effort or persistence (Pintrich, 1999). Despite the existence of a wide range of value conceptualisations, two elements appear as being particularly relevant: academic goals and the value assigned to tasks.

Chapter 9 - Studies related to alcohol and drug use in healthcare students, namely nursing, pharmacy, and medicine suggest that drug and alcohol abuse continues to be a growing problem among health profession students. A review of the more recent literature involving pharmacy students, has noted higher levels of alcohol and drug use when compared to the undergraduate student population. Interestingly, the use and/or abuse of tobacco have largely been overlooked in studies involving substance abuse in pharmacy students. This study documented the current alcohol and tobacco use in pharmacy students and conducted a lecture series on the use and abuse of alcohol and tobacco. The lecture series was successful in increasing the awareness of the use and potential abuse of alcohol in the students. Attitudinal changes in students following the lecture series were also assessed.

In: Anxiety in College Students
Editor: Benjamin Ayres and Michelle Bristow

ISBN: 978-1-60692-282-8

Short Communication

Self-Concept Disturbances in Eating-Disordered Female Students Compared to Normal Controls

Laurence Claes, Joke Simons & Walter Vandereycken
Catholic University of Leuven, Department of Psychology,
Tiensestraat 102, B-3000 Leuven, Belgium

Abstract

Self-concept disturbances have been considered to play a determining role in the development of eating disorders. However, questions remain unanswered about the aspects of self-concept that distinguish eating-disordered women from other populations, and about the mechanisms that link the self-concept to the disordered behaviors. Referring to Markus' self-schema model (1977), a limited collection of positive self-schema available in memory, in combination with a chronically and inflexibly accessible schema about body weight, may contribute to the development of an eating disorder. To test this model, two multidimensional self-concept questionnaires, the Self Description Questionnaire III and the Physical Self Description Questionnaire, were administered to two groups of female high school students: 125 eating-disordered (both anorexic-like and bulimic-like) students and 103 normal controls. No significant differences emerged in the academic-related aspects of the self-concept. However, nonacademic-related dimensions, particularly body-weight/appearance aspects, revealed significantly differences between the eating-disordered students and their normal peers. Less differences appeared between the anorexic-like and bulimic-like subgroups. Disturbances in body-weight/appearance aspects of the self-concept may be useful as early signals in the detection of students at risk for developing an eating disorder.

Introduction

For both anorexia nervosa and bulimia nervosa distortions in the self-concept have been thought to play an important role in the development of these eating disorders (ED). Stein (1996) has given a comprehensive overview of models that link ED to self-concept deviations. Three types of self-concept deviations have been addressed by Stein (1996, p. 97), including (1) deficits in identity formation, (2) distortions in body image, and (3) body dissatisfaction and low self-esteem.

The first approach to the self-concept in ED focuses on the process of identity formation in childhood and adolescence (Stein, 1996). According to several authors (e.g., Bruch, 1973), difficulties in the parent-child relationship make it difficult for the child to develop a separate and stable sense of the self. Such family dysfunctions include too low/high cohesion, lack of emotional expressiveness, patterns of high conflict among family members, as well as over-concern about physical appearance, and high need for achievement (for an extensive overview, see Leung, Schwartzman, & Steiger, 1996). For example, overprotective mothers find it difficult to let their adolescent girls become autonomous, and to reinforce dependence instead of autonomy. Hence, these youngsters fail to develop a sense of self, and the weight-control and food-restriction actions become alternative ways to define the self (i.e., they form a pseudo-self or pseudo-identity).

The second approach to the self-concept in ED addresses body-image disturbances (Stein, 1996). By body-image disturbance we understand the presence of value judgments about one's body that do not coincide with the real characteristics (Sepúlveda, Botell, & León, 2002, p. 83). According to Rosen (1990), the disordered eating behaviors stem from the subjective experience of one's body as being larger and fatter than it objectively is. In AN patients, a lower weight appears to be associated with greater body overestimation, indicating a greater cognitive bias in the appreciation of their body (Stein & Corté, 2007).

The third approach addresses the link between ED and negative attitudes toward the self, namely body dissatisfaction and a global negative self-esteem (Stein, 1996). Women with ED evaluate their bodies and their global self-esteem more negatively than women with other psychiatric disorders (Jacobi, Paul, de Zwaan, Nutzinger, & Dahme, 2004) and women without ED (Cash & Brown, 1987; Stein & Corte, 2007; Rosen, 1990).

Although considerable research has been carried out, several questions about the mechanisms linking the self-concept disturbances to ED remain unanswered. Stein (1996) proposed Markus' self-schema model (1977) as a theoretical approach to explore the role of the self-concept in ED. More specifically, it is assumed that a limited collection of positive self-schema available in memory (due to identity disturbance and lack of self-definition), in combination with a chronically and inflexibly accessible body-weight self-schema (linked to feelings of fatness and body size overestimations), lead to the disordered behaviors associated with ED.

Referring to Markus' self-schema model (1977), we would like to test the following three hypotheses concerning the link between ED and self-concept:

1) ED persons, in comparison with normal controls, will show lower scores on measures of positive self-concept dimensions (e.g., academic self-concept) and

higher scores on measures of negative self-concept dimensions (e.g., body fat). No significant differences are expected between the different ED subtypes. To test this hypothesis we make use of Marsh's (1992a) Self Description Questionnaire (SDQ-III), which was designed to measure multiple dimensions of self-concept for college students and other adults.

2) The self-concept dimensions concerning body weight/physical appearance will be more important for ED persons than for normal controls. This question will be answered by making use of the items of the SDQ-III that were developed to measure the importance of each of the self-concept dimensions.
3) Finally, we will check whether only the weight-related dimensions of the physical self-concept discriminate between ED subjects and normal controls. For this purpose we use the Physical Self Description Questionnaire (PSDQ; Marsh & Redmayne, 1994), measuring different dimensions of the physical self-concept.

Method

Subjects

Data of 338 first-year female high school students (nurses, teachers) were collected during a regular course in the scope of participation in scientific research. No information about the research purposes was given in advance. The subjects were divided into three subgroups based on their scores on the Eating Disorder Evaluation Scale (EDES; Vandereycken, 1993) and their Body Mass Index [BMI = weight in kilogram / (length in meter)^2]. As summarized in Table 1, the EDES subscales revealed an unexpectedly high number of ED characteristics. For reasons of comparability in group size the number of normal controls was reduced at random (without differences between the smaller subsample and the original group of normal controls with respect to the the self-concept measures). We ended up with 92 "anorexic-like" (AN-like) students, 33 "bulimic-like" (BN-like) students, and 103 students without any sign of ED ("normal controls"). Of course, we were not able to make diagnostic conclusions with respect to the presence of a full-blown clinical picture of ED (based upon DSM-IV criteria). Nevertheless, the distinction into subgroups was confirmed by the results of the BMI: an average low weight in AN-like students (16.56, SD=1.26), overweight in BN-like students (31.09, SD=2.37), and normal weight for the controls (22.09, SD=1.20); these results all differed significantly from each other ($F(2,225)=1251.30$; $p<.001$). It is important to note that we were able to check whether students had been honest in giving information about their weight: the correlation between their self-reported weight and their weight as measured during a standard medical examination – being part of a routine assessment of all students – was almost perfect ($r=0.99$, $p<.001$). The mean age of the students was 19.24 (SD=0.92) and there were no significant differences between the three subgroups.

Table 1. Means (M) and Standard Deviations (SD) of the three subgroups for each of the EDES subscales

	Group 1 AN N=92		Group 2 BN N=33		Group 3 Controls N_{min}=102		F[a]	Scheffé's Post Hoc Tests
	M	(SD)	M	(SD)	M	(SD)		
Total score[b, c]	41.15	(7.51)	40.31	(8.93)	76.31	(4.35)	819.84***	AN<C, BN<C
Anorectic Preoccupation	9.45	(3.90)	7.15	(3.24)	23.62	(2.49)	590.64***	AN<C, BN<C, BN<AN
Real/Ideal Weight	3.13	(1.15)	0.18	(1.04)	5.29	(1.18)	261.63***	AN<C, BN<C, BN<AN
Weight Fluctuations	3.19	(2.07)	3.75	(1.92)	5.32	(0.95)	42.58***	AN<C, BN<C,
Strict Dieting	0.67	(0.95)	2.12	(0.69)	5.51	(0.86)	761.03***	AN<C, BN<C, AN<BN
Food Preoccupation	1.54	(1.32)	0.54	(0.90)	3.49	(0.87)	128.02***	AN<C, BN<C, BN<AN
Weight Preoccupation	0.91	(1.00)	0.54	1.03	4.01	(0.90)	313.01***	AN<C, BN<C
Bulimic Behavior	12.67	(2.89)	5.87	(2.11)	17.33	(0.94)	392.50***	AN<C, BN<C, BN<AN
Vomiting	2.78	(2.11)	2.18	(0.76)	6.00	(0.00)	172.05***	AN<C, BN<C
Bingeing	5.67	(0.74)	0.18	(0.58)	5.33	(0.94)	593.34***	C<AN, BN<AN, BN<C
Laxatives Abuse	4.21	(2.08)	3.51	(1.66)	6.00	(0.00)	53.63***	AN<C, BN<C
Sexuality	6.58	(2.16)	9.00	(2.68)	15.16	(2.14)	369.74***	AN<C, BN<C, AN<BN
Regular Menstruation	2.63	(1.02)	5.87	(0.70)	4.81	(0.98)	187.42***	AN<C, C<BN, AN<BN
Attitude to Sexuality	1.89	(1.16)	2.36	(0.92)	5.47	(0.88)	332.91***	AN<C, BN<C,
Active Sexuality	2.06	(1.52)	0.90	(1.66)	4.87	(1.10)	153.27***	AN<C, BN<C, BN<AN
Psychosocial Adjustment	12.43	(2.61)	18.96	(3.71)	20.19	(2.40)	210.69***	AN<C, AN<BN
Attitude to	2.50	(1.81)	4.00	(0.50)	4.15	(0.72)	44.75***	AN<C,

Family								AN<BN
Attitude to Friends	3.34	(0.98)	5.87	(0.69)	5.74	(0.77)	220.42***	AN<C, AN<BN
Attitude to Work/School	3.91	(1.80)	5.09	(1.12)	4.79	(1.06)	13.02***	AN<C, AN<B
Other Psychiatric Symptoms	2.67	(2.67)	4.00	(2.00)	5.49	(1.44)	43.95***	AN<C, BN<C, AN<BN

[a] *: p<.05, **: p<.01, ***: p<.001

[b] The lower the scores on the EDES subscales, the more pathological the results

[c] Normative values in Flemish population (Vandereycken, 1993): EDES-Total ($M_{Normals}$=67.16, $M_{Patients}$=29.63, Cut-off score=55); Anorectic Preoccuation ($M_{Normals}$=18.68, $M_{Patients}$=5.94); Bulimic Behavior ($M_{Normals}$=16.49, $M_{Patients}$=11.43); Sexuality ($M_{Normals}$=10.94, $M_{Patients}$=3.01); Psychosocial Adjustment ($M_{Normals}$=21.05, $M_{Patients}$=9.25).

As summarized in Table 1, both ED-like subgroups showed pathological scores on the Anorectic Preoccupation scale of the EDES: for the AN-like students mostly due to "strict dieting behavior" and "weight preoccupation", and the BN-like students due to their "bad real weight/ideal weight ratio" and their "food and weight preoccupations". Furthermore, of the Bulimic Behavior scale, the items "bingeing" and "vomiting" revealed pathological scores for both the AN-like and BN-like students. With respect to the Sexuality scale of the EDES, AN-like students most often reported irregular menstruation, probably due to their underweight. With respect to the Psychosocial Adjustment scale, AN-like students showed more relational problems than BN-like students and normal controls.

Instruments

To measure the different dimensions of the (physical) self-concept, we made use of the Self Description Questionnaire III (SDQ-III; Marsh, 1992a) and the Physical Self Description Questionnaire (PSDQ, Marsh & Redmayne, 1994), both of which have been shown to be reliable and valid self-reporting instruments (Byrne, 1996).

The *SDQ-III* was designed to measure multiple dimensions of self-concept for college students and other adults. Its multidimensional structure is firmly rooted in the theoretical model of self-concept put forward by Shavelson et al. (1976). The SDQ-III is a 136-item self-report scale with 13 subscales related to eight nonacademic areas (Physical Ability, Physical Appearance, Peer Relations-Same Sex, Peer Relations-Opposite Sex, Parent Relations, Emotional Stability, Honesty/Thrustworthiness, and Spiritual Values/Religion), four academic areas (Verbal, Mathematics, Problem Solving, and General-Academic), and a single global perception of self (i.e., General Self-Concept). The items are structured on a 8-point Likert-type scale; some subscales are composed of 10 items, whereas others contain 12 items. To disrupt acquiescence response biases, half of the items in each subscale are worded negatively. Respondents also provide self-ratings on 12 single item scales called "summary descriptions". These were designed to represent 12 of the SDQ-III scales – all but the General Self-Concept scale. Subjects have to judge the "importance" of the statement associated with each scale as a self description, and report their judgement on a 9-point scale response scale (from 1, very unimportant, to 9, very important).

The PSDQ (Marsh & Redmayne, 1994) is a 70-item self-reporting questionnaire that assesses nine specific components of physical self-concept (strength, body fat, activity, endurance/fitness, sports competence, coordination, health, physical appearance, and flexibility), a single global physical self-concept, and overall general self-esteem. Items constituting the PSDQ are structured in a 6-point Likert-type scale; two subscales comprise 8 items (Health and Global Self-Esteem), whereas the remainder have 6 items each. Development of the PSDQ evolved from construct validity research related to both the hierarchical model of self-concept by Shavelson et al. (1976) and the Self Description Questionnaire-II (SDQ-II; Marsh, 1992b). In particular, the PSDQ reflects three subscales from the SDQ-II: Physical Ability, Physical Appearance, and General Self-Concept.

Analyses

One way analyses of variance (ANOVAs) have been used to evaluate whether the three subgroups of students (AN-like, BN-like, controls) differed significantly from each other with respect to the multiple dimensions of self-concept. When the ANOVAs showed significant results, Scheffe's post hoc tests were applied to find out which subgroups differed from each other.

Self Description Questionnaire III (SDQ-III)

The SDQ-Total score revealed significant differences between the eating-disordered students and the normal controls (see Table 2). However, no significant differences were found between AN-like and BN-like students. In general, controls had a more positive self-image than ED students. The differences can mainly be due to differences in the Non-Academic Self-Concept, more specifically the Physical Appearance dimension. ED students perceived themselves as more ugly than normal controls. Further, AN-like students reported more difficulties in their interaction with males (SDQ-Opposite Sex Relations) compared to BN-like students and controls. BN-like students, on the other hand, described themselves as more dishonest, compared to both AN-like students and controls. No significant differences emerged between the normal controls and the ED subgroups with respect to the Academic Self-Concept and its different components (Maths, Verbal, Academic, Problem Solving). With respect to the ratings of importance for each of the self-concept dimensions, only two significant differences appeared: AN-like students found their Physical Appearance more important than controls ($F(2,225)=9.64$; $p<.001$), and they appreciated Physical Activity more than BN-like students ($F(2,225)=3.96$; $p<.05$).

Results

Table 2. Means (M) and Standard Deviations (SD) of the three subgroups for eachof the SDQ-III subscales

	Group 1 AN-like N=92		Group 2 BN-like N=33		Group 3 Controls N=103		F(2, 225)[a]	Scheffé's Post Hoc Tests
	M	(SD)	M	(SD)	M	(SD)		
Total[b]	704.47	(79.30)	692.51	(68.60)	733.42	(86.46)	4.67**	AN<C, BN<C
Academic	209.35	(33.85)	200.93	(29.88)	207.89	(39.01)	0.68	n.s.
Mathematic	52.30	(15.75)	52.09	(17.95)	50.07	(19.57)	0.41	n.s.
Verbal	56.53	(10.41)	52.87	(11.90)	57.20	(9.94)	2.18	n.s.
Academic	47.63	(12.73)	45.30	(11.37)	48.84	(12.91)	1.00	n.s.
Problem Solving	52.89	(6.94)	50.66	(5.76)	51.76	(7.49)	1.37	n.s.
Non Academic	424.82	(53.33)	420.96	(46.68)	455.05	(56.01)	9.62***	AN<C, BN<C
Physical Ability	55.81	(12.81)	50.63	(8.11)	55.70	(12.39)	2.54	n.s.
Phys. Appearance	38.11	(14.71)	42.30	(10.83)	57.49	(12.43)	55.29***	AN<C, BN<C
Same Sex	59.52	(11.06)	60.00	(10.62)	59.72	(11.34)	0.02	n.s.
Opposite Sex	48.38	(12.39)	54.63	(8.41)	57.93	(11.59)	16.80***	AN<BN, AN<C
Parents	56.06	(15.54)	50.57	(15.71)	53.97	(15.73)	1.54	n.s.
Religion	32.38	(12.44)	34.42	(14.26)	35.12	(16.67)	0.86	n.s.
Honesty	79.95	(8.19)	75.33	(9.96)	80.45	(8.73)	4.52**	BN<AN, BN<C
Emot. Stability	54.58	(14.71)	53.06	(13.49)	54.64	(13.53)	0.17	n.s.
Self-Concept	70.29	(15.94)	70.60	(6.85)	70.47	(5.76)	0.00	n.s.

[a] *: p<.05, **: p<.01, ***: p<.001

b The higher the scores on the SDQ-III subscales, the more positive the particular self-concept dimensions

Table 3. Means (M) and Standard Deviations (SD) of the three subgroups for each of the PSDQ subscales

	Group 1 AN-like N=92		Group 2 BN-like N=33		Group 3 Controls N=103		F(2, 225)[a]	Scheffé's Post Hoc Tests
	M	(SD)	M	(SD)	M	(SD)		
General Self-Concept	40.86	(3.73)	41.45	(3.96)	42.79	(3.23)	7.34***	AN<C
Health	37.67	(5.68)	40.15	(4.53)	40.89	(4.37)	10.20***	AN<C
Strength	22.02	(7.68)	24.96	(6.58)	27.19	(6.62)	13.02***	AN<C
Coordination	21.90	(5.71)	22.60	(3.82)	25.86	(5.12)	15.03***	AN<C, BN<C
Flexibility	20.65	(7.36)	20.18	(5.50)	26.39	(6.60)	21.19***	AN<C, BN<C
Sport	17.03	(9.64)	20.54	(8.34)	26.17	(8.31)	26.06***	AN<C, BN<C

Table 3. (Continued)

	Group 1 AN-like N=92		Group 2 BN-like N=33		Group 3 Controls N=103		F(2, 225)[a]	Scheffé's Post Hoc Tests
	M	(SD)	M	(SD)	M	(SD)		
Global Physical	20.76	(5.61)	21.93	(5.07)	27.03	(5.48)	34.01***	AN<C, BN<C
No Body Fat	22.05	(5.27)	22.21	(3.15)	29.80	(3.78)	87.70***	AN<C, BN<C
Physical Activity	24.77	(3.31)	16.42	(3.88)	22.97	(6.40)	33.77***	C<AN, BN<C, BN<AN
Phys. Appearance	25.25	(4.69)	27.30	(2.53)	29.44	(1.94)	37.09***	AN<C, BN<C, AN<BN
Endurance	22.26	(7.00)	16.33	(5.04)	24.65	(7.91)	16.72***	BN<C, BN<AN

[a] *: p<.05, **: p<.01, ***: p<.001

[b] The higher the scores on the PSDQ subscales, the more positive the particular physical self-concept dimensions

Physical Self Description Questionnaire (PSDQ)

AN-like students, compared to controls, had lower scores on the General Self-Concept scale, and the Health and Strength dimensions (see Table 3). They also reported a lower self-image and described themselves as less healthy and strong than normal controls. Further, both ED subgroups scored lower than the controls on the dimensions Coordination, Flexibility, Sport, Global Physical Self-Concept, No Body Fat, and Physical Appearance. Although underweight, the AN-like students perceived themselves as "fat" as the overweight BN-like students, and fatter than normal controls. Compared to BN-like peers, AN-like students described themselves as physically more active and less attractive. Again, dimensions related to physical appearance and body weight, seem the most important self-concept dimensions (highest F values) to differentiate ED students from normal controls.

Conclusion

The sample we have studied is an interesting one because of the relatively large numbers, the clear and consistent distinction between "eating-disordered" students and "normal" controls, and the reliability of the given information (for example almost perfect correlation between self-reported body weight and objectively measured weight). Inspired by Markus' (1977) self-schema model we have tested three hypotheses.

We expected that the ED groups would have lower scores on the different (positive formulated) self-concept dimensions of the SDQ-III compared to normal controls. Our findings partially confirm this hypothesis. With respect to the Academic Self-Concept and its dimensions, no significant results appeared among the different groups. However, with respect to the Non-Academic Self-Concept, the Physical Appearance dimension revealed the most significant difference between the ED groups and the normal controls. No difference emerged between the AN-like and BN-like subgroups with respect to the SDQ-Physical Appearance Scale. Furthermore, AN-like students admitted to have more problems with interactions with male peers than BN-like students, and the latter described themselves as more dishonest than AN-like students, perhaps referring to their "secretive" eating-disordered behaviors (bingeing and purging).

Next, we expected that ED students, who are supposed to deal with chronically and inflexibly accessibly body-weight self-schemas, would evaluate weight and physical appearance dimensions as more important than normal controls. Using the SDQ-III importance ratings for each of the self-concept dimensions, Physical Appearance was significantly more important for the AN-like group than for the normal controls. Also the PSDQ-scales related to physical appearance (PSDQ-Appearance, PSDQ-Global Physical Self-Esteem) and body weight (PSDQ-No Body Fat) revealed significant differences between the ED students and normal controls. The former considered themselves to be more "fat" and less physical attractive than normal controls.

Finally, we checked whether only the weight-related and physical appearance related dimensions of the physical self-concept enable distinction between the ED subgroups and the normal controls. Our findings confirm indeed that these dimensions have the highest discriminating power (highest F values), but also other physical self-concept dimensions (such as health, physical strength, coordination, sport, and flexibility) revealed differences between one or both ED subgroups and the normal controls. The fact that AN-like students reported more physical activity than the BN-like students and normal controls is quite understandable because it is often used as a means for losing weight in AN. On the contrary, the fact that BN-like students showed less endurance than their AN-like peers and than normal controls might be due to their overweight.

Furthermore, as shown by Rosen (1990), we found that persons with ED students experienced more body-image disturbances than normal controls, given their scores on all subscales referring to negative bodily appearance (PSDQ-Appearance, PSDQ-Global Physical Self-Esteem) and body fat (PSDQ-Body Fat). Certainly, the AN-like students perceived themselves as thicker ("fatter") than that they objectively are, indicating a greater cognitive bias in the appreciation of the body as typically found in ED patients Stein & Corté, 2007). Cash and Brown (1987) found that ED patients evaluate their bodies more negatively than women without ED, and that they report lower global self-esteem than women without ED. However, in our sample these differences occurred only in non-academic related aspects of the self-concept, and not in the academic related domains.

In summary, we can conclude that there is a significant association between ED related behaviors and disturbances in non-academic related self-concept dimensions, especially aspects linked to body weight and appearance. These aspects of the self-concept may be early signs of female students at risk for developing ED. As such they may be very important in the early detection and (secondary) prevention of ED and related problems.

References

Bruch, H. (1973). Eating disorders: Obesity, anorexia nervosa, and the person within. New York: Basic Books.

Bruch, H. (1982). Anorexia nervosa: Therapy and theory. American Journal of Psychiatry, 139, 1531-1538.

Byrne, B.M. (1996). Measuring self-concept across the life span: Issues and instrumentation. Washington, DC: American Psychological Association.

Cash, T.F., & Brown, T.A. (1987). Body image in anorexia nervosa and bulimia nervosa: A review of the literature. Behavior Modification, 11, 487-521.

Gordon, R.A. (1990). Anorexia and bulimia: Anatomy of a social epidemic. Cambridge, MA: Basil Blackwell.

Jacobi, C., Paul, T., de Zwaan, M., Nutzinger, D.O., & Dahme, B. (2004). Specificity of self-concept disturbances in eating disorders. International Journal of Eating Disorders, 38, 204-210.

Leung, F., Schwartzman, A., & Steiger, H. (1996). Testing a dual-process family model in understanding the development of eating pathology: A structural equation modelling analysis. International Journal of Eating Disorders, 20, 367-375.

Markus, H. (1977). Self-schemata and processing information about the self.

Journal of Personality and Social Psychology, 35, 63-78.

Marsh, H.W. (1992a). Self Description Questionnaire (SDQ) III. A theoretical and empirical basis for the measurement of multiple dimensions of adult self-concept. An interim test manual and research monograph. Macarthur (NSW, Australia): University of Western Sydney, Faculty of Education.

Marsh, H.W. (1992b). Self Description Questionnaire (SDQ) II. A theoretical and empirical basis for the measurement of multiple dimensions of adolescent self-concept. An interim test manual and research monograph. Macarthur (NSW, Australia): University of Western Sydney, Faculty of Education.

Marsh, H.W., & Redmayne, R.S. (1994). A multidimensional physical self-concept and its relations to multiple components of physical fitness. Journal of Sports and Exercise Psychology, 16, 43-55.

Rosen, J.C. (1990). Body-image disturbances in eating disorders. In T.F. Cash, & T. Pruzinsky (Eds.), Body images: Development, deviance, and change (pp. 190-213). New York: Guilford Press.

Sepúlveda, A.R., Botella, J., & León, J.A. (2002). Body-image disturbance in eating disorders: a meta-analysis. Psychology in Spain, 6, 83-95.

Shavelson. R.J., Hubner, J.J., & Stanton, G.C. (1976). Self-concept: Validation of construct interpretations. Review of Educational Research, 46, 407-441.

Smeets, M. & Panhuysen, G. (1995). What can be learned from body size estimation? It all depends on your theory. Eating Disorders: The Journal of Treatment and Prevention, 3, 101-114.

Stein, K. F. (1996). The self-schema model: A theoretical approach to the self-concept in eating disorders. Archives of Psychiatric Nursing, 10, 96-109.

Stein, K.F. & Corte, C. (2007). Identity impairment and the eating disorders: Content and organization of the self-concept in women with anorexia nervosa and bulimia nervosa. European Eating Disorders Review, 15, 58-69.

Vandereycken, W. (1993). The Eating Disorders Evaluation Scale. Eating Disorders: The Journal of Treatment and Prevention, 1, 115-122.

Research and Review Studies

In: Anxiety in College Students
Editor: Benjamin Ayres and Michelle Bristow
ISBN: 978-1-60692-282-8

Chapter I

LINKING STUDENT BEHAVIOURS AND ATTITUDES TOWARDS INFORMATION AND COMMUNICATION TECHNOLOGY WITH LEARNING PROCESSES, TEACHER INSTRUCTION AND CLASSROOM ENVIRONMENT

Robert F. Cavanagh and Joseph T. Romanoski
Curtin University of Technology, Perth, Australia

Abstract

This chapter describes how the Rasch model was applied to construct an interval-level scale measuring student use and disposition towards information and communication technology (ICT). Scale development was based upon an hypothesised model of classroom ICT learning culture comprising self and collective values, attitudes and behaviours. Specifically, the study aimed to produce a scale that: Measured student self-reported learning behaviours and attitudes towards use of ICT; had calibrated item difficulties and self-reported learning behaviours and attitudes towards ICT measures on the same scale; and elicited data to fit the theoretical model. A 126 item Likert scale type instrument was developed, administered to 439 primary and secondary school students, and then refined and validated by Rasch analysis. The validated data comprised 62 items on five aspects of ICT learning culture. These five aspects were: Student reported learning attitudes and behaviours; student reported teacher attitudes and behaviours; student reported attitudes and behaviours towards ICT networks; student reported home ICT attitudes and behaviours; and student reported values towards ICT use at school. Examination of the psychometric properties of the data identified common and uncommon attitudes and behaviours. This illustrated how students viewed their classroom ICT learning culture.

Keywords: information and communication technology, learning, classroom environment, teacher instruction, students, attitude, behaviour, Rasch measurement.

Introduction

The methodology applied in the study was quantitative and the research method was basically hypothesis testing. The efficacy of the study relied upon development of a theoretical model that was both a valid representation of the phenomenon under investigation as well was amenable to empirical validation. Consequently, the first stage of the study was to clarify epistemological issues - that is, to develop a theoretical understanding as to how students view and use information and communications technology (ICT). A preliminary review of literature on ICT and student learning through use of ICT showed that this field of research was epistemologically complex due to the variety of rationales applied in the research. Much of this research was predicated on the postulation that ICT is an integral part of post-modern knowledge society and consequently education. Thus, ICT is presumed to have utility in schools, it should lead to improvements in student learning and research should support these presumptions. However, it was recognised that there is arguably a bifurcation in the motives for applying and researching ICT use in schools. On one hand, there is a demand for justifying ICT innovation in schools per se; on the other hand, for viewing ICT application within a broader scheme based upon assumptions about the purpose and aims of education. Whether one or the other, or perhaps both viewpoints, are accepted, depends on how the relationship between technology and education is interpreted.

The methodological decision to apply quantitative methods required specification of the uni-dimensional trait to be measured. The theoretical model needed to comprise constructs that are inter-related and would collectively constitute this trait. So the previously identified dichotomy in conceptualising ICT application and the intentions of the educative processes in classrooms had to be resolved. This matter is addressed in the following section of the chapter.

Background

The Western Australian curriculum, the *Curriculum Framework* (Curriculum Council, 1997) is underpinned by five *Core Values*. These are pursuit of knowledge and achievement of potential, self-acceptance and self-respect, respect and concern for the rights of others, social and civic responsibility, and environmental responsibility. These values are consistent with the expectations of national and international educational policies, nationally in the *Adelaide Declaration on National Goals for Schooling in the Twenty-first Century* (MCEETYA, 2000), and internationally by the *UNESCO International Commission on Education for the Twenty-first Century* (Stoll, MacBeath & Mortimore, 2001). Implicit in the explication of values in these curriculum policies is the expectation that education systems and schools will assume responsibility for enculturation and values development. The values incumbent in social culture should also be present in schools and be evidenced by the culture of schools and classrooms. From this perspective, the psycho-sociological environment of the school can be viewed as school culture and that of the individual classroom as classroom culture.

School and Classroom Culture

The term school culture has been defined as comprising: The common values, beliefs, behaviours, rules, products, signs and symbols which provide a community with cohesion (Donahoe, 1993); a reflection of shared values, norms, symbols and traditions (Mitchell & Willower, 1992); the social dimension of the school concerned with belief systems, values, cognitive structures and meaning (Anderson, 1982); and as a combination of processes and shared value systems expected to make schools educationally effective (Stoll & Mortimer, 1995). Ideas, beliefs and values are developed to give meaning to the behaviours of groups and individuals and in turn, these behaviours are an expression of a specific culture (Maxwell & Thomas, 1991). The beliefs, values, attitudes and behaviours constituting school and classroom culture should reflect general societal norms and mores, but equally importantly, exemplify the educative mission of schools and the pedagogical processes within classrooms (Cavanagh & Dellar, 2003).

The development and maintenance of school and of classroom culture can be viewed as a process of social constructivist learning. This emphasises the importance of the social environment on the acquisition and development of knowledge (Blumenfield, Marx, Patrick, Krajcik, & Soloway, 1997; Good & Brophy, 2000; McCarthy, 1994). Adoption of a social constructivist view of classroom culture and student learning supports the instructional importance of the social processes occurring within the classroom for learning. This is consistent with cooperative learning instructional methods (Johnson, Johnson & Stanne, 2000), and also propositions about the effectiveness of caring learning environments (Battistitch, Solomon, Watson & Schaps, 1997; Pena & Amrein, 1999). In addition, the home and family also influence the dispositions and behaviours of students within the classroom. The effect of family and home on student achievement is well established (Coleman, 1998; Lingard, 2001; McCall, Smith, Stoll, Thomas, Sammons, Smees, MacBeath, Boyd & MacGilchrist, 2001; Waugh & Cavanagh, 2002; 2003). Accepting the social constructivist view of learning in educational research involves investigating classroom learning and teaching in relation to the factors influencing students' mental construction of the socio-psychological environment that constitutes classroom culture.

The notions of school and classroom culture are also applicable in conceptualising educational change and innovation. Indeed, school improvement and the more recent of notion school renewal, have been portrayed as a process of re-culturing to change belief and value systems throughout the school (Dalin, Rolff & Kleekamp, 1993; Fullan, 1993; Glickman, 1992; Hargreaves, 2003; Harris, 2001; Sergiovanni, 1992 & 2000). Transforming the culture of a school requires teachers to develop new beliefs, attitudes and values about instructional processes that will lead to change in classroom practice and improved educational outcomes for students (Halsall, 1998). Classroom culture can be considered as the result of curriculum implementation or of educational innovation. From this perspective, data obtained by empirical investigations of classroom cultures profiles the extent of innovation adoption. Alternatively, classroom culture can also be viewed as the vehicle for facilitating curriculum implementation and educational innovation. In this instance, data on classroom culture can inform management of the change and innovation implementation.

In 2001, the Australian *Department of Science, Education and Training* (DEST) reported a national study of innovation and best practice in Australian schools. The study found that educational change needed to "… affect the practices, culture and structure of schools by restructuring roles and re-organising responsibilities, including those of students and parents" (DEST, 2001 p.2). The study also revealed that successful innovation implementation focused on "creating learning environments that could meet the learning needs of individual students, which, in most cases, involved a more student-centred approach" (DEST, 2001 p.20). These findings resulted from investigating the four most prevalent areas of innovation in schools. These areas were literacy in the early years, 'schooling' in the middle years (middle schooling), and mathematics and information and communication technologies across all years.

The subject of this investigation was the application of information and communication technology (ICT) in improving student learning. The national importance of ICT innovation in schools is reflected in the local curriculum. The Western Australian *Curriculum Framework* articulates 13 *Major Learning Outcomes* that express the long-term generic aims of kindergarten, elementary and secondary schooling. Particular reference is made to students being able to "select, use and adapt technologies" and to "recognise when and what information is needed, locate and obtain it from a wide range of sources and evaluate, use and share it with others" (Curriculum Council, 1997 p.17).

ICT application in classrooms should be viewed as a tool for supporting and complementing the school program (Anderson & Dexter, 2000; Latham, 1998). Thus researching ICT application needs to be undertaken with concurrent attention given to the situation and the purpose of this application. This study needed to be contextually and intentionally grounded within an internally coherent and cohesive theoretical framework. While the immediate locus of ICT application in schools is clearly the classroom, identification of the intent of application is not so evident. Reynolds, Cavanagh and Dellar (2003) applied philosophical methods to clarify distinctions between the purpose, outcomes, mission and visions of schools, curricula and school programs. They suggested the nub of the matter was precise specification of the 'aims' of education and this required a philosophical rather than pragmatic approach. In cognisance of their recommendation, this study viewed the purpose of ICT application to be development and reinforcement of the value systems that provide the rationale for local curriculum policies. That is viewing ICT as an instrument of learning and values development. As was previously noted, identification and expression of values is a fundamental aspect of school and classroom culture. Accordingly, the conceptual framework for the empirical investigation was based upon propositions about school and classroom culture. In particular, values, attitudes and resulting behaviours identified in school effectiveness research as a means toward a general improvement in student learning.

This discussion has focussed on the importance of classroom culture as a crucial consideration in curriculum implementation, school improvement and enhancing educational outcome attainment. The following section examines how application of ICT has been associated with improving student learning.

Information and Communication Technology and Student Learning

Literature connecting ICT with learning presents a multifarious view of ICT application and student learning. The mode of participation of students in the learning process is varied. Students can work independently, or in groups. Alternatively, they can interact virtually. The cognitive processes constituting learning are also varied. These include constructivist activities such as problem solving, creativity, self-regulation and meta-cognition. The outcomes or product of ICT usage are multidimensional. ICT can affect the quality of schoolwork and the pace of completing tasks. Accessibility to ICT in the classroom can be an incentive for learning and ICT use can influence general motivation and engagement. In addition, confidence and commitment to working with ICT can be considered a desirable outcome in its own right.

The following discussion of examples of ICT application in classrooms is organised into three sections. These concern modes of participation, learning processes and learning outcomes.

ICT Modes of Participation

Independent student learning utilising ICT has been an ongoing investigative concern at all three educational levels - primary, secondary, and tertiary. Some studies focus on the effectiveness of particular software programs or web sites on individual student learning. Recently, programs such as *Espresso* (Watts, Lloyd & Jackson, 2001), *Flash* (Chan, Hodgkiss & Chan, 2002), *kar2ouche* (Davies & Birmingham, 2002), *WebDeGrator* (Sung & Ou, 2002), *WEAR* (Moundridou & Virvou, 2002), and *ActivStats* (Morris, Joiner & Scanlon, 2002), and web sites such as *Xref* (Young & Ramsden, 2002) have been recently described and evaluated. Other studies have concerned the individual knowledge or skill acquisition that ensues as a direct result of the individual activities of the student on the computer (Goodison, 2002; Morris et al., 2002). Still others focus on improved individual outcomes resulting from independent learning via the computer in such diverse disciplines as physics (Tolmie, 2001), spelling (Torgerson & Elbourne, 2002), and history (Hillis, 2002).

Learning also occurs when groups of students use computers. Positive learning outcomes that result from embedded collaborative activities with a computer have been demonstrated in health education (Lockyer, Patterson & Harper, 2001), primary science (Tolmie, Howe, Duchak-Tanner & Rattray, 1999), and secondary science (Chiu, 2002). Chiu (2002) demonstrated that students completing a science report assignment with the support of network technology in a team setting learned as well as those who were in an individual setting. The criterion applied was the acquisition of scientific process skills and the development of positive attitudes toward science and using computers. Chiu (2002) noted, that diffusion of responsibility, also called the 'free-rider' effect, often occurs in team learning. Studies regarding gender differences and interactions within a collaborative ICT learning environment and their subsequent impact on learning have likewise been conducted. Tolmie (2001) observed that the female and male students possessed well-established patterns of interaction (or non-interaction) with each other, especially with respect to conflict management. Volman and van Eck (2001) noted that, in collaborative ICT activities, boys appeared to be more task-oriented while girls were more process-oriented. Individual knowledge acquisition obtained mainly through group use of ICT has also been investigated in conjunction with activity theory models. These provide a language for describing and understanding the changes and difficulties that arise in the development of websites (Issroff & Scanlon, 2002).

Virtual reality (VR) environments also enable collaborative learning. In the last few years, new computer games have emerged that enable people to link up online to game together. This has fostered both co-operative and competitive elements within a strategic context. It may well be the case that online games are more educationally useful than traditional games in which a player competes against the machine only (Griffiths & Davies, 2002). Other examples of online-learning involving social interaction is the creation and use of alternative personae (avatars) in chat rooms (Turkle, 1995), self-expression through the use of text-based communication, and discursive discussion and argument in electronic environments (Wheeler, Waite & Bromfield, 2002). Individual knowledge acquisition obtained mainly through communicating and interacting with others electronically has also been investigated in conjunction with asynchronous text-based communication. Active knowledge generation occurs through informal peer-to-peer discussion between students (Popolov, Callaghan & Luke, 2002).

ICT Learning Processes

Constructivists believe that learning involves constructing knowledge from one's own experiences rather than directly receiving information from the outside world (Resnick, 1987; Brown, Collins & Duguid, 1989; Collins, Brown & Newman, 1989; Collins & Green, 1992). Constructivism refers to a learning approach that emphasises the importance of experiential exploratory learning. It evolved from the writings of Piaget and Bruner who together focused on the relevance of direct meaningful knowledge construction through experience of the world (Collins & Green, 1992; Collins et al., 1989). Constructivism dovetails with VR learning environments in a fundamental and significant manner. The learning that occurs in VR is qualitatively experiential and direct. Students explore their environment and construct meaningful knowledge acquired from the virtual environment (Cronin, 1997). Hence, students can determine the extent to which ICT enhances or detracts from learning and how computers enhance the quality of learning (Goodison, 2002). ICT-mediated communication contributes to the cognitive development of students by stimulating them to articulate ideas, ask questions, participate in discussion and work together, and receive feedback on their ideas from their classmates (Harasim, 1996). This fosters the active construction of knowledge and promotes the development of knowledge from other perspectives (Volman & van Eck, 2001).

Problem solving may be observed in a variety of online activities including behaviour resulting from lateral or divergent thinking. These include expert manipulation of text and graphics; creative use of colour, animation and effects to convey particular messages; and economic navigation through complex web-based resources (Wheeler et al., 2002). The objective of inquiry-based learning with ICT is to help students to find problems, seek answers, generate solutions, and build their own theories and ideas about the world through explorations (Zhang, 2002). In addition, ICT contributes to creating learning environments in which students can actively work on solving real problems encountered in daily life (Volman

& van Eck, 2001). Goodison (2002) has advised that, if ICT were indeed an effective way of promoting the formal or informal devising of algorithms or strategies, it would be worthwhile to find ways of allowing children to explore software for themselves in a structured supportive environment.

Computers can help students develop their creativity. Creativity is the ability to come up with new ideas that are surprising, yet intelligible, and also valuable in some way (Boden, 2001). Creative thinking involves the representation in meaning derived from a dialogue between children and their work (Loveless, 2000). Examples of creative ICT learning include the development and management of a personal website, personal writing using a word-processor, and discovering and adapting to new ways of working and studying using electronic environments (Wheeler, et al., 2002). Also, the use of hypertext technology has been positively associated with empowering students to do original and creative work (Dreher, 1997).

Teaching children to develop creativity in using ICT also encourages responsibility for learning and self-regulation (Wheeler et al., 2002). Likewise, the way to decrease the opportunity for diffusion of responsibility in collaborative learning with ICT is to have individual accountability (Slavin, 1983). This, major researchers seem to agree, is necessary for effective learning in conventional classrooms (Watson, 1992). Responsibility for learning can be understood as recognition, on the part of the student, of personal individual accountability. This is being accountable for the results of those nominated educational ICT processes or activities presented to and/or initiated on behalf of the individual student for the specific purpose of facilitating the student's acquisition of knowledge or skills.

Metacognitive awareness is a key element in successful learning (Bransford, Donovan & Pellegrino, 2000). The idea of particular software tools being suited to particular tasks has important implications for the development of students' metacognitive awareness. For example, the software program *Smartboard*, promotes quite a sophisticated level of metacognitive reflection (Goodison, 2002). This encourages children to think about their own thinking can enhance the ICT learning process (Wheeler et al., 2002). A major contribution of ICT to the teaching-learning process is found in the ease with which teachers can give students feedback and with which students can correct their own work. This stimulates students to reflect on their experiences (Volman & van Eck, 2001). The flexibility afforded by an asynchronous web-based environment also supports student reflection (Lockyer et al., 2001; Sung & Ou, 2002).

ICT Learning Outcomes

Many students enjoy using computers and this increases motivation, engagement, and generally enhances the learning experience (Moundridou & Virvou, 2002). Student use of software programs such as *kar2ouche* (Davies & Birmingham, 2002) and *Espresso* (Watts, et al., 2001) takes on the appearance of game playing and thereby adds the motivational element of fun to the learning experience. Likewise, software programs provide imagery that appeals to different ages and the different genders provide an additional stimulus towards individual utilization of ICT (Volman & van Eck, 2001). Younger students in particular seem to develop more positive attitudes towards learning as a result of using ICT (Volman & van Eck, 2001). Improvement in tertiary students' outlooks has also been noted (Chan et al., 2002; Gardner,

Sheridan & White, 2002). Access to ICT in the classroom provides an incentive for learning and engagement.

Increased student work output can result from ICT use. Recent studies (Smeets & Mooij, 2001; Tolmie, 2001; Watts, et al., 2001; Zandvliet, 1999) have noted marked student productivity improvements as a direct result of ICT usage. Alternatively, Goodison (2002) found only marginal improvement in student productivity as a result of computer use. One aim of the ImpaCT2 (http://www.becta.org.uk/impact2/) study in the UK was to analyse the relationship between students' use of ICT and their performance in National Tests and GCS examinations. In almost every case, the study found evidence of a positive relationship between ICT use and educational attainment.

Computer use can develop self-efficacy. Self-efficacy determines how much effort an individual will expend towards execution of a behaviour to accomplish a particular outcome, the length of persistence toward goal accomplishment in the face of obstacles, and resilience to failure. Self-efficacy or persistence levels of students, also influence the amount of learning that occurs during computer-based instruction (Hooper, 2003). The cognitive processes that develop self-efficacy require acquisition of knowledge gained through prior experiences (Cassidy & Eachus, 2002). Learning how to learn thus is not simply a matter of cognitive ability. It is also the self-confidence to face the challenge of learning something new, and the belief in learning as an incremental process (Seltzer & Bentley, 2001). There is a spectrum of confidence in using ICT in the classroom (Watts, et al., 2001). Evidence exists that ICT increases the confidence of lower attaining students (Wheeler, Waite & Bromfield, 2002). However, some studies have shown that girls appear to be less self-confident than boys regarding their computer skills, even when experience is taken into account (Comber, Colley, Hargreaves & Dom, 1997; Volman, 1997; Durndell, Glissov & Siann, 1995; Huber & Schofield, 1998).

Summary

It was previously indicated that the theoretical basis for the study was propositions about school and classroom culture. In keeping with the aim of the study, the incumbent values and disposition constituting this culture needed to concern ICT learning. Consequently, the theoretical model guiding the empirical investigation was based upon a classroom learning culture framework that was modified to focus on ICT learning. The aspects of ICT application in classrooms just discussed were situated within a classroom culture frame. The dominant trait investigated was classroom ICT learning culture.

Research Objectives

The study sought to apply the Rasch Model to construct an interval-level scale to measure student values, attitudes and behaviours towards use of information and communication technology (ICT). Scale development was based upon a hypothesised model comprised by one ICT educational outcome component and four ICT behaviours and attitudes components (four in-school and one out-of-school). Specifically, the study aimed to apply a scale development process to produce a scale that:

1. Measured student self-reported learning behaviours and attitudes towards use of ICT;
2. Calibrated item difficulties and self-reported learning behaviours and attitudes towards ICT measures on the same scale; and
3. Elicited data to fit the theoretical model.

Theoretical Model

ICT application in classrooms was viewed within the broader schema of curriculum policy expectations and the role of classroom culture in realising these expectations. The values upon which the curriculum is grounded are an expression of the aims of education in Western Australia and of the purpose of schooling. A classroom culture conducive to attainment of the aims would be characterised by these values. The classroom attitudes and behaviours of students would be shaped by these values. Such a culture would express the aims or outcomes of learning and also apply social and pedagogical processes to enable these goals to be attained. Cavanagh (1997) described school culture as being manifested by the sharing of values and norms concerning commonality of purpose and actions intended to improve the learning of students and teachers. Application of this conception in multiple local studies of school and classroom culture has identified five elements of school and classroom culture often cited as characteristics of effective schools, classrooms, teaching and learning (Cavanagh, Dellar, Ellett & Rugutt, 2000; Cavanagh, Waugh, & Dellar, 2003; Waugh, & Cavanagh, 2002). These are:

- Improved educational outcomes;
- An emphasis on learning;
- Mutual empowerment and caring;
- Collaboration; and
- Partnerships (home and local community).

The elements provide a framework for describing prevailing cultural values and can also be viewed as vehicles for building or transforming the culture. For example, *an emphasis on learning* is an expression of values concerning the importance of learning. It can also be viewed as a process in which learning is continually emphasised within the classroom environment. Similarly, *improved educational outcomes* concerns the importance of educational outcome attainment and in turn, attainment of outcomes provides motivation for subsequent engagement in the further learning.

In this study of ICT and learning, the five-element model was applied as a frame for structuring aspects of ICT application pertaining to learning. ICT-specific constructs were identified from the examination of literature on ICT and learning discussed previously. These constructs were defined operationally and classified within the five-element model of classroom culture. The defining and classification process clarified understanding of the constructs and differentiated between constructs with similar meaning. It also revealed additional constructs considered relevant for the study that had not been identified in the ICT literature. For example, the influence of the home environment on ICT learning at school was deemed to be important. At the completion of this process, 21 constructs were identified, operationally defined and classified. These constructs are presented in Table 1.

While the content of Table 1 provides sufficient conceptual detail for instrument sub-scale development and item writing, the conceptual structure does not constitute a theoretical model that could be subject to empirical validation. Relationships between variables are not specified and the dominant trait to be measured is also not made sufficiently explicit. Consequently the uni-dimensional concept of classroom ICT learning culture was defined tentatively and a model of classroom ICT learning culture was proposed (see Figure 1).

Classroom ICT learning culture was proposed to constitute student attitudes, behaviours and values concerning ICT that lead to achievement of generic and ICT-specific educational outcomes. The model presented in Figure 1 assumes classroom ICT learning culture is comprised of five components. These are *ICT learning*, *ICT empowerment and caring*, *ICT collaboration*, *ICT use outside of school*, and *improved educational outcomes*. The double arrows in Figure 1 show these five components were expected to be mutually influential. The particular attitudes, behaviours and values comprising the five components were hypothesised to collectively constitute and influence classroom ICT learning culture.

Table 1. ICT learning constructs, operational definitions and classroom culture elements

ICT learning constructs		Operational definitions	Classroom culture elements
1.	Self -regulation	Improvement in acceptance of responsibility for the learning process through use of ICT	Improved educational outcomes
2.	Productivity	Improvement in individual student work output from use of ICT	
3.	Incentivisation	Improvement in outlook, attitude, demeanour, or overall motivation through use of ICT	
4.	Self-efficacy	Conviction and belief in personal capacity to successfully use ICT	
5.	Disposition towards independent learning	Learning through individual use of ICT.	An emphasis on learning
6.	Disposition towards problem-solving	Application of ICT to answer questions	
7.	Disposition towards creativity	Use of ICT for self-expression and developing original ideas and views	
8.	Disposition towards meta-cognition	Reflecting upon and evaluating the effectiveness of own learning through use of ICT	
9.	Peer support	Helping each other use ICT	Mutual empowerment and caring
10.	Peer caring	Caring for others when using ICT	

Table 1. (Continued)

ICT learning constructs	Operational definitions	Classroom culture elements
11. Virtual relationships	Developing and maintaining friendships on the Internet	
12. Student centred teaching	Teacher concern for individual learning needs in implementation of ICT activities	
13. Teacher caring	Teacher concern for student personal needs in implementation of ICT activities	
14. Group collaboration	Discussing learning in group use of ICT	Collaboration
15. Instructional design	Teacher-student discussion about ICT learning	
16. Teacher – student negotiation	Teacher-student discussion about ICT learning outcomes and assessment	
17. School intranet collaboration	Discussion about schoolwork on the school intranet	
18. Internet collaboration	Discussion about schoolwork on the Internet.	
19. Parental involvement	Parents and students working together with ICT	Partnerships
20. Home ICT environment	Use of ICT in the home	
21. Website associations	Membership of Internet groups	

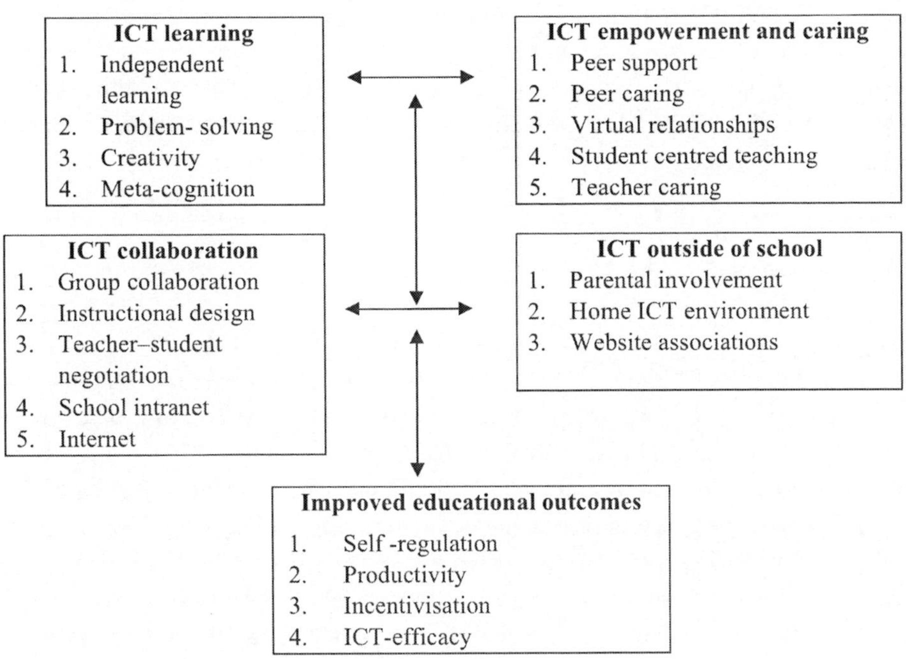

Figure 1. Model of classroom ICT learning culture

Each component is comprised of between three and five sub-components. For example *learning through use of ICT* is evidenced by engagement in independent learning, problem solving, creativity, and meta-cognition. The presence of support and caring from fellow students, development of virtual relationships, and the teacher being responsive to the needs of individual students and caring for students in the classroom were expected to lead to students experiencing *empowerment and caring*. Similarly, *Collaborative use of ICT* would occur by students working in groups, being involved in the design of ICT instructional activities, the teacher negotiating the goals of ICT activities and their assessment with students, and students working with others on the Internet and school intranet. How students use *ICT outside of the school* will also influence ICT use within the classroom. ICT use outside of school includes parental involvement in ICT learning, the home ICT environment and students becoming affiliated with and subscribing to particular Internet websites.

The fifth proposed component of classroom ICT learning culture was *improved educational outcomes*. Differentiating between classroom learning processes and the outcomes of the processes of learning is fraught with difficulty. Indeed it would not be unreasonable to view the presence of the previously explicated four components and respective sub-components of classroom ICT learning culture as legitimate educational outcomes of ICT use. This is an example of a paradox that cannot be resolved by rational argument or the normal application of logic. So student proclivity for self-regulation, productivity, incentivisation, and ICT-efficacy were arbitrarily hypothesised as educational outcomes that could be attained through use of ICT.

Prior to explaining how the model was applied for instrument development, it is worthwhile to reiterate the reasons for proposing the model. First, the model provided the study with a conceptual grounding based upon previous assertions and research about classroom culture and ICT learning. Second, the model provided a conceptual structure to be subjected to empirical investigation and the psychometric properties of data generated during instrument development and refinement would be evaluated by reference to the model. Third, the statistical methods applied to develop and refine the instrument were based upon hypothesis testing, whereby the model provided these hypotheses.

Research Methods

Survey items were developed to elicit student perceptions of the 21 sub-components in the hypothesised model. Six items were written for each sub-component. The respective sets of items were designed to have internal semantic similarity by eliciting data on only one construct and to have internal discriminant capacity by the items being written in differing levels of anticipated difficulty. All the sets of items were further developed by a pilot study with three primary school classes. Problems with ambiguity and reading level were identified and approximately one quarter of the items were re-written. The 126 items were then incorporated in a survey instrument utilising a four point Likert response scale. Items were answered on a four point Likert scale from strongly agree, agree, disagree and strongly disagree. These were scored from 4 to 1.

The instrument was administered to a sample of 439 students from two secondary schools and four primary schools. The primary sample comprised 284 students from Years Six and Seven. The secondary sample comprised 155 students from Years Eight to Twelve and included classes from core curriculum areas and also computing-related electives (e.g. Year Eleven Business Studies).

Data were recorded in an Excel spreadsheet and then transferred into the Rasch Unidimensional Measurement Models program (RUMM) (Andrich, Sheridan, Lyne & Luo,

2000). Un-centralised item thresholds were calculated and items with disordered thresholds were identified and discarded. These items had elicited illogical or inconsistent responses from the students. Data from items with ordered thresholds were retained for further analysis. The criteria for further instrument refinement included retaining items with low residuals. The residual for an item is the difference between the actual student response and the expected response, as specified by the model. A low residual value ($< \pm 2.0$) shows the data for an item fit the model well. Also, items with high Chi Square probability values were retained. The Chi-square test estimates the probability that an item's data fit the model and a low probability value ($p < 0.05$) shows the fit is poor.

The RUMM computer program was then applied to examine the overall fit between the students and the items. The items were calibrated against the students so that the distribution of students and their respective scores was matched by the distribution of items. This process is analogous to using item response theory to calibrate an achievement test. The students perform at differing levels and the items have differing levels of difficulty for these students. The range and distribution of scores should be matched by the range and distribution of item difficulties. Calculating RUMM item-person interaction statistics in this way shows the extent of the fit between the items and the range of perceptions of the students of their classroom ICT learning culture. Item-trait interaction was then examined. The item-trait interaction indicates the consistency of the item 'difficulties' across the range of different student classroom culture measures on the scale; that is how well students agree on the 'difficulties' of the items along the scale. When the data fit the model, the item-trait interaction (a Chi-square) has a probability greater than 0.05. This interaction also evidences the degree to which the scale is measuring a uni-dimensional trait. Finally, RUMM power of test-of-fit statistics were calculated. The separation index indicates how closely the data fit the model with a high value indicating a tight fit.

Results

Following examination of decentralised item thresholds for the original 126 items, 27 items with disordered thresholds (illogical responses) were identified and data from these items were not used in subsequent analyses. Individual item-fit statistics were then calculated for the remaining 99 items and the items that elicited data with either low residuals or high Chi-square probability were identified. Of the 99 items, 37 had not elicited data that satisfied these criteria. Data from the other 62 items were retained and scrutinised further.

Individual item-fit statistics for the 62 items were calculated to show item difficulty locations that were measured in logits (logarithmic units based on the logarithmic odds of answering positively). These locations were considered in conjunction with individual item semantics to examine the structure of the data from both psychometric and conceptual perspectives. As a result, the items were classified into five sub-groups and items within these sub-groups wherever possible, were organised hierarchically (Guttman patterns) according to item logits. The results of this process are presented in 'Appendix A: Item locations, standard errors, residuals and fit to the model'. The individual item-fit statistics presented in Appendix A (i.e. residuals and Chi-square probabilities) also show that the majority of the items fit the model well. It should be noted that the reductionist process applied in scale refinement leads to the psychometric properties of the remaining data differing slightly from that for the larger data-set previously analysed. Hence, some of the residuals and Chi-square probability values in the final analysis do not meet the criteria applied earlier in identifying these items from the 99-item data (e.g. items 11, 14, 24, 31 & 48).

(Appendix A provides a summary of some of the psychometric properties of the data but it does not include the wording of the 62 items. The item statements and the respective item locations are presented in 'Appendix B: The Questionnaire'). RUMM was then applied to generate summary test-of-fit statistics (see Table 2). These analyses included item-student interaction, item-trait interaction and the power of the tests-of-fit.

The item-student interaction indicates the degree to which students answer items of different 'difficulty' in a logical and consistent manner. When the data fits the model, the fit statistic has a mean near zero and a standard deviation near 1. A negative fit statistic indicates that data fitted the model very closely. A positive fit statistic indicates that some 'noise' is present. In this case the means of 0.39 and –0.69 indicate the students were logical and consistent in their responses to items of different 'difficulty'. The standard deviations of 0.88 and 3.20 indicate the variance in item data was acceptable but variance in student data was somewhat lower than would be observed in an ideal data to model fit. For item-trait interaction, the total Chi-square probability was 0.21 ($p > 0.05$). This result indicates that for these data, the scale was uni-dimensional. The proportion of observed variance considered true should be close to 1. In this case the proportion of observed variance considered true (a Cronbach Alpha) was 0.93. The power of the tests-of-fit statistic showed the overall fit between the data and the model was excellent with a separation index of 0.95.

Table 2. Summary of Rasch psychometric statistics for the 62 item scale of classroom ICT learning culture (n = 439)

Item-Student Interaction				
	Items		Students	
	Location	Fit Statistic	Location	Fit Statistic
Mean	0.00	0.39	0.41	-0.69
SD	0.50	0.88	0.71	3.20
Item-Trait Interaction				
Total Item Chi Sq	394.1			
Total Degree Freedom	372			
Total ChiSq Probability	0.21			
Proportion of observed variance considered true for the scale is 0.93 (93%)				
Cronbach Alpha is 0.93				
Power of Tests-of-Fit				
Power is EXCELLENT				
(Separation Index of 0.93)				

The degree of fit between students and items can be represented diagrammatically in a RUMM item map (see Figure 2). In an ideal fit, the distribution of student scores would mirror the distribution of item scores. The scale in Figure 2 is in logits and each 'X' represents 4 students. The student scores (left of scale) range from –1.4 (low) to +2.2 logits (high). The Item threshold locations (right of the scale) range from –3.2 ('easy'/common) to +1.6 logits ('difficult'/uncommon). The range of item thresholds 'covers' the range of student scores showing the items were well targeted at the students.

```
------------------------------------------------------------------------------------------------
LOCATION              PERSONS        ITEMS [un-centralised thresholds]
------------------------------------------------------------------------------------------------
                High classroom ICT   'Difficult' items/uncommon ICT attributes

3.0                                 |
                                    |
                                    |
                                    |
                                   X|
2.0                                X|
                                   X|
                                   X| 34.3 31.3 30.3 22.3 21.3 35.3
                                XXXX| 04.3 47.3 58.3 46.3 27.3
                                  XX| 15.3 19.3 44.3 26.3 48.2 23.3 48.3 54.3 42.3 45.3 20.3 58.2 40.3
1.0                            XXXXX| 25.3 38.3 22.2 53.3 57.3 21.2 14.3 60.3 56.3 43.3 29.3 37.3 10.3
                                      33.3
                             XXXXXXX| 11.3 51.3 41.2 47.2 61.3 18.3 41.3 42.2 59.3 09.3 39.3
                        XXXXXXXXXXXX| 32.3 14.3 01.3 19.2 02.3 54.2 62.3 12.3 55.3 06.3 07.3
                        XXXXXXXXXXXX| 32.2 62.2 16.3 53.2 27.2 08.3 36.3 03.3 05.3 45.2 51.3 39.2 44.2
                    XXXXXXXXXXXXXXXX| 38.2 04.2 15.2 37.2 17.3 43.2 50.3 13.3 46.2 40.2 57.2
0.0             XXXXXXXXXXXXXXXXXXXX| 56.2 20.2 54.1 61.2 18.2 48.1 28.3
                      XXXXXXXXXXXXXX| 43.1 14.2 42.1 34.2 22.1 58.1 45.1 47.1 20.1 53.1 51.2 49.3 46.1
                          XXXXXXXXXX| 30.2 40.1 61.1 17.2 62.1 36.2 31.2 26.2 59.2 21.1 33.2 41.1
                                XXXX| 35.1 50.1 13.2 29.2 52.1 49.2 52.2 12.2 36.1 37.1 44.1 50.2 39.1
                                      60.2
                                   X| 55.1 13.1 06.2 49.1 60.1 08.2 57.1 32.2 55.2 51.1 10.2 09.2 25.2
                                      28.2 38.1 11.2
-1.0                               X| 27.1 24.2 18.1 07.2 23.2 56.1 08.1
                                   X| 07.1 19.1 33.1 30.1 34.1 05.2 16.2 24.1 29.1
                                   X| 03.2 26.1 14.1 23.1 01.2 09.1 31.1 25.1 17.1 15.1 02.2 59.1
                                    | 28.1 32.1
                                    | 12.1 16.1 06.1 03.1
-2.0                                | 04.1 11.1 05.1
                                    |
                                    | 02.1
                                    | 01.1
                                    |
-3.0                                |
                                    | 10.1
                                    |
                                    |
                                    |
-4.0                                |

                Low classroom ICT    'Easy' items /common ICT attributes
------------------------------------------------------------------------------------------------
```

Figure 2. Student attitudes towards information and communications technology with student measures and item thresholds calibrated on the same scale

Note to figure 2

01.1 is the threshold between categories 1 and 2.

01.2 is the threshold between categories 2 and 3, and so on.

Discussion of the Classroom ICT Learning Culture Scale

The scale development process commenced with a rigorous examination of previous research into classroom learning culture and how the application of information and communications technology can improve student learning. This provided information for the proposal of a preliminary theoretical model of the phenomenon. However, the rigour applied in the scale development and refinement process, particularly the requirement that the data fitted a uni-dimensional trait, necessitated that some of the initially hypothesised attributes of the phenomenon would not be included in the refined scale. Since measurement criteria were applied stringently in scale refinement, only those attributes empirically proven to be measurable were retained in the scale. As a result, the refined scale did not have the capacity to measure the original 21 constructs comprising the hypothesised model. However it was shown to be measuring a slightly smaller but conceptually similar range of classroom ICT learning culture attributes.

The scale was a calibrated measure of classroom ICT learning culture. The calibration process identified the logits (item location) for individual items and examination of the relative logits of data from items comprising the postulated sub-groups provides information about how students viewed their ICT learning. Highly negative logits for item data indicates that the students perceived the attribute being measured was a comparatively common aspect of ICT learning. Alternatively, highly positive logits for item data shows they perceived the respective attribute to be relatively uncommon. The following discussion of ICT learning culture is based upon the sub-groups of items and the respective item logits presented in the Appendices. It should be noted that logits are standardised measures and the zero point in a scale of item logits does not equate to students being equally divided between affirmation and non-affirmation.

Student Reported Learning Attitudes and Behaviours

Learning attitudes and behaviours were hypothesised to include information retrieval, cooperative learning, responsibility for learning, self-expression and assessment.

As part of their schoolwork, students use computers to find and retrieve information of relevance to particular topics they are investigating or questions they seek to answer. The range of logits for the four items on *information retrieval* was from –1.0 to –0.10. Students affirmed that computers were useful for information retrieval and that they frequently used computers for this purpose.

Students often work together when using computers and the success of this activity depends upon cooperative attitudes and behaviours. The range of logits for the five items on *cooperative learning* was from –0.82 to –0.33. Students were disposed positively towards cooperative learning with computers. The suggestion here is that they communicated with one another, shared knowledge and were caring of their classmates.

Development of confidence in students to monitor, evaluate and control their own learning is an important aspect of the learning process. The range of logits for *responsibility for learning* was from -0.87 to +0.08. Students indicated that they reflected upon their use of computers and made decisions about when and how to use computers. They also acknowledged that this use included making mistakes.

Computer use by students can enable self-expression. The range of logits for *self-expression* was from –0.80 to +0.25. The students perceived that computer use provided them with choice and freedom to work on topics of interest that were not boring. However they were less certain about how this use affected their life and view of the world. There is a strong indication that expressive and creative use of computers in the classroom may not necessarily equate with self-expression and creativity outside of the classroom.

Assessment is a fundamental aspect of learning and how work produced with computers is assessed can be different from traditional assessment methods. The range of logits for *assessment* was from +0.43 to +0.88. The positive logits show students considered that the teacher marking work stored electronically, marking each other's computer work and marking their own computer work were not common practices in their classrooms.

In general, students were positive about how computers were used in learning and affirmed that computers were used in classrooms for this purpose. They were more certain about retrieving information, cooperative learning and taking responsibility for learning than for self-expression and assessment procedures.

Student Reported Teacher Attitudes and Behaviours

Teacher attitudes and behaviours towards ICT instruction were hypothesised to comprise teacher-student negotiation of computer use, teacher recognition of student ability and teacher encouragement of students. When students are working on computers, they are engaged with the computer and are somewhat independent of the teacher. This independence can allow more flexible learning but too much independence could be viewed as lack of teacher concern and support for individual students and their learning.

Decisions about how computers are used in the classroom can be negotiated between the teacher and the students. The range of logits for *teacher-student negotiation of computer use* was from –0.31 to +0.33. The students considered that teachers should involve them in deciding about computer use and that their teachers did listen to their views on this matter. However they were less certain about teachers actively seeking these views.

The range of activities available in computer learning is diverse and requires varying levels of student ICT competence and motivation. It is important for teachers to understand the level of competence of each student and to ensure that the difficulty of computer tasks assigned to individual students does not exceed their competence. The range of logits for *teacher recognition of student ability* was from –0.69 to +0.04. The students indicated that their teachers were aware of their ICT ability and provided work that was of personal interest. On the other hand, they were less sure about whether this work actually suited their own specific capabilities and needs.

Teacher support and encouragement of students should be an integral part of instruction, particularly when students are using new technology or new ICT applications. The range of logits for *teacher encouragement of students* was from –0.51 to +0.53. The students expected that teachers would ensure that computer work was enjoyable. The students affirmed that their teachers did ensure that this work was enjoyable. While they recognised that teachers were generally supportive, they did not affirm that this support was necessarily provided for individual students.

The overall view of teacher attitudes and behaviours towards ICT instruction is that teachers were aware of the need to negotiate with students, aware of student computer competence and interests, and provided encouragement for students. The students considered their teachers to know how to tailor instruction to meet student needs. However they did not affirm that this knowledge was applied to meet the specific needs of individual students.

Student Reported Attitudes and Behaviours towards ICT Networks

The computers in most local schools and many classrooms are part of school and global communication networks. These networks provide increased opportunities for learning and interaction with others. Use of ICT networks within the classroom has the capacity to dissolve the physical boundaries around the classroom. In turn and this may influence the social dynamics within the classroom in various comprehensive ways. The hypothesised elements of attitudes and behaviours towards ICT networks were intranet use, Internet relationships and Internet collaboration.

In schools with intranets, the connections between computers within the classroom, in other classrooms, in specialist facilities such as resource centres, and in offices are used for communication and information sharing. The logits for the two *intranet use* items were –0.07 and +0.36. Students were slightly positively disposed towards using computers for communication in schools but not sure about this leading to more effective communication.

Internet relationships can be developed by participation in Internet ‘chat rooms’ and using email. While these facilities are freely available to the public, their use in schools is usually restricted. The range of logits for *Internet relationships* was +0.20 to +0.70. Students did not affirm using the Internet for personal reasons such as developing friendships and mutually supportive relationships. Whether or not this result is due to the restrictions on this communication or to students being negatively disposed towards Internet relationships cannot be ascertained from these results.

Internet collaboration concerns students using the Internet for learning and instructional purposes, to find useful information and to share information with others. The range of logits for *Internet collaboration* was from +0.44 to +0.88. Students did not affirm that they needed to use this facility and their use of it was not seen to be common.

The general finding about student attitudes and behaviours towards ICT network use is that the students were negatively disposed towards using these networks.

Student Reported Home ICT Attitudes and Behaviours

The home ICT environment and the support of parents for their child’s ICT learning at home were hypothesised to constitute the home influence on ICT learning. The home ICT environment includes the availability of computers and the use and attitudes towards using computers. The range of logits for the *home ICT environment* items was from –0.43 to +0.68. Students considered that having this technology in the home was important for their family but were less sure about their family fully exploiting the potential applications of the technology. They did not affirm that progress at school was related to parental interest in their computer use or that successful students came from homes with computers.

The *parent support of ICT learning* items provided more information on parental involvement. The range of logits for these items was from -0.24 to +0.91. While students expected their parents to take an interest in their computer work, they did not affirm that their parents encouraged them to complete homework on the computer, helped them with this homework, or required them to use the computer for homework.

The general finding therefore, is that whilst students considered having ICT in the home was important, they did not acknowledge the availability of this home technology to be related to success at school, or that their parents expected them to use this technology for completing homework.

Student Reported Values Towards ICT at School

Two of the items on valuing ICT use at school sought student views on whether computers improved the quality and rate of completion of their schoolwork. The logits for these items were -0.17 and 0.00. This shows that students were uncertain about the utility of computers for improving their schoolwork. The other two items concerned the preference for more time on computers at school and the use of computers in making school less boring. The logits for these items were +0.19 and +0.29. The students did not affirm that more computer use at school would make school better for them or that school would be less boring without computers. These findings question assumptions about computer use increasing student productivity and student interest in school.

Conclusion

The study sought to develop a measure of classroom ICT learning culture incorporating attitudes, behaviours and educational outcomes. The scale development process was rigorous as evidenced by the initial conceptualisation of the phenomenon and the multiple tests used in scale refinement and validation. As a result, the items were calibrated, the scale was interval level, the data fitted the hypothesised model, and the trait being measured was uni-dimensional.

Examination of the psychometric properties of the data provided information on how students viewed their classroom ICT learning culture. Students generally affirmed positive attitudes and behaviours towards the use of computers in their learning. Students affirmed that teachers had an awareness of their obligation to meet student needs but did not affirm that teachers always did this. The students were not positively disposed towards ICT networks or towards their use of these networks. Students affirmed that homes should have ICT facilities but did not affirm the importance of this home technology for success at school. They also failed to affirm the involvement of parents in using computers for homework. The final finding was that students were uncertain about computer use at school improving their schoolwork and did not affirm that this use made school more interesting for them.

Further development of the scale could include writing and testing new items to replace items eliciting data that did not fit the model. Also, the generalisability of the findings about classroom ICT learning culture could be improved by replicating the study with a larger sample.

References

Anderson, C.S. (1982) The search for school climate: a review of the research. *Review of Educational Research*, 52(3), 368-420.

Anderson, E.E. & Dexter, S.L. (2000). School technology leadership: Incidence and impact. Berkley, California: Center for Research on Information Technology and Organizations. [Online] *Available http:/www.crito.uci.edu/tlc/html/findings/html*

Andrews, R. (2002). A hard road to measure. *The Times Educational Supplement*, 4478, 16.

Andrich, D., Sheridan, B., Lyne, A. & Luo, G. (2000). *RUMM: a windows-based item analysis program employing Rasch unidimensional measurement models*. Perth: Murdoch University.

Anonymous. (2002). ICT used to promote pupils' creativity across the curriculum. *Micromath*, 18(2), 19-20.

Anonymous. (2002). Editorial: the impact of ICT on learning. *Journal of Computer Assisted Learning*, 18(1), 1.

Baggott la Velle, L. (2002). 'Virtual' teaching, real learning? *Journal of Biological Education,* 36(2), 56-57.

Bandura, A. (1977). Self-Efficacy: Toward a unified theory of behavioural change. *Psychological Review*, 84, 191-215.

Battistitch, V., Solomon D., Watson, M. & Schaps, E. (1997). Caring school communities. *Educational Psychologist*, 32(3), 137-151.

Blumenfield, P.C., Marx, R.W., Patrick, H., Krajcik, J., & Soloway, E. (1997). Teaching for understanding. Biddle, B.G., Good, T.L. & Goodson, I. F. (eds), *International handbook of teachers and teaching*. Dordrecht; Boston: Kluwer Academic Publishers.

Boden, M. (2001). Creativity and Knowledge. Creativity in Education Craft, A.B., Jeffrey, B. & Leibling, M.(eds). *Creativity in Education*. London, UK: Continuum Press.

Bradshaw, L.K. (2002). Technology for Teaching and Learning: Strategies for Staff Development and Follow-Up Support. *Journal of Technology and Teacher Education*, 10(1), 131 -150.

Bransford, J.D., Donovan, S.M. & Pellegrino, J.W. (2000). *How people Learn: Brain, Mind, Experience and School*. Washington, DC: National Academy Press.

Brown, J.S., Collins, A. & Duguid, P. (1989). Situated cognition and the culture of learning. *Educational Researcher*, 18, 1, 32–42.

Cavanagh, R. F. (1997). *The culture and improvement of Western Australian senior secondary schools*. Unpublished doctoral dissertation. Curtin University: Western Australia.

Cavanagh, R. F., Dellar, G. B., Ellett, C. D. & Rugutt, J.K. (2000). *Development of an instrument for investigating classroom culture. Paper presented at the 2000 Annual Meeting of the American Educational Research Association.*

Cavanagh, R.F. & Dellar, G.B. (2003). Organisational and learning community conceptions of schools: implications for understanding and researching school improvement. In: *On the Forefront of educational psychology*, R.F.Waugh (Ed.). New York: Nova Science.

Cavanagh, R.F., Waugh, R.F. & Dellar, G.B. (2003). *The culture, outcomes and improvement of secondary school classrooms. Paper presented at the 2003 Annual Meeting of the American Educational Research Association: Chicago.*

Chan, B.K.K., Hodgkiss, I.J. &Chan, R.Y.P. (2002). A distributed learning model for freshwater ecology practical classes. *Journal of Computer Assisted Learning*, 18(3).

Chiu, C.H. (2002). The effects of collaborative teamwork on secondary science. *Journal of Computer Assisted Learning*, 18(3).

Coleman, P. (1998). *Parent, student and teacher collaboration: the power of three*. Corwin Press Inc: California.

Collins, A., Brown, J.S. & Newman, S.E. (1989). *Cognitive Apprenticeship: Teaching the crafts of reading, writing and mathematics. Resnick, L. (ed). Knowing, learning and instruction: Essays in honor of Robert Glaser. Mahwah, NJ: Lawrence Erlbaum.*

Collins, E. & Green, J.L. (1992). Learning in classroom settings: making or breaking a culture. Marshall, H.H. (ed). *Redefining student learning: Roots of educational change.* Norwood, N.J: Ablex.

Comber, C., Colley, A., Hargreaves, D.J., & Dom, L. (1997). The effects of age, gender and computer experience upon computer attitudes. *Educational Research*, 39(2), 123-133.

Conlon, T. (1999). Critical thinking required or seven deadly sins of information technology. *Scottish Affairs*, 28.

Cronin, P. (1997). *Report on the applications of virtual reality technology to education. Doctoral dissertation*. University of Edinburgh.

Curriculum Council. (1997). *Curriculum Framework. Perth: Curriculum Council of Western Australia.*

Dalin, P., Rolff, H. & Kleekamp, B. (1993). *Changing the school culture*. London: Cassell.

Davies, C. & Birmingham, P. (2002). Using ICT to enhance the learning experience in the classroom. *Education Libraries Journal*, 45(1), 17.

DEST. (2001). School innovation pathway to the knowledge society. [On-line] Available *http://www.dest.gov.au/schools/publications/2001/innovation/index.htm*

Donahoe, T. (1993). Finding the way: structure, time and culture in school improvement. *Phi Delta Kappan*, 75(4), 298-306.

Dreher, H. (1997). *Empowering human cognitive activity through hypertext technology. Doctoral dissertation, Curtin University of Technology, Perth, Western Australia.*

Durndell, A., Glissov, P., & Siann, G. (1995). Gender and computing: Persisting differences. *Educational Research*, 37(3), 219-227.

Ewing, J. (2000). Enhancement of online and offline student learning. *Educational Media International*, 37(4), 205-217.

Foote, K. E. (1999). Bringing faculty online: Inspiring and sustaining innovation in information and computer technologies (ICT). *Journal of Geography in Higher Education*, 23(1), 5-7.

Fullan, M.G. (1993). *Change forces probing the depths of educational reform*. London: The Falmer Press.

Gardner, L., Sheridan, D. & White, D. (2002). A web-based learning and assessment system to support flexible education. *Journal of Computer Assisted Learning*, 18(2).

Glickman, C.D. (1992). The essence of school renewal: The prose has begun. *Educational Leadership*, 50 (1).

Good, T. L. & Brophy, J. E. (2000). *Looking in classrooms* (8th ed.). New York, NY: Addison Wesley.

Goodison, T.A. (2002). Learning with ICT at primary level: pupils' perceptions. *Journal of Computer Assisted Learning*, 18(3).

Griffiths, M.D. & Davies, M.N.O. (2002). Research note: Excessive online computer gaming: implications for education. *Journal of Computer Assisted Learning*, 18(3).

Halsall, R. (1998). School improvement: an overview of key findings and messages. Halsall, R. (ed). *Teacher research and school improvement: opening doors from the inside*. Buckingham: Open University press.

Harasim. L.M. (1996). Computer networking for education. De Corte, E. & Weinert, F.E. (eds.). *International Encyclopedia of Developmental and Instructional Psychology*. New York, NY: Pergamon Press.

Hargreaves, A. (2003). *Teaching in the knowledge society: Education in the age of insecurity*. New York: Teachers College Press.

Harris, A. (2001). Contemporary perspectives on school effectiveness and school improvement. Harris, A. & Bennett, N. (eds). *School effectiveness and improvement: alternative perspectives*. London: Continuum.

Hillis, P. (2002). Using ICT to enhance the teaching and learning of history in Scottish schools. *History Computer Review*, 18(1), 11-16.

Huber, B. & Schofield, J.W. (1998). "I like computers, but many girls don't": Gender and the sociocultural context of computing. In Bromley, H. & Apple, M.W. (eds.), *Education/Technology/Power: Educational computing as a social practice*, (pp. 103-132). Albany, NY: State University of New York Press.

Issroff, K. & Scanlon, E. (2002). Using technology in higher education: An activity theory perspective. *Journal of Computer Assisted Learning*, 18(1).

Jeronen, Eila (2001). Assessing technology based instruction in biology and geography. *Computers in the Schools*, 18(4), 199-212.

Johnson, C. (2002). And the lesson today is… *The Times Educational Supplement*, 4467, 18.

Johnson, D.W., Johnson, R.T. & Maruyama, G. (1983) Interdependence and interpersonal attraction among heterogeneous individuals: A theoretical formulation and a meta-analysis of the research. *Review of Educational Research*, 53(1), 5–54.

Johnson, D.W., Johnson, R.T. & Stanne, M.B. (2000). Cooperative learning methods: A meta-analysis. Minneapolis: Cooperative Learning Center. [On-line] Available *http://www.clcrc.com/pages/cl-methods.html*

Kenny, J. (2002). Suite success in the primaries. *The Times Educational Supplement*, 4481, T26-T27.

Latham, A. (1998). Strategic information systems planning: a necessary evil for schools? *Journal of Applied Management Studies*, 7(2), 267-275.

Law, N., Lee, Y. & Chow, A. (2002). Practice characteristics that lead to 21st century learning outcomes. *Journal of Computer Assisted Learning*, 18(4).

Lingard, B. (2001). Some lessons for educational researchers: repositioning research in education and education in research. *The Australian Educational Researcher*, 28(3), 1-46.

Lockyer, L., Patterson, J. & Harper, B. (2002). ICT in higher education: evaluating outcomes for health education. *Journal of Computer Assisted Learning*, 17(3).

Loveless, A. (2000). *Creativity, visual literacy and information and communications technology.* Watson, D.M & Downes, T. (eds). Communications and Networking in Education: Learning in a Networked Society. Norwell, MA: Kluwer Academic Press.

Lynch, W., Hobbs, B. & Hollanders, H. (1999). Dancing on quicksand: The role of the ICT co-ordinator in the primary school. *Research in Education*, 62, 32.

Mavers, D., Somekh, B. & Restorick, J. (2002). Interpreting the externalized images of pupils' conceptions of ICT: methods for the analysis of concept maps. *Computers and Education*, 38(1/3), 187-207.

Maxwell, T. W. & Thomas, A. R. (1991). School climate and school culture. *Journal of Educational Administration*, 29(2), 72-82.

McCall, J., Smith, I., Stoll, L., Thomas, S., Sammons, P., Smees, R., MacBeath, J., Boyd, B. & MacGilchrist, B. (2001). *Views of pupils, parents and teachers: vital indicators of effectiveness and for improvement.* MacBeath, J. & Mortimore, P. (eds). Improving school effectiveness. Buckingham: Open University press.

McDougall, A. (2002). Guest editorial: Assessing learning with ICT. *Journal of Computer Assisted Learning*, 17(3).

MCEETYA. (2000). *The Adelaide Declaration on National Goals for Schooling in the Twenty-first Century. Carlton South, Victoria: MCEETYA.*

Mitchell, J. T. & Willower, D. J. (1992). Organisational culture in a good high school. *Journal of Educational Administration*, 30(1), 6-16.

Morris, E.J., Joiner, R., & Scanlon, E. (2002). The contribution of computer-based activities to understanding statistics. *Journal of Computer Assisted Learning*, 18(2).

Moundridou, M. & Virvou, M. (2002). Evaluating the persona effect of an interface agent in a tutoring system. *Journal of Computer Assisted Learning*, 18(3).

NCET (1994). Information Technology works. Coventry: NCET.

Newton, D. P. & Newton, L. D. (2001). Choosing and judging teachers: What heads and student teachers think matters. *Research in Education*, 66, 54.

Oliver, M., MacBean, J., Conole, G. & Harvey, J. (2002). Using a toolkit to support the evaluation of learning. *Journal of Computer Assisted Learning*, 18(2).

Openheimer, Todd (1997). The computer delusion. The Atlantic Monthly, Digital Edition. [On-line] *Available http:www.theatlantic.com/issues/97jul/computer.htm.*

Pelgrum, W.J. (2001). Obstacles to the integration of ICT in education: results from a worldwide educational assessment. *Computers and Education*, 37(2), 163-178.

Pena, R.A. & Amrein, A.L. (1999). Classroom management and caring: a primer for administrators and teachers. *International Electronic Journal for Leadership in Learning*, 3(24).

Popolov, D., Callaghan, M., & Luke, P. (2002). Tying models of learning to design of collaborative learning software tools. *Journal of Computer Assisted Learning*, 18(1).

Ralston, L. (2002). Online skills program preps students for IT training. *What Works in Teaching and Learning*, 34(16), 1-2.

Resnick, L.B. (1987). *Education and learning to think*. Washington, DC: National Academy Press.

Reynolds, P., Cavanagh, R.F. & Dellar, G.B. (2003). *Orienting dialogues concerning school renewal. Paper presented at the 2003 Annual Meeting of the Australian Association for Research in Education: Auckland.*

Seltzer, K. & Bentley, T. (2001). *The creative age: Knowledge and skills for the new economy*. London, UK: Demos Publishing.

Selwyn, N. (2000). Creating a "connected" community? Teachers' use of an electronic discussion group. *Teachers College Record*, 102(4).

Selwyn, N., Marriott, N. & Marriott, P. (2002). Home computers and university ICT use. *Journal of Computer Assisted Learning*, 18(1).

Sergiovanni, T. J. (1992). Why we should seek substitutes for leadership. *Educational Leadership.* 49(5), 41-45.

Sergiovanni, T.J. (2000). *The life world of leadership: creating culture, community, and personal meaning in our schools*. San Francisco: Jossey-Bass Publishers.

Slavin, R.E. (1983). *Cooperative learning*. New York, NY: Longman Publishing.

Smeets, E. & Mooij, T. (2001). Pupil-centred learning, ICT, and teacher behaviour: observations in educational practice. *British Journal of Educational Technology*, 32(4), 403-417.

SPSS. (2001). *SPSS version 11. Chicago: SPSS Inc.*

Stoll, L. & Mortimer, P. (1995). *Viewpoint no 2: School effectiveness and school improvement.* London: Institute of Education.

Stoll, L., MacBeath, J. & Mortimore, P. (2001). *Beyond 2000: where next for effectiveness and improvement*. MacBeath, J. & Mortimore, P. (eds). Improving school effectiveness. Buckingham: Open University press.

Sung, W.T. & Ou, S.C. (2002). Web-based learning in the computer-aided design curriculum. *Journal of Computer Assisted Learning*, 18(2).

Tolmie, A. (2002). Examining learning in relation to the contexts of use of ICT. *Journal of Computer Assisted Learning*, 17(3).

Tolmie, A., Howe, C.J., Duchak-Tanner, V., & Rattray, C. (1999) *Explicit and implicit support for procedural learning within collaborative group work in science. Ninth European Conference on Developmental Psychology: Spetses, Greece.*

Torgerson, C.J. & Elbourne, D. (2002). A systematic review and meta-analysis of the effectiveness of informat communication technology (ICT) on the teaching of spelling. *Journal of Research in Reading*, 25(2), 129-143.

Turkle, S. (1995). *Life on the Screen: Identity in the Age of the Internet*. New York, NY: Simon and Shuster, Inc.

Volman, M. (1997). Gender-related effects of information and computer literacy education. *Journal of Curriculum Studies*, 29(3), 315-328.

Volman, M. (2001). Gender equity and information technology in education: The second decade. *Review of Educational Research*, 71(4), 613-634.

Watson, S.B. (1992). The essential elements of cooperative learning. *American Biology Teacher*, 54(2), 84-86.

Watts, M., Lloyd, C. & Jackson, C. (2001). ICT in the literacy hour: Studying a classroom innovation. *Research in Education*, 66 (84).

Waugh, R.F. & Cavanagh, R.F. (2002). Measuring parent receptivity towards the classroom environment using a Rasch measurement model. *Journal of Learning Environments Research,* 5 (3), 329-352.

Waugh, R.F. & Cavanagh, R.F. (2003). Linking classroom environment with educational outcomes using a Rasch measurement model. In: *On the Forefront of Educational Psychology*, R.F. Waugh (Ed.), (pp.257-283). New York: Nova Science Publishers.

Wheeler, S., Waite, S.J., & Bromfield, C. (2002). Promoting creative thinking through the use of ICT. *Journal of Computer Assisted Learning*, 18(3).

Wild, M. (1989). *History and new technologies in schools: Problems, possibilities and the way forward.* Denley, P. Fogelvik, S. & Harvey, C. (eds.), History and Computing II. Manchester: Manchester University Press.

Young, R, & Ramsden, A. (2002). ICT on line. *Teaching Business and Economics*, 6(1), 34.

Zandvliet, D.B. (1999). *The physical and psychological environment associated with classrooms using information technologies: a cross-national study. Doctoral dissertation, Curtin University of Technology, Perth, Western Australia.*

Zhang, J. (2002). Incorporating ICT into K-12 schools: China's perspective in the global backgrounds. *TechTrends,* 46(4), 49.

Appendix A. Item Locations, Standard Errors, Residuals and Fit to the Model

Item	Location	SE	Residual	DegFree	DatPts	Chi Sq	Prob
Sub-group: Student reported learning attitudes and behaviours (22 items)							
Information retrieval							
1	-1.00	0.07	0.63	428.9	439	10.5	0.11
2	-0.95	0.07	-0.09	428.9	439	3.9	0.68
3	-0.84	0.07	0.09	428.9	439	5.1	0.53
4	-0.10	0.06	1.75	428.9	439	3.4	0.75
Cooperative learning							
5	-0.82	0.07	1.42	428.9	439	8.8	0.19
6	-0.58	0.07	1.30	428.9	439	5.9	0.43
7	-0.45	0.06	1.01	428.9	439	4.8	0.56
8	-0.35	0.06	1.76	428.9	439	2.8	0.84
9	-0.33	0.06	-0.23	428.9	439	4.7	0.58

Appendix A. (Continued)

Item	Location	SE	Residual	DegFree	DatPts	Chi Sq	Prob
Sub-group: Student reported learning attitudes and behaviours (22 items)							
Responsibility for learning							
10	-0.87	0.07	-0.16	428.9	439	2.1	0.91
11	-0.56	0.07	2.07	428.9	439	20.4	0.00
12	-0.50	0.06	1.33	428.9	439	5.8	0.44
13	-0.32	0.06	0.96	428.9	439	6.4	0.38
14	-0.29	0.06	2.11	428.9	439	15.8	0.01
15	0.08	0.06	0.19	428.9	439	8.1	0.23
Self-expression							
16	-0.80	0.07	0.30	428.9	439	6.0	0.42
17	-0.42	0.06	1.50	428.9	439	6.1	0.41
18	0.03	0.06	-0.30	428.9	439	7.2	0.30
19	0.25	0.06	-0.24	428.9	439	7.5	0.27
Assessment							
20	0.43	0.05	1.60	428.9	439	5.8	0.44
21	0.85	0.06	1.46	428.9	439	3.8	0.70
22	0.88	0.06	1.61	428.9	439	5.0	0.55
Teacher-student negotiation of computer use							
23	-0.31	0.07	0.49	428.9	439	6.7	0.35
24	-0.31	0.06	-1.05	428.9	439	20.1	0.00
25	-0.30	0.06	0.64	428.9	439	2.9	0.82
26	-0.12	0.06	0.73	428.9	439	2.0	0.92
27	0.35	0.06	0.84	428.9	439	5.2	0.51
Teacher recognition of student ability							
28	-0.69	0.06	1.62	428.9	439	5.9	0.43
29	-0.14	0.06	0.73	428.9	439	2.7	0.84
30	0.04	0.06	0.50	428.9	439	6.0	0.42
31	0.04	0.06	2.08	428.9	439	0.7	0.99
Teacher encouragement of students							
32	-0.51	0.06	0.17	428.9	439	3.0	0.81
33	-0.06	0.06	-0.25	428.9	439	4.9	0.56
34	0.12	0.06	0.69	428.9	439	4.8	0.57
35	0.53	0.06	1.48	428.9	439	4.9	0.55
Sub-group: Student reported attitudes and behaviours towards ICT networks (13 items)							
Intranet use							
36	-0.07	0.05	0.27	428.9	439	5.6	0.47
37	0.36	0.05	0.04	428.9	439	7.5	0.28

Appendix A. (Continued

Internet relationships							
38	0.20	0.06	0.82	428.9	439	0.9	0.99
39	0.38	0.05	0.08	428.9	439	2.2	0.90
40	0.46	0.06	-0.46	428.9	439	4.2	0.65
41	0.51	0.05	0.59	428.9	439	4.2	0.65
42	0.70	0.06	0.48	428.9	439	2.8	0.83
Internet collaboration							
43	0.44	0.05	-0.23	428.9	439	6.1	0.41
44	0.45	0.06	-0.81	428.9	439	3.6	0.73
45	0.60	0.05	-1.32	428.9	439	4.9	0.56
46	0.64	0.05	0.62	428.9	439	11.0	0.09
47	0.72	0.06	-0.10	428.9	439	6.5	0.37
48	0.88	0.06	-0.10	428.9	439	13.3	0.04
Sub-group: Student reported home ICT attitudes and behaviours (10 items)							
Home ICT environment							
49	-0.43	0.06	0.45	428.9	439	3.3	0.77
50	-0.22	0.05	0.27	428.9	439	3.0	0.80
51	-0.06	0.05	-0.14	428.9	439	6.2	0.40
52	-0.05	0.06	-0.83	428.9	439	3.4	0.75
53	0.50	0.05	-1.19	428.9	439	10.9	0.09
54	0.68	0.05	-0.42	428.9	439	8.6	0.20
Parent support for ICT learning							
55	-0.24	0.06	-0.66	428.9	439	15.7	0.02
56	0.11	0.06	-0.85	428.9	439	7.8	0.25
57	0.26	0.06	0.30	428.9	439	5.2	0.52
58	0.91	0.06	-0.98	428.9	439	8.5	0.21
Sub-group: Student reported values towards ICT at school (4 items)							
Valuing ICT use at school							
59	-0.17	0.06	-0.58	428.9	439	9.3	0.15
60	0.00	0.06	-0.01	428.9	439	8.0	0.24
61	0.19	0.05	-0.17	428.9	439	7.3	0.29
62	0.29	0.05	0.57	428.9	439	4.1	0.66

Notes

1. Location (degree to which students provided affirmation) is measured in logits (log odds of answering positively).
2. SE is the standard error in logits.
3. Residual is the difference between the actual student response and the expected response, according to the model. The closer to zero the residual, the better the fit to the model.
4. The probability of fit to the model is tested statistically with a Chi-square. Chi-square is sensitive to sample size and is not to be taken too literally with a large sample of 439.

Appendix B. Questionnaire: Student Views of Learning Through Use of Information and Communications Technology

This questionnaire is anonymous. Please don't put your name or any identification on it. Please read the consent and cover page.

Please rate the 62 items according to the following response format and place a number corresponding to the format on the appropriate line opposite each statement:

Response categories

Strongly agree	put 4
Agree	put 3
Disagree	put 2
Strongly disagree	put 1

Appendix B. Questionnaire

Sub-group: Student reported learning attitudes and behaviours (22 items)		
Information retrieval		
1	Using the computer helps me find the right answers to questions	-1.00
2	I use the computer to find answers to questions	-0.95
3	I enjoy using the computer to find answers to questions	-0.84
4	Using the computer gives the best answers to questions	-0.10
Cooperative learning		
5	Working together on computers should be a happy experience for everyone	-0.82
6	Learning on computers works best when students show care for each other	-0.58
7	We talk about what we are doing on the computer	-0.45
8	The best learning with computers happens when students work together	-0.35
9	We share our computer knowledge	-0.33
Responsibility for learning		
10	Using the computer lets me learn in different ways from other types of schoolwork	-0.87
11	By working alone, I find new ways to use the computer	-0.56
12	I think about how I use the computer	-0.50
13	I need to be able to use computers	-0.32
14	I never start work on the computer until I am sure about what I will be doing	-0.29
15	I rarely make mistakes using computers	+0.08
Self-expression		
16	Using the computer gives me freedom to do what pleases me	-0.80
17	The computer lets me escape from things that are boring or not interesting	-0.42
18	My life has become more interesting by using the computer.	+0.03
19	I see the world differently when I use the computer	+0.25

Appendix B. Questionnaire (Continued)

Sub-group: Student reported learning attitudes and behaviours (22 items)		
Assessment		
20	The teacher marks my work while it is still in the computer	+0.43
21	We mark each other's computer work	+0.85
22	We mark our own computer work	+0.88
Sub-group: Student reported teacher attitudes and behaviours (13 items)		
Teacher-student negotiation of computer use		
1	Students should be asked by the teacher in deciding how computers will be used	-0.31
2	Students can help the teacher plan how computers will be used	-0.31
3	We talk with the teacher about what is required in computer work	-0.30
4	The teacher listens to our views on marking our computer work	-0.12
5	In this class, the teacher asks the students how they would like to use computers	+0.35
Teacher recognition of student ability		
6	My teacher should know what I can do and can't do on the computer	-0.69
7	The work the teacher asks me to do on the computer is interesting for me	-0.14
8	The work the teacher asks me to do on the computer is just right for me	+0.04
9	The work the teacher asks me to do on the computer meets my own needs	+0.04
Teacher encouragement of students		
10	Teachers must make sure all students enjoy computer work	-0.51
11	The teacher makes sure I enjoy using the computer	-0.06
12	The teacher makes me feel good when I use the computer	+0.12
13	The teacher gives me special help with the computer	+0.53
Sub-group: Student reported attitudes and behaviours towards ICT networks (13 items)		
Intranet use		
1	Schools should make more use of computers for communication	-0.07
2	Communication within the school is improved by using computers	+0.36
Internet relationships		
3	Everyone should use the Internet to communicate with friends	+0.20
4	I use the Internet to share my ideas and feelings with others	+0.38
5	I use the Internet to help others	+0.46
6	Everyone should use the Internet to find new friends	+0.51
7	I use the Internet to share my problems with others	+0.70
Internet collaboration		
8	I need information that can only come from special groups or organisations on the Internet	+0.44
9	Everyone should use the Internet to find new people to work with	+0.45
10	I provide information to others on the Internet	+0.60
11	I often receive messages from groups or organisations on the Internet	+0.64
12	I share information with others who belong to groups or organisations on the Internet	+0.72
13	Being a member of groups or organisations on the Internet is important for me	+0.88
Sub-group: Student reported home ICT attitudes and behaviours (10 items)		
Home ICT environment		
1	Having a computer at home is important for my family	-0.43
2	Every family should have at least one computer	-0.22
3	My parent(s) use a home cmputer	-0.06
4	My family is finding new ways to use computers	-0.05
5	Students who do well at school have parents who take an interest in their computer work	+0.50
6	Students who do well at school come from homes with computers	+0.68

Parent support for ICT learning		
7	My parent(s) should take an interest in my computer work	-0.24
8	My parent(s) encourage me to complete homework on a computer	+0.11
9	My parent(s) help me to use a computer to complete homework	+0.26
10	My parent(s) make me use a computer for homework	+0.91
Sub-group: Student reported values towards ICT at school (4 items)		
Valuing ICT use at school		
1	Computers improve the quality of my schoolwork	-0.17
2	Computers help me get my work done more quickly	+0.00
3	More time using computers would make school better for me	+0.19
4	School would be boring without computers	+0.29

Notes:

1. Item difficulties on the RHS are in logits.
2. The difficulties of the items in each sub-group increase vertically down in correspondence with the conceptual design of the items from anticipated 'common' to 'uncommon' student views (in nearly all cases).
3. The standard errors vary from 0.05 to 0.07 logits.

In: Anxiety in College Students
Editor: Benjamin Ayres and Michelle Bristow
ISBN: 978-1-60692-282-8

Chapter II

Social Anxiety in the College Student Population: The Role of Anxiety Sensitivity

*Angela Sailer and Holly Hazlett-Stevens**
University of Nevada,
Reno Nevada, USA

Abstract

Most college students experience some degree of social anxiety on occasion. However, many suffer chronic anxiety across social situations coupled with a strong fear of negative evaluation. In addition to impaired occupational and social functioning, severe social anxiety or social phobia can carry profound consequences for college students. Social anxiety is a prominent motivation for college student drinking (Burke and Stephens, 1999). In addition to social isolation, social anxiety is associated with depressogenic cognitions, both of which leave socially anxious students at an increased risk for depression (Johnson et al., 1992). Anxiety sensitivity – fear of anxiety-related sensations due to perceived consequences of physical, mental, or social harm – might play an important role in the development of social anxiety (Hazen et al., 1995). Unlike panic disorder, in which individuals typically fear anxiety symptoms out of fear of physical harm or loss of mental control, socially anxious individuals fear perceived social consequences of others noticing their anxiety. Socially anxious college students also judge others who appear anxious more negatively than do college students without social anxiety (Purdon et al., 2001). Although panic disorder treatments target anxiety sensitivity directly with interoceptive exposure strategies, this approach is just beginning to receive attention for the treatment of social anxiety. After a brief review of the literature describing the nature of social anxiety among college students, this chapter will

* Correspondence concerning this article should be addressed to Holly Hazlett-Stevens, University of Nevada, Department of Psychology/298 Reno, NV 89557, or the author can be reached via email at: hhazlett@unr.edu

examine the specific role of anxiety sensitivity in its development and maintenance. Finally, results from a preliminary investigation comparing the effects of interoceptive exposure delivered in a social context to social context exposure without the interoceptive component will be presented and discussed.

Introduction

Many college students find interpersonal relationships stressful (Santiago-Rivera, Gard, and Bernstein, 1999) and anywhere from twenty to fifty percent of college students report shyness (Durand and Barlow, 2006). A smaller percentage of students suffer from a more serious clinical condition known as social phobia. Lifetime prevalence estimates for this anxiety disorder are as high as 13.3% in the general population (Kessler et al., 1994). Diagnostic criteria for social phobia, generalized type (also known as social anxiety disorder) include a "marked and persistent fear" of social situations in which the individual fears acting in a way that will be humiliating or embarrassing (DSM-IV-TR; American Psychiatric Association, 2000). Exposure to feared social situations almost always provokes an anxiety response. These situations are either endured with intense discomfort or avoided altogether, resulting in significant functional impairment and/or distress.

Social anxiety is maintained by unreasonably high standards for social performance coupled with views that others perceive oneself as inadequate and that such perceptions are valid (Clark and Wells, 1995; Rapee and Heimberg, 1997). Individuals with social phobia also tend to rely heavily upon internal cues as an indication of whether or not a social situation is going well (Clark and Wells, 1995). Thus, individuals assume that if they feel anxious in a social interaction, this is indicative of poor performance. When compared to control samples, individuals with social anxiety disorder experience higher negative affect and judge their quality of life lower (Davidson, Hughes, George, and Blazer, 1994; Safren, Heimberg, Brown, and Holle, 1997). Ineffective coping strategies such as drinking and social isolation may be especially problematic in the college setting.

We begin this chapter with a literature review examining the nature and impact of social anxiety among college students. We then turn to an important construct in the anxiety disorders literature, anxiety sensitivity, which may play an important role in the development and maintenance of social phobia. An original research investigation comparing two different exposure approaches for socially anxious college students will be described, and suggestions for treatment and future research will be discussed.

Literature Review

Social Anxiety among College Students

Purdon, Antony, Monteiro, and Swinson (1999) investigated the nature of social anxiety in the college student population. In addition to the frequency of social anxiety symptoms experienced, they examined how the perception of anxiety in others influences immediate impressions of personal characteristics such as attractiveness and intelligence. A total of 81 undergraduate college students completed self-report measures of social anxiety and social desirability and rated how much their impressions of others are influenced when the other person appears anxious. Of the 81 college students surveyed, 15 reported elevated levels of social anxiety on clinical social phobia scales. Thirteen percent of the student participants experienced all 24 social anxiety symptoms listed on the Social Anxiety Symptoms Scale at least "rarely." In addition, a substantial majority of students experienced many of these anxiety symptoms in social situations at least once. Stomach "butterflies," general tension, desire to avoid the situation, trouble expressing oneself, and blushing were the most frequently reported social anxiety symptoms.

When asked about specific personal characteristics of those appearing anxious, most students indicated that if they noticed someone was anxious, their perception of the other's attractiveness, intelligence, compassion, ambition, reliability, and mental health would not be influenced. Over half the student participants did, however, indicate that their perception of an individual's leadership abilities and strength of character would be negatively influenced if the person in question was visibly anxious. Interestingly, the students reporting elevated social anxiety themselves were more likely to perceive others who show signs of anxiety as having less strength of character and as less attractive. Students with high levels of social anxiety also indicated that other individuals appearing anxious would be more compassionate than individuals who did not appear anxious. Overall, results from this investigation suggested that most college students experience social anxiety symptoms now and then and that negative attitudes towards those with social anxiety are prevalent, even among socially anxious individuals (Purdon et al., 1999). These authors also noted that individuals who are highly socially anxious may underestimate how often others become anxious as well as how visible the signs of anxiety are in others.

Another self-report study of social anxiety in college students was conducted by Lesure-Lester (2001). Questionnaire measures of social anxiety, dating competence, and social assertion were collected from 217 college students from different ethnic groups (African American, Asian American, European American, Mexican American, and multiracial). Relationships between dating competence, social assertion, and social anxiety as well as ethnic differences in these constructs were examined. Measures included the Dating and Assertion Questionnaire (DAQ; Levenson and Gottman, 1978), the Social Anxiety Thoughts Questionnaire (SAT; Hartman, 1984), and the Social Avoidance and Distress Scale (SAD; Watson and Friend, 1969). College students reporting greater competence at dating also reported a tendency to be more assertive in social situations and less socially anxious. No differences in reported dating competence and dating assertion were found among the various ethnic groups. Although these results suggested that low levels of social anxiety were associated with improved social assertiveness and competence, the relationship between social anxiety and actual social performance was not addressed with behavioral measures. Nevertheless, these results are consistent with previous research finding a negative relationship between self-reported social anxiety and self-reported assertiveness among college students (Chambless, Hunter, and Jackson, 1982). It is important to note that Chambless et al. also found that this observed relationship was weaker in their college student sample than their clinical social phobic sample.

Kashdan and Roberts (2004) investigated the impact of self-focused attention on affective, cognitive, and motivational disturbances during a reciprocal self-disclosure task. College students reporting either high or low levels of social anxiety were included to determine if high levels of self-focused attention and social threat would have more detrimental effects for students with high levels of social anxiety than for students reporting low levels of social anxiety. Ninety-one college students completed social anxiety measures prior to their participation in a reciprocal self-disclosure social interaction task. Participants were required to answer personal questions with a video camera pointed at them as well as to ask such questions while the camera pointed at a confederate. Results indicated that students reporting high levels of social anxiety experienced more negative and less positive affect than students with low social anxiety during both phases of the task. These group differences were greater when the camera was pointed at the participant. These findings suggested that the level of social threat as well as the degree of self-focused attention may contribute to the cognitive and affective difficulties reported by so many socially anxious individuals (Kashdan and Roberts, 2004).

The nature of "irrational" anxiety-provoking thoughts about social situations was examined with a small sample of socially anxious (n = 8) and nonanxious control (n = 15) undergraduate college students (Davison and Zighelboim, 1987). Socially anxious students articulated more irrational thoughts during a simulated social situation task than during a neutral task, and these students articulated more irrational thoughts than control participants during the experiment.

Social anxiety among college students may also be associated with more general cognitive distortions. Johnson, Johnson, and Petzel (1992) collected self-report measures of social anxiety as well as the Cognitive Distortion Questionnaire (CDQ; Krantz and Hammen, 1979) from 114 undergraduate psychology students. Results indicated that students reporting high levels of social anxiety endorsed more distressed-distorted responses than less socially anxious students even after depression and trait anxiety measures were used as covariates. Thus, cognitive disturbances for socially anxious college students may not be limited to the domain of social performance and interpersonal relationships. Depressed thinking about other areas of one's life, such as achievement, also appears to be elevated for these students. Not surprisingly, Johnson et al. concluded that social anxiety among young college students may be an important risk factor for the later development of clinical depression.

Results from these studies suggest that while most college students experience some symptoms of social anxiety from time to time, socially anxious college students exhibit negative beliefs about social situations and their social performance to a greater degree than their less socially anxious peers. Although it is unclear to what degree these beliefs reflect actual social performance deficits, socially anxious students may also hold more general negative beliefs about themselves and others. These students may be vulnerable to depression, not only because of the social isolation resulting from avoidance of social situations but also due to elevated general cognitive distortions associated with the development of depression.

One additional consequence of social anxiety may be particularly problematic for the college student population. In their review of the literature on social anxiety and drinking among college students, Burke and Stephens (1999) found that social anxiety is indeed a prominent motivation for college student heavy drinking. This relationship appears to be moderated by cognitive variables such as alcohol expectancies and social situation self-efficacy. As a result, these authors outlined a social cognitive model of college student drinking in which expectations about the effects of alcohol and beliefs in one's ability to avoid heavy drinking in the face of anxiety-provoking social situations are central. This model also suggests that social anxiety treatments may be crucial to the prevention and reduction of excessive drinking on college campuses.

In this next section, we discuss an important construct in anxiety disorders research known as *anxiety sensitivity*. A widely used self-report measure of this construct, the Anxiety Sensitivity Index (ASI; Reiss, Peterson, Gursky, and McNally, 1986), will be described. Anxiety sensitivity has received the most attention in panic disorder research. However, anxiety sensitivity may play a pivotal role in other anxiety disorders as well, including social anxiety disorder. We therefore review empirical investigations of anxiety sensitivity and social anxiety among college students before presenting our own empirical investigation.

Anxiety Sensitivity

Anxiety sensitivity – fear of anxiety-related sensations due to perceived consequences of physical, mental, or social harm – is considered an imperative factor in the maintenance and development of anxiety disorders (Reiss and McNally, 1985). This construct is much more specific than the previously proposed anxiety-related construct of *trait anxiety*. There is much variability in how prone people are to experience anxiety. Some individuals experience anxiety when minimally provoked, and others require much more stressful circumstances. Individual differences in how prone one is to experience anxiety is considered *trait anxiety* (Taylor, 1999). The tendency to see the world as dangerous or threatening or the tendency to become anxious across situations sums up the broad definition of trait anxiety (Beck and Emery, 1985). A more sophisticated conceptualization was offered in a hierarchical model of trait anxiety (Lilienfeld, Turner, and Jacob, 1993). In this model, anxiety consists of one higher-order factor, the general concept of trait anxiety, and three lower-order factors: anxiety sensitivity, fear of negative evaluation, and fear of illness or injury sensitivity. This model later received empirical support (Taylor, 1995). Anxiety sensitivity is conceptually different from trait anxiety in that anxiety sensitivity represents the tendency to fear or respond anxiously to arousal symptoms whereas trait anxiety refers to the tendency to have an anxious response to any stressor or stressors in general (Holloway and McNally, 1987). In sum, the development and severity of a variety of anxiety conditions is determined by three fundamental fears: negative evaluation, fear of injury or death, and anxiety sensitivity (Reiss and McNally, 1985; Reiss, 1991). According to the sensitivity theory of motivation, anxiety sensitivity is a genetically based aversion to anxiety that is combined with beliefs about the negative consequences of anxiety (Reiss and Havercamp, 1996).

Similar to how individuals vary in their proneness to experience anxiety, there is also variability in their fear of experiencing these symptoms. The construct of anxiety sensitivity represents the individual differences associated with the fear of anxiety (Reiss and McNally, 1985). Anxiety sensitivity is considered a predisposition that is a stable and trait-like characteristic (Taylor, 1999). Anxiety sensitivity refers to a fear of anxiety-related symptoms resulting from distressing thoughts or beliefs about the possible negative consequences of experiencing anxious sensations (Scott, Heimberg, and MacAndrew, 2000). For example, an individual with high anxiety sensitivity may view heart palpitations as an indication that he or she is having a heart attack, while an individual with low anxiety sensitivity would consider such an experience to be just uncomfortable or unpleasant (Taylor, 1999). In addition to fearing anxiety-related sensations because of feared imminent physical or mental complications, other individuals may fear these sensations out of social evaluative concerns.

Anxiety Sensitivity Index

The Anxiety Sensitivity Index (ASI; Reiss, Peterson, Gursky, and McNally, 1986; Peterson and Reiss, 1992) was developed to measure and test the theory of anxiety sensitivity. The ASI consists of 16-items asking about the degree to which an individual finds anxiety sensations fearful or catastrophic in outcome (Peterson and Reiss, 1992). Individuals respond to each question on a five-point Likert scale ranging from 0 ("very little") to 4 ("very much"). A recent psychometric analysis of the ASI was conducted by Zinbarg, Barlow, and Brown (1997). They found that the ASI is made up of a hierarchy of subscales. The lowest first-order factors assess three areas: physical concerns, mental incapacitation concerns, and social concerns. Most of the items on the ASI address the fear of physical harm resulting from anxious sensations, as reflected in the first factor. Examples of items targeting an individual's beliefs about mental incapacitation include "When I cannot keep my mind on a task, I worry that I might be going crazy" and "When I am nervous, I worry that I am mentally ill." Finally, items measuring the feared social consequences of anxiety sensations include "Other people notice when I feel shaky" and "It is important to me not to appear nervous."

Taylor (1995) expressed concern that this third lower-order social concerns ASI factor may be conceptualized more appropriately as negative evaluation sensitivity than anxiety sensitivity. However, Zinbarg, Mohlman, and Hong (1999) argued that the social concern items of the ASI are conceptually different from negative evaluation sensitivity. These authors proposed that the construct of anxiety sensitivity taps into negative evaluation concerns resulting from publicly displaying observable symptoms of anxiety whereas negative evaluation sensitivity refers to fears of negative evaluation resulting from a wide variety of other behaviors.

The question of where the social concerns component of the ASI belongs was investigated by McWilliams, Stewart, and MacPherson (2000). An exploratory factor-analytic approach was used to determine if this third ASI component would be better conceptualized in the domain of negative evaluation sensitivity or in the domain of anxiety sensitivity. Factors were obtained that represented the construct of negative evaluation sensitivity as well as the three lower-order constructs that make up the ASI (i.e., physical, psychological, and social concerns). Subscales derived from these four factors were positively correlated with one another within the ASI and the Brief Fear of Negative Evaluation scale (BFNE; Leary, 1983). Contrary to the speculation that ASI social concerns belong to a higher-order anxiety sensitivity factor that is separate from a higher-order negative evaluation sensitivity factor, anxiety sensitivity and negative evaluation sensitivity were positively and significantly correlated with a single higher-order factor labeled Threat Sensitivity. Thus, the social concerns component of the ASI does appear distinct from the other two components of anxiety sensitivity (i.e., physical and psychological) as well as from negative evaluation sensitivity. However, results from correlation and higher-order principal components analyses suggested that the ASI social concerns factor represents a blend of anxiety sensitivity and negative evaluation sensitivity in addition to something unique and separate from global negative evaluation sensitivity and anxiety sensitivity constructs (McWilliams et al., 2000).

The ASI has been used to study a range of anxiety disorders, including the development of panic attacks and anxiety. Anxiety sensitivity as measured by the ASI is elevated in individuals with anxiety disorders when compared to normal control groups (Reiss et al., 1986; Taylor, Koch, and Crockett, 1991). Furthermore, ASI scores are often elevated among individuals with panic disorder compared to individuals with other anxiety disorders (Taylor, Koch, and McNally, 1992). For this reason, anxiety sensitivity has received the most attention in panic disorder research.

Anxiety Sensitivity and Panic Disorder

Anxiety sensitivity appears to predispose individuals to panic disorder. Lilienfeld (1997) found that anxiety sensitivity predicts a history of panic attacks above and beyond indicators of more general trait anxiety or negative affect. Anxiety sensitivity measures differentiated individuals who experience panic attacks but do not have panic disorder from those who have never had a panic attack (Norton, Cox, and Malan, 1992). Individuals high in anxiety sensitivity are considered to be at greater risk to experience panic attacks and develop panic disorder than individuals with low levels of anxiety sensitivity.

Anxiety sensitivity may develop from direct experience with aversive events such as serious illness or injury. Alternatively, exposure to the serious illness or death of a family member or the influence of an overprotective parent may also contribute to an individual's vulnerability to anxiety sensitivity (Craske, 1999). Anxiety sensitivity is associated with a heightened level of attention paid to internal physical cues. Individuals who experience panic appear to have an elevated awareness or an increased ability to identify and detect bodily sensations associated with arousal. This increased ability to detect physical cues may predispose an individual for the development of panic disorder (Craske, 1999).

Initial panic attacks occur in a variety of settings. These locations are often outside of the home (Craske, Miller, Rotunda, and Barlow, 1990), such as while at work or school, while driving, on a plane or bus, in public in general, or in a situation that is socially evaluative (Craske, 1999). Craske and Rowe (1997) proposed that initial panic attacks are most likely to occur in situations where feared physical sensations are perceived as especially threatening because of possible impairment. Examples include driving, fear of being trapped, fear of negative evaluation, or fear of being in an unfamiliar location. Certain situations or contexts are more likely to be linked with negative personal consequences of experiencing anxiety (Craske, 1999).

An intense fear of specific bodily sensations related to panic attacks often develops after an individual experiences the initial panic attack. Following a panic attack, this "fear of fear" is considered a sensitization of the individual's predisposing trait of anxiety sensitivity. Reiss (1991) described a vicious cycle in which anxiety sensitivity increases the risk of panic attacks and panic attacks increase the levels of anxiety sensitivity. There is considerable evidence demonstrating that panic disordered individuals hold powerful beliefs and fears of mental or physical harm occurring from bodily sensations associated with panic attacks (Craske, 1999).

One study looked specifically at anxiety sensitivity as a predictor of panic attacks. Struzik, Vermani, Duffin, and Katzman (2004) reasoned that if anxiety sensitivity is an intrinsic and independent factor in panic development as opposed to a learned fear of earlier panic (Goldstein and Chambless, 1978), then anxiety sensitivity should be a predictor of panic that is both provoked and unprovoked. Struzik et al. tested the predictive value of the ASI when panic was induced in the laboratory. Participants with panic disorder as well as healthy nonanxious volunteers were included. Only two items on the ASI ("It is important to me not to appear nervous" and "It is important to me to stay in control of my emotions") correlated with panic attacks experienced by the group with panic disorder. Total ASI scores as well as subscale scores and individual ASI item scores were not effective in predicting the elicitation of panic in either population. Thus, the hypothesis that anxiety sensitivity plays a causal role in the elicitation of panic attacks was not supported by Struzik et al. Nevertheless, anxiety sensitivity appears to predict a number of process variables involved in both physiological and psychological panic symptoms (Brown, Smits, Powers, and Telch, 2003; Perna, Romano, Caldirola, Cucchi, and Bellodi, 2003; Shipherd, Beck, and Ohtake, 2001; Rassovsky, Kushner, Schwarze, and Wangensteen, 2000).

Holloway and McNally (1987) examined the effects of anxiety sensitivity on the response to hyperventilation. They predicted that anxiety sensitivity would increase responses to the biological challenge of hyperventilation. Individuals with low and high anxiety sensitivity were selected for participation. Results indicated that participants with high anxiety sensitivity reported more frequent and intense hyperventilation and anxiety sensations in response to the hyperventilation challenge than those with low anxiety sensitivity. Interestingly, individuals with high anxiety sensitivity also reported a greater number of other sensations not related to the physiological effects of hyperventilation. These results suggested that anxiety sensitivity may intensify the anxious responses of individuals who experience panic during biological challenge tests (Holloway and McNally, 1987).

Anxiety Sensitivity and Other Anxiety Disorders

The role of anxiety sensitivity has been in examined in other anxiety disorders, particularly social anxiety. However, anxiety sensitivity appears to play a different role in the maintenance of social anxiety disorder than it does in panic. Different anxiety disorders are associated with different patterns of responding on the ASI. For example, Hazen, Walker, and

Stein (1995) compared ASI scores of individuals with social phobia to those of individuals with panic disorder. Results suggested a different manner of responding between the two groups, with the social phobia group having significantly higher scores than the panic disorder group on three items ("Other people notice when I am shaky", "It is important to me not to appear nervous", and "It embarrasses me when my stomach growls"), all of which reflect concern for social consequences.

Along similar lines, Taylor et al. (1992) examined how anxiety sensitivity varies across anxiety disorders. A total of 313 patients recruited from a medical school and hospital completed the ASI. All participants received an anxiety disorder diagnosis according to DSM-III-R criteria (American Psychiatric Association, 1987). Diagnostic groups consisted of panic disorder (PD), post-traumatic stress disorder (PTSD), generalized anxiety disorder (GAD), obsessive compulsive disorder (OCD), social phobia, and simple phobia. As expected, ASI scores were elevated for all anxiety disorder groups when compared to normal controls with the exception of simple phobia. Taylor et al. noted that simple phobia participants may not have shown elevated levels of anxiety sensitivity because their panic was situationally bound and thus more predictable. ASI scores were significantly higher for individuals with PD than those of all other anxiety disorders with the exception of PTSD. There was a nonsignificant trend in which the PD group had higher scores than the PTSD group. The PD group also scored significantly higher than the PTSD group on 7 out of 16 items assessing fears of fainting, heart palpitations, unusual body sensations, and the subjective experience of anxiety. There were no differences between the groups on items targeting fears of difficulty concentrating or trembling.

Taylor et al. (1992) conducted further analyses by grouping together the remaining anxiety disorders for comparison with panic disorder patients. The PD group had higher ASI item scores than the other anxiety disorder patients except for two items, suggesting that PD is characterized by greater anxiety sensitivity than the other anxiety disorders. However, this difference may simply reflect the amount of distress associated with each anxiety disorder (Taylor et al., 1992).

The direction of the relationship between anxiety sensitivity and anxiety disorder symptoms is not entirely clear. Anxiety sensitivity is viewed by some as a risk factor for panic disorder as well as other anxiety disorders. This causal interpretation of the data was articulated by Reiss and McNally (1985; Reiss, 1991). In contrast, earlier views of a related construct known as "fear of fear" proposed that a fear of anxious bodily sensations resulted from panic attacks through the process of interoceptive conditioning (Goldstein and Chambless, 1978). Indeed, Donnell and McNally (1990) found that individuals with high anxiety sensitivity were more likely to report both a personal and a family history of panic when compared to individuals with low anxiety sensitivity. However, they also found that two thirds of the individuals with high anxiety sensitivity had never experienced a panic attack. Thus, anxiety sensitivity is not only a consequence of panic but also precedes the onset of panic attacks in a number of cases (Donnell and McNally, 1990).

Anxiety Sensitivity and Social Anxiety in College Students

Given that anxiety sensitivity was elevated in individuals with social anxiety (Taylor et al., 1992), researchers have begun to examine anxiety sensitivity and social anxiety in the college student population. Gore, Carter, and Parker (2002) collected self-report measures including the Social Interaction Anxiety Scale and the Social Phobia Scale (SIAS and SPS; Mattick and Clarke, 1998), Anxiety Sensitivity Index-Physical Scale (ASI; Peterson and Reiss, 1992), and the State-Trait Anxiety Inventory (STAI-T; Speilberger, Gorsuch, and Lushene, 1970) from 37 university students enrolled in psychology courses. All participants were also presented with a laboratory social challenge task instructing them to ask an "aloof" confederate on a date. Gore et al. (2002) found that while trait anxiety significantly predicted anxiety responses to the social challenge task, social anxiety measures were better predictors than either the ASI-physical subscale or the STAI-T. Thus, the SIAS and SPS combined accounted for more variance than either the STAI-T or the ASI-physical scale when predicting all social challenge task-related state measures. In addition, the higher the individual's social anxiety measure scores, the greater the state social anxiety as well as physical symptoms reported after interacting in the social challenge. In regards to anxiety sensitivity, individuals with higher ASI-physical scores did report greater fear during the social challenge. A surprising finding noted by Gore et al. was that the ASI-physical scale was nearly as good at predicting anxiety response as the SIAS and SPS combined. The ASI-physical scale significantly predicted all dependent measures, including the Beck Anxiety Inventory (BAI; Beck, Brown, Epstein, and Steer, 1988), the Fear of Physical Sensations Questionnaire (FPSQ) which is a modified version of the Agoraphobic Cognitions Questionnaire (ACQ; Chambless, Caputo, Bright, and Gallagher, 1984), and Social State (SocS) which is a state measure adapted from a version of the Fear of Negative Evaluation scale (Watson and Friend, 1969).

Roth, Coles, and Heimberg (2002) investigated the relationship between memories for childhood teasing and anxiety and depression in college students. These researchers examined the impact of childhood teasing on later social anxiety exhibited during the college years, whereas most of the previous research on "bullying" examined immediate effects on depressive symptoms and social anxiety among children. This line of research has found that children experiencing higher levels of victimization by their peers displayed higher levels of social anxiety (Craig, 1998; Walter and Inderbitzen, 1998) and depression (Callaghan and Joseph, 1995), as well as lower levels of social acceptance (Callaghan and Joseph) than children with lower levels of victimization. Victimized children may learn to perceive the world as a dangerous place in which they always need to be on alert, thereby leading to problems with anxiety, especially in social situations. Direct experience with such situations reinforces the perception that social situations are dangerous and are expected to end in failure, a well-known characteristic of social anxiety (Clark and Wells, 1995; Rapee and Heimberg, 1997). Avoidance of social situations often results and prevents individuals from having experiences that disconfirm their beliefs (Francis and Radka, 1995).

Roth et al. (2002) measured social anxiety, worry, and anxiety sensitivity in a college student sample to investigate the relationship between memory for teasing in childhood and levels of depression and anxiety in early adulthood. A Teasing Questionnaire was developed to measure the extent to which participants remembered having been teased about 20 different topics during childhood. Positive correlations between scores on the Teasing Questionnaire and anxiety and depression measures were predicted. In addition, social anxiety was expected to have the strongest relationship with memories of teasing. Finally, the authors predicted that the stronger the memories of teasing as a child, the higher the levels of anxiety and depression as an adult. As expected, statistically significant and positive correlations were found between the Teasing Questionnaire and all of the anxiety and depression measures. Anxiety sensitivity and social anxiety were more strongly related to a reported history of childhood teasing than was worry. The authors noted surprise that the strength of the link between childhood teasing and social anxiety did not differ from the strength of association between teasing and anxiety sensitivity.

A couple of research studies have examined relationships between social anxiety, anxiety sensitivity, and alcohol consumption in the college setting. Consistent with the tension reduction hypothesis, Lewis and Vogeltanz-Holm (2002) proposed that individuals often consume or abuse alcohol out of an expectation that drinking will reduce unpleasant sensations and cognitions, thus serving as a way to self-medicate anxious feelings. This view is consistent with the Burke and Stephens (1999) model described above and is supported by research showing that socially anxious individuals are more likely to report alcohol-related problems than nonanxious individuals (Kessler, Crum, Warner, Nelson, Schulenberg, and Anthony, 1997; Kushner, Sher, and Beitman, 1990) and that both placebo and alcoholic drinks reduced speech anxiety in a diagnosed social phobia sample (Himle, Abelson, Haghightgou, Hill, Nesse, and Curtis, 1999).

Lewis and Vogeltanz-Holm (2002) also suggested that this tension-reduction effect of alcohol differs among individuals with varying levels of anxiety sensitivity. Lewis and Vogeltanz-Holm examined the interaction between anxiety sensitivity, social anxiety, and the effects of alcohol by measuring subjective and physiological responses to a social stressor. ASI (Peterson and Reiss, 1992) scores were obtained from a sample of college women who were subsequently separated into groups of low or moderate anxiety sensitivity. All participants performed a "body image speech" social stressor task in which they presented a speech about what they liked and disliked about their bodies in front of a mirror. Results indicated that participants in the moderate anxiety sensitivity group who consumed alcohol experienced a greater dampening of heart rate compared to participants who did not consume alcohol during the anticipatory phase. This result suggested that individuals with elevated levels of anxiety sensitivity are highly responsive to the stress-reduction effects of alcohol when anticipating a stressor. Results from this Lewis and Vogeltanz-Holm study were consistent with a previous investigation in which a burst of loud noise served as the stressor (Stewart and Pihl, 1994). Stewart and Pihl assigned female college students to low, moderate, and high anxiety sensitivity groups based on their Anxiety Sensitivity Index scores (ASI; Peterson and Reiss, 1992). All participants were presented with the loud burst of noise when they were sober and again after they had consumed alcohol. All experienced lower anxiety levels when intoxicated than when sober. Greater anxiety reductions were displayed by the participants in the high anxiety sensitivity group when compared to the low anxiety sensitivity group (Stewart and Pihl, 1994). Thus, anxiety sensitivity may heighten the tension-reducing effects of alcohol in both social and nonsocial stressful situations.

Anxiety sensitivity, particularly the fear of negative social consequences resulting from anxiety sensations, appears to be an important component of social anxiety. However, social anxiety treatments rarely address this facet directly. In this next section, we describe original research investigating whether an additional interoceptive exposure component provides any additional clinical benefit over social situation exposure alone.

Research Investigation

Effects of Interoceptive Exposure on Social Anxiety

Interoceptive exposure was originally developed to treat the fears of anxious bodily sensations seen in panic disorder. This treatment involves repeated exposure to feared bodily sensations (Barlow, Craske, Cerny, and Klosko, 1989) and effectively reduced the number of panic attacks as well as the fear of bodily sensations when delivered as a sole treatment (Beck and Shipherd, 1997; Beck, Shipherd, and Zebb, 1997). As discussed above, panic disorder individuals typically fear anxiety-related sensations because they misinterpret these sensations as signs of imminent physical or mental complications. However, individuals may also fear these sensations based on concerns of negative social evaluation. Indeed, socially anxious people tend to report high anxiety sensitivity due to feared social consequences rather than perceived physical harm such as a heart attack (Hazen et al., 1995). Individuals with social phobia interpret the same anxiety-related sensations as a sign of embarrassment or social rejection. For example, a socially anxious individual with high anxiety sensitivity might consider sensations of feeling hot or flushed dangerous because others will see that he or she is anxious and therefore judge them negatively. In contrast, an individual with low anxiety sensitivity would not interpret these sensations as problematic. This conceptualization of social anxiety has led clinical researchers to study interventions that target feared bodily sensations directly.

A couple clinical studies have investigated exposure to bodily sensations as a treatment component for social phobia. For example, socially anxious participants exposed to somatic symptoms in a paradoxical treatment showed improvement (Mersch, Hidlebrand, Lavy et al., 1992). However, it was unclear whether improvements resulted from exposure to feared physiological sensations or other treatment factors. Similarly, Plotkin (2002, unpublished dissertation) investigated the effects of interoceptive exposure on public speaking anxiety compared to guided imagery relaxation in a sample of socially anxious college students. While some empirical support for the efficacy of interoceptive exposure was found, again it was not clear if exposure to physiological sensations was the active treatment component responsible for decreases in anxiety. Alternatively, some other component of the intervention, such as social exposure to the group setting, may have accounted for treatment effects.

The current study investigated whether interoceptive exposure effectively reduced speech anxiety for college students reporting general social phobia. Unlike these previous studies, we controlled for exposure to the group setting by including a control treatment in which participants performed tasks that did not directly induce specific physiological sensations. We predicted that socially anxious students receiving a group session of interoceptive exposure would display greater reductions in distress during a public speaking behavioral assessment test than socially anxious students receiving only social situation exposure. We also expected that students randomized to the interoceptive exposure condition would experience greater reductions in self-report measures of anxiety sensitivity and fear of bodily sensations than students randomized to the social exposure only condition.

Method

Approximately 600 undergraduate college students completed the Anxiety Sensitivity Index (ASI; Reiss et al., 1986) and the Social Phobia Diagnostic Questionnaire (SPDQ; Newman et al., 2003) during a mass screening session conducted in their psychology courses. The SPDQ is a 15 item self-report diagnostic questionnaire of social phobia according to DSM-IV criteria. Participants also rated their fear of giving a speech and their fear of anxiety symptoms during a speech. Students endorsing DSM-IV diagnostic criteria for generalized social phobia on the SPDQ, reporting moderate to extreme fear of giving a speech as well as of their heart racing, sweating, shaking, or some other physical sign of anxiety during a speech were eligible for participation.

A total of 41 eligible students agreed to participate in the two-hour experimental session for extra credit in their psychology class. Students were randomly assigned to either the interoceptive exposure (IE) condition or the social exposure only condition. In order to ensure that these randomly assigned groups were equivalent on a number of measures before the exposure intervention, all participants completed the following measures both beforehand and afterward: the Anxiety Sensitivity Index (ASI; Reiss et al., 1986), the Body Sensations Questionnaire (BSQ; Chambless et al., 1984), the Social Avoidance and Distress Scale (SADS; Watson and Friend, 1969), the Brief Fear of Negative Evaluation (BFNE; Leary, 1983), and the Personal Report of Confidence as a Speaker Personal Report of Confidence as a Speaker (PRCS; Paul, 1966). These measures were administered at the beginning of the experimental session prior to the intervention and immediately following the intervention at the end of the experimental session.

In addition to these self-report measures, all participants completed a behavioral assessment test (BAT) of speech anxiety before and after the exposure intervention. Participants were instructed to speak for one minute in front of two other participants and a video camera, choosing from one of three topics: "Your favorite foods and restaurants"; "How you would like to spend your next vacation"; or "What you like to do for fun when you are not studying". Subjective units of distress (SUDS; 0-100) were recorded immediately before and after this public speaking BAT task.

Participants randomized to the interoceptive exposure (IE) condition were led through three interoceptive exposure exercises conducted in small groups. The interoceptive exposure treatment exercises of overbreathing (i.e., hyperventilation), running in place, and muscle tension were conducted as described by Barlow and Craske (2000). Next, these participants selected the interoceptive exposure exercise that was most anxiety provoking for them and most similar to what they typically experience in feared social situations. IE participants then repeated the selected exercise until habituation occurred, operationally defined as a SUDS rating of 25 or less on two consecutive trials. All of these interoceptive exposure exercises were performed in front of the other group members as well as in front of a video camera.

The second condition involved tasks not designed to directly induce physiological arousal. To control for the performance of novel physical tasks in front of a group seen in the IE condition (e.g., hyperventilating and running in place), similar tasks not expected to induce sensations of physiological arousal were developed for this control condition. Specifically, students randomized to this control condition were instructed to stick out their tongue, say ahhh, and stand awkwardly in lieu of the interoceptive exposure exercises performed by IE participants. Following the same procedure as the IE condition, participants chose which task was most anxiety provoking for them and performed this exercise repeatedly until habituation occurred. These tasks were also performed in the presence of the other group members as well as a video camera.

For both conditions, participants rated how willing they were to perform each exercise immediately after the exercise was described. After the participants performed each exercise, a SUDS rating, two state measures, and two social anxiety ratings were collected. State measures consisted of autonomic arousal scale items from the Mood and Anxiety Symptom Questionnaire-Anxious Arousal Scale (MASQ-AA; Watson and Clark, 1991) and an abbreviated state version of the State-Trait Anxiety Inventory (STAI-S; Marteau and Bekker, 1992) consisting of 6 statements reflecting one's level of anxiety "at the moment." The first social anxiety rating was collected in response to the question "How embarrassed were you during this task?" Level of embarrassment was rated from 0 ("not embarrassed at all") to 8 ("extremely embarrassed"). The second social anxiety rating was collected in response to the question "How self-conscious did you feel during this task?" Participants rated how self-conscious they felt on a scale of 0-8, with 0 indicating "not at all self-conscious" and 8 indicating "extremely self-conscious."

Results

A one-way MANOVA including all pre-experimental measures yielded no significant group differences before the exposure intervention (all univariate p's greater than .22), suggesting that random assignment was successful. A series of between-group repeated measures ANOVAs were then conducted on each of the outcome measures. Means and standard deviations for SUDS ratings collected during each BAT as well as for ASI, BSQ, and BFNE scores collected at baseline and following the exposure intervention are presented in Table 1.

A between-group repeated measures ANOVA was conducted on SUDS ratings collected during the baseline BAT performed before the exposure intervention and on SUDS ratings collected during the post-intervention BAT performed after the exposure intervention. A main effect for time reflected that BAT SUDS ratings decreased after the exposure intervention for the participants overall, $F(1, 39) = 10.87$, $p < .01$. No main effect for group $F(1, 39) = 1.89$, ns, or interaction effect $F(1, 39) = 0$, ns was found.

A between-group repeated measures ANOVA was also conducted on total ASI scores collected at baseline and after the exposure intervention. A main effect for time showed that total ASI scores reduced for the sample as a whole, $F(1, 39) = 5.09$, $p < .05$, but no main effect for group, $F(1, 39) = .13$, ns was found. An interaction effect approached significance, $F(1, 39) = 3.86$, $p = .057$, reflecting a greater decrease in ASI scores for the social exposure only group than the IE group.

Table 1. Means and Standard Deviations for Measures Collected Pre and Post Exposure Intervention

Measure	Interoceptive Exposure Condition		Social Exposure Only Condition	
	Pre	Post	Pre	Post
BAT SUDS	58.45 (34.64)	43.55 (30.28)	72.01 (31.54)	57.18 (41.53)
ASI	21.30 (11.44)	21.10 (11.11)	21.38 (12.23)	18.48 (10.71)
BSQ	43.15 (13.74)	44.90 (15.47)	42.05 (14.75)	37.76 (14.50)
BFNE	39.40 (8.93)	41.25 (8.55)	38.40 (12.00)	26.75 (11.63)

A between-group repeated measures ANOVA was then conducted on pre and post exposure intervention BSQ scores. A significant interaction effect was found $F(1, 39) = 3.86$, $p < .01$, in which only the social exposure control group exhibited a decrease. No main effects of time $F(1, 39) = 1.47$, ns, or of group $F(1, 39) = .86$, ns were found.

A between-group repeated measures ANOVA conducted on pre and post exposure intervention BFNE scores also yielded a significant interaction effect $F(1, 38) = 10.05$, $p < .01$, in which only the social exposure control group showed a decrease. No main effect of time $F(1, 38) = .03$, ns, or of group $F(1, 38) = .72$, ns were found. Between-group repeated measures ANOVAs conducted with SADS and PRCS scores yielded no significant main or interaction effects for either measure.

Given the unexpected nature of these results, we conducted a series of post-hoc group comparisons. Independent samples t-tests between the two groups were performed on three task variables. No significant group differences were found for ratings of how embarrassing the tasks were, $t(39) = .30$, $p < .76$, or for ratings of how self-conscious participants felt while performing the tasks, $t(39) = -.53$. $p < .60$. The MASQ-AA, our self-report measure of physiological arousal, was significantly higher for the IE group than the social exposure only control group $t(36) = 3.27$, $p <.01$. As intended, the IE group reported more physiological arousal during their exposure tasks than the control group.

Discussion

As expected, both exposure groups experienced reductions in social anxiety following the exposure intervention as measured by subjective distress ratings (SUDS) during a public speaking behavioral assessment task. However, this reduction was not more pronounced for the IE group than the social exposure only group. Both groups also reported reductions in anxiety sensitivity following the exposure intervention, but interoceptive exposure did not lead to greater reductions in anxiety sensitivity than social exposure alone. Perhaps most surprising was our finding that only the social exposure control group exhibited reductions in a related construct measured by the Body Sensations Questionnaire. In contrast, the interoceptive exposure group failed to show decreases on this measure. Fears of negative evaluation also reduced for the social exposure only control group but not for the IE group. Thus, the addition of interoceptive exposure exercises designed to elicit specific feared bodily sensations does not appear necessary in the treatment of college student social anxiety. Follow up data analysis suggested that feared physiological symptoms were effectively induced during interoceptive exposure, as interoceptive exposure produced greater self-reported physiological arousal than the social exposure only tasks. However, participants in the social exposure only condition appeared to benefit *more* from this experimental control intervention on a couple of outcome measures when compared to participants in the interoceptive exposure intervention. There were no differences between groups on the ratings of embarrassment and self-consciousness experienced during the exposure tasks. Thus, it does not appear that participants in the social exposure only condition received more intensive social situation exposure than participants in the IE condition. However, IE participants may have been distracted from the social context in which the tasks were performed more so than control participants, given the focus of interoceptive task instructions on the induction of specific bodily sensations. The students who performed the social exposure only tasks may have had more attentional resources available for the social exposure component of that intervention.

Conclusion

Social anxiety is a common clinical problem across college campuses. Socially anxious college students report reduced assertiveness and feelings of competence in social situations, particularly in dating relationships (Chambless et al., 1982; Lesure-Lester, 2001). In addition to common physical symptoms such as "butterflies" in the stomach, general tension, and blushing (Purdon et al., 1999), social anxiety among college students can lead to behavioral avoidance, social isolation, and depression (Johnson et al., 1992). Excessive drinking to self-medicate anxiety and tension in social situations appears to be a particularly problematic coping strategy for these students (Burke and Stephens, 1999).

Ironically, socially anxious students are more likely than nonanxious students to judge visible signs of anxiety in others negatively (Purdon et al., 1999). For this reason, experiencing anxious sensations in the presence of others may be especially threatening for the socially anxious. Indeed, socially anxious individuals report elevated levels of anxiety sensitivity, or fear of anxious bodily sensations, due to perceived threatening social consequences of such sensations (Hazen et al., 1995). Available research suggests that anxiety sensitivity plays an integral role in the development and maintenance of social anxiety among college students (Gore et al., 2002), possibly interacting with other important factors such as a history of childhood teasing (Roth et al., 2002). Furthermore, anxiety sensitivity may augment a socially anxious individual's response to the stress-reduction effects of alcohol (Lewis and Vogeltanz-Holm, 2002).

Social anxiety researchers have begun to investigate the possible clinical benefit of interoceptive exposure, the direct induction of feared physiological sensations first developed for panic disorder treatment. Although promising, previous research (Mersch et al., 1992.

Plotkin, 2002) did not control for the social situation exposure inherent in conducting interoceptive exposure exercises in front of others. In our own original research investigation, we randomly assigned socially anxious college students to receive a session of either group interoceptive exposure or group social exposure only. Results indicated that interoceptive sensations were effectively produced for interoceptive exposure participants and that both treatments were largely beneficial. However, the social exposure only group showed additional improvements not exhibited by the interoceptive exposure group. Thus, inducing physiological sensations did not seem to have any clinical benefit above and beyond mere exposure to a social situation. Given that no group differences were found on task-related measures of embarrassment and self-consciousness, the nature of the specific tasks conducted in the social exposure only condition do not seem to account for these results.

The question of whether or not socially anxious individuals would benefit from induction of physiological sensations remains. Limitations of the current study include a small sample size, use of a brief single session intervention, and lack of direct physiological arousal measures. Future research is needed to develop relevant interoceptive exposure exercises that effectively target the fears of socially anxious individuals before this approach can be recommended for the treatment of social phobia. The traditional cognitive-behavioral exposure approach, such as Cognitive-Behavioral Group Therapy developed by Heimberg and colleagues (Turk, Heimberg, and Hope, 2001), is still the psychological treatment of choice for social anxiety disorder.

References

American Psychiatric Association (1987). *Diagnostic and statistical manual of mental disorders* (3rd ed., rev.). Washington, DC: Author.

American Psychiatric Association (2000). *Diagnostic and statistical manual of mental disorders* (4th ed.). (Text Revision). Washington, DC: Author.

Barlow, D.H., and Craske, M.G. (2000). Mastery of your anxiety and panic, 3rd Ed. (MAP-3). New York: Oxford University Press.

Barlow, D. H., Craske, M.G., Cerny, J., and Klosko, J. (1989). Behavioral treatment of panic disorder. *Behavior Therapy, 20*(2), 261-282.

Beck, A. T., Brown, G., Epstein, N., and Steer, R. A. (1988). An inventory for measuring clinical anxiety: psychometric properties. *Journal of Consulting and Clinical Psychology, 56,* 893-897.

Beck, A. T., and Emery, G. (1985). *Anxiety disorders and phobias.* New York: Basic Books.

Beck, J. G., and Shipherd, J. C. (1997). Repeated exposure to interoceptive cues: Does habituation of fear occur in panic disorder patients? A preliminary report. *Behaviour Research and Therapy, 35*(6), 551-557.

Beck, J. G., Shipherd, J. C., and Zebb, B. J. (1997). How does interoceptive exposure panic disorder work? An uncontrolled case study. *Journal of Anxiety Disorders, 11,* 541-556.

Brown, M., Smits, J. A., Powers, M. B., and Telch, M. J. (2003). Differential sensitivity of the three ASI factors in predicting panic disorder patients' subjective and behavioural response to hyperventilation challenge. *Anxiety Disorders, 17,* 583-591.

Burke, R. S., and Stephens, R. S. (1999). Social anxiety and drinking in college students: A social cognitive theory analysis. *Clinical Psychology Review, 19*(5), 513-530.

Callaghan, S., and Joseph, S. (1995). Self-concept and peer victimization among school children. *Personality and Individuals Differences, 18,* 161-163.

Chambless, D. L., Caputo, G. C., Bright, P., and Gallagher, R. (1984). Assessment of fear of fear in agoraphobics: the Body Sensations Questionnaire and the Agoraphobic Cognitions Questionnaire. *Journal of Consulting and Clinical Psychology, 52,* 1090-1097.

Chambless, D. L., Hunter, K., and Jackson, A. (1982). Social anxiety and assertiveness: A comparison of the correlations in phobic and college student samples. *Behaviour Research and Therapy, 20*(4), 403-404.

Clark, D. M., and Wells, A. (1995). A cognitive model of social phobia. In R. G. Heimberg, M. R. Liebowitz, D. A. Hope, and F. R. Schneier (Eds.), *Social phobia: diagnosis, assessment, and treatment* (pp. 69-93). New York: Guilford Press.

Craig, W. M. (1998). The relationship among bullying, victimization, depression, anxiety, and aggression in elementary school children. *Personality and Individual Differences, 24,* 123-130.

Craske, M. G. (1999). *Anxiety disorders: Psychological approaches to theory and treatment.* New York: Basic Books.

Craske, M. G., Miller, P. P., Rotunda, R., and Barlow, D. H. (1990). A descriptive report of features of initial unexpected panic attacks in minimal and extensive avoiders. *Behaviour Research and Therapy, 33,* 197-203.

Craske, M. G., and Rowe, M. K. (1997). Nocturnal panic. *Clinical Psychology: Science and Practice, 4,* 153-174.

Davidson, J. R. T., Hughes, D. L., George, L. K., and Blazer, D. G. (1994). The boundary of social phobia: Exploring the threshold. *Archives of General Psychiatry, 51,* 975-983.

Davis, D. (1982). Determinants of responsiveness in dyadic interaction. In W. Ickes and E. S. Knowles (Eds.), *Personality, roles, and social behavior* (pp. 85-139). New York: Springer-Verlag.

Davison, G. C. and Zighelboim, V. (1987). Irrational beliefs in the articulated thoughts of college students with social anxiety. *Journal of Rational-Emotive Therapy, 5*(4), 238-254.

Donnel, C. D. and McNally, R. J. (1990). Anxiety sensitivity and panic attacks in a nonclinical population. *Behaviour Research and Therapy, 28,* 83-85.

Durand, M. V. and Barlow, D. H. (2006). *Essentials of abnormal psychology.* (4th ed.). Pacific Grove, CA: Thomson-Wadsworth.

Francis, G., and Radka, D. F. (1995). Social anxiety in children and adolescents. In: M. B. Stein (Ed.), *Social phobia: clinical and research perspectives* (pp. 119-143). Washington, DC: American Psychiatric Press.

Goldstein, A. J. and Chambless, D. L. (1978). A reanalysis of agoraphobia. *Behavior Therapy, 9,* 47-59.

Gore, K. L., Carter, M. M., and Parker, S. (2002). Predicting anxious response to a social challenge: the predictive utility of the social interaction anxiety scale and the social phobia scale in a college population. *Behaviour Research and Therapy, 40,* 689-700.

Hartman, L. M. (1984). Cognitive components of anxiety. *Journal of Clinical Psychology, 40,* 137-139.

Hazen, A. L., Walker, J. R., and Stein, M. B. (1997). Comparison of anxiety sensitivity in panic disorder and social phobia. *Anxiety, 1,* 298-301.

Himle, J. A., Abelson, J. L., Haghightgou, H., Hill, E. M., Nesse, R. M., and Curtis, G. C. (1999). Effect of alcohol on social phobic anxiety. *American Journal of Psychiatry, 156,* 1237- 1243.

Holloway, W. and McNally, R. J. (1987). Effects of anxiety sensitivity on the response to hyperventilation. *Journal of Abnormal Psychology, 96(4),* 330-334.

Johnson, K. A., Johnson, J. E., and Petzel, T. P. (1992). Social anxiety, depression, and distorted cognitions in college students. *Journal of Social and Clinical Psychology, 11*(2), 181-195.

Kashdan, T. B. and Roberts, J. R. (2004). Social anxiety's impact of affect, curiosity, and social self-efficacy during a high self-focus social threat situation. *Cognitive Therapy and Research, 28*(1), 119-141.

Kessler, R. C., Crum, R. M., Warner, L. A., Nelson, C. B., Schulenberg, J., and Anthony, J. C. (1997). Lifetime co-occurrence of DSM-III-R alcohol abuse and dependence with other psychiatric disorders in the national comorbidity survey. *Archives of General Psychiatry, 54,* 313-321.

Kessler, R. C., McGonagle, K. A., Zhao, S., Nelson, C. B., Hughes, M., Eshleman, S., Wittchen, H.-U., and Kendler, K. S. (1994). Lifetime and 12-month prevalence of DSM-III-R psychiatric disorders among persons aged 15-54 in the United States: Results from the national comorbidity survey. *Archives of General Psychiatry*, *51,* 8-19.

Krantz, S., Hammen, C. (1979). Assessment of cognitive bias in depression. *Journal of Abnormal Psychology, 88,* 611-619.

Kushner, M. G., Sher, K. J., and Beitman, B. D. (1990). The relation between alcohol problems and the anxiety disorders. *American Journal of Psychiatry, 147,* 685-695.

Leary, M. (1983). A brief version of the Fear of Negative Evaluation Scale. *Personality and Social Psychology Bulletin, 9,* 371-375.

Lesure-Lester, E. G. (2001). Dating competence, social assertion, and social anxiety among college students. *College Student Journal, 35*(2), 317-321.

Levenson, R. W., and Gottman, J. M. (1978). Toward the assessment of social competence. *Journal of Consulting and Clinical Psychology, 46,* 453-462.

Lewis, B. A., and Vogeltanz-Holm, N. D. (2002). The effects of alcohol and anxiousness on physiological and subjective responses to a social stressor in women. *Addictive Behaviors, 27,* 529-545.

Lilienfeld, S. O. (1997). The relation of anxiety sensitivity to higher and lower order personality dimensions: Implications for the etiology of panic attacks. *Journal of Abnormal Psychology, 106*(4), 539-544

Lilienfeld, S. O., Turner, S. M., and Jacob, R. G. (1993). Anxiety sensitivity: An examination of theoretical and methodological issues. *Advances in Behaviour Research and Therapy, 15,* 147-183.

Marteau, T. M., and Bekker, H. (1992). The development of a six-item short-form of the state scale of the Spielberger State-Trait Anxiety Inventory (STAI). *British Journal of Clinical Psychology, 31,* 301-306.

Mattick, R. P., and Clarke, J. C. (1998). Development and validation of measures of social phobia scrutiny fear and social interaction anxiety. *Behaviour Research and Therapy, 36*(4), 455-470.

McWilliams, L. A., Stewart, S. H., and Macpherson, P. S. R. (2000). Does the social concerns component of the Anxiety Sensitivity Index belong to the domain of anxiety sensitivity or the domain of negative evaluation sensitivity? *Behaviour Research and Therapy, 38,* 985-992.

Mersch, P. P., Hildebrand, M., Lavy, E. H., Wessel, I., et al. (1992). Somatic symptoms in social phobia: A treatment method based on rational emotive therapy and paradoxical interventions. *Journal of Behavior Therapy and Experimental Psychiatry, 23,* 199-211.

Newman, M. G., Kachin, K. E., Zuellig, A. R., Constantino, M. J., and Cashman, L. (2003). The social phobia diagnostic questionnaire: Preliminary validation of a new self-report diagnostic measure of social phobia. *Psychological Medicine, 33,* 623-635.

Norton, G. R., Cox, B. J., and Malan, J. (1992). Nonclinical panickers: A critical review. *Clinical Psychology Review, 12,* 121-139.

Perna, G., Romano, P., Caldirola, D., Cucchi, M., and Bellodi, L. (2003). Anxiety sensitivity and 35% CO^2 reactivity in patients with panic disorder. *Journal of Psychosomatic Research, 54,* 573-577.

Peterson, R. A., and Reiss, S. (1992). *Anxiety Sensitivity Index Revised Manual.* Worthington, OH: International Diagnostic Systems Publishing Corporation.

Paul, G. (1966). *Insight versus desensitization in psychotherapy.* Standford, CA: Standford University Press.

Plotkin, D. P. (2002, unpublished dissertation). The effects of interoceptive exposure on public speaking anxiety.

Purdon, C., Antony, M., Monteiro, S., and Swinson, R. P. (2001). Social anxiety in college students. *Anxiety Disorders, 15,* 203-215.

Rapee, R. M., and Heimberg, R. G. (1997). A cognitive-behavioral model of anxiety in social phobia. *Behaviour Research and Therapy, 35,* 741-756.

Rassovsky, Y., Kushner, M. G., Schwarze, N. J., and Wangensteen, O. D. (2000). Psychological and physiological predictors of response to carbon dioxide challenge in individuals with panic disorder. *Journal of Abnormal Psychology, 109,* 616-623.

Reiss, S. (1991). Expectancy model of fear, anxiety, and panic. *Clinical Psychology Review, 11,* 201-214.

Reiss, S., and Havercamp, S. H. (1996). The sensitivity theory of motivation: Implications for psychopathology. *Behaviour Research and Therapy, 34,* 621-632.

Reiss, S., and McNally, R. J., (1985). Expectancy model of fear. In S. Reiss and R. R. Bootzin (Eds.), *Theoretical issues in behavior therapy.* San Diego, CA: Academic Press.

Reiss, S., Peterson, R. A., Gursky, D. M., and McNally, R. J. (1986). Anxiety sensitivity, anxiety frequency and the prediction of fearfulness. *Behaviour Research and Therapy, 24,* 1-8.

Roth, D. A., Coles, M. E., and Heimberg, R. G. (2002). The relationship between memories for childhood teasing and anxiety and depression in adulthood. *Anxiety Disorders, 16,* 149- 164.

Safren, S. A., Heimberg, R. G., Brown, E. J., and Holle, C. (1997). Quality of life in social phobia. *Depression and Anxiety, 4,* 126-133.

Santiago-Rivera, A. L., Gard, T., and Bernstein, B. (1999). The importance of achievement, intimacy, autonomy, and life events among first year college students. *Journal of College Student Psychotherapy, 13,* 57-73.

Scott, E. L., Heimberg, R. G., and MacAndrew, S. L. (2000). Anxiety sensitivity in social phobia: comparison between social phobics with and without panic attacks. *Depression and Anxiety, 12,* 189-192.

Shipherd, J. C., Beck, J. G., and Ohtake, P. J. (2001). Relationships between the Anxiety Sensitivity Index, the Suffocation Fear Scale, and responses to CO^2 inhalation. *Anxiety Disorders, 15,* 247-258.

Speilberger, C. D., Gorsuch, R. W., and Lushene, R. E. (1970). *State-Trait Anxiety Inventory.* Palo Alto, CA: Consulting Psychologists Press.

Stewart, S. H., and Pihl, R. O. (1994). Effects of alcohol administration of psychophysiological and subjective emotional responses to aversive stimulation in anxiety sensitive women. *Psychology of Addictive Behaviors, 8,* 29-42.

Struzik, L., Vermani, M., Duffin, J., and Katzman, M. A. (2004). Anxiety sensitivity as a predictor of panic attacks. *Psychiatry Research, 129,* 273-278.

Taylor, S. (1995). Anxiety sensitivity: theoretical perspectives and recent findings. *Behaviour Research and Therapy, 33,* 243-258.

Taylor, S. (1999). *Anxiety sensitivity: Theory, research, and treatment of the fear of anxiety.* Lawrence Erlbaum Associates: Mahwah, NJ

Taylor, S., Koch, W. J., and Crockett, D. J. (1991). Anxiety-sensitivity, trait anxiety, and the anxiety disorders. *Journal of Anxiety Disorders, 5,* 293-311.

Taylor, S., Koch, W. J., and McNally, R. J. (1992). How does anxiety sensitivity vary across the anxiety disorders? *Journal of Anxiety Disorders, 6,* 249-259.

Turk, C.L., Heimberg, R.G., and Hope, D.A. (2001). Social anxiety disorder. In D.H. Barlow (Ed.), *Clinical handbook of psychological disorders: A step-by-step treatment manual* (3rd ed.). New York: Guilford.

Walter, K. S., and Inderbitzen, H. M. (1998). Social anxiety and peer relations among adolescents: testing a psychobiological model. *Journal of Anxiety Disorders, 12,* 183-198.

Watson, D., and Clark, L. A. (1991). The Mood and Anxiety Symptom Questionnaire. (Unpublished manuscript, University of Iowa, Department of Psychology, Iowa City.)

Watson, D., and Friend, R. (1969). Measurement of social-evaluative anxiety. *Journal of Consulting and Clinical Psychology, 33,* 48-457.

Zinbarg, R. E., Barlow, D. H., and Brown, T. A. (1997). Hierarchical structure and general factor saturation of the Anxiety Sensitivity Index: Evidence and implications. *Psychological Assessment, 9,* 277-284.

Zinbarg, R. E., Mohlman, J, and Hong, N. N. (1999). Dimensions of anxiety sensitivity. In:Taylor, S. (Ed.), Anxiety Sensitivity: Theory, Research, and Treatment of the Fear of Anxiety. Mahwah, NJ: Lawrence Erlbaum Associates.

In: Anxiety in College Students
Editor: Benjamin Ayres and Michelle Bristow
ISBN: 978-1-60692-282-8

Chapter III

Test Anxiety and Its Consequences on Academic Performance among University Students

Mohd Ariff Bin Kassim[1a], Siti Rosmaini Bt Mohd Hanafi[1b] and Dawson R. Hancock[2c]

[1]Universiti Tenaga Nasional, 26700 Muadzam Shah, Pahang, Malaysia
[2]University of North Carolina at Charlotte, 9201 University City Boulevard, Charlotte, North Carolina, U.S.A.

Abstract

Some educators have failed to acknowledge the prevalence of test anxiety and its effect on academic performance among university students. This study addresses this issue at the university level using data collected through the Revised Test Anxiety (RTA) instrument and Sarason's four-factor model as a basis for measuring test anxiety. The study also investigates the effect of demographic factors on test anxiety. Findings reveal that test anxiety is significantly and negatively related to academic performance. Reasons for these findings are addressed.

Although testing is an important and widely used means for evaluating ability and achievement of individuals, many motivated and talented college students suffer from test anxiety (Austin & Patridge, 1995). Students often experience increased testing as they progress from primary school to post-secondary levels. Although most students experience normal nervousness during tests, others experience severe anxiety.

[a] E-mail address: ariff@kms.uniten.edu.my. Telephone: 012-6097503
[b] E-mail address: rosmaini@kms.uniten.edu.my. Telephone: 09-4552043
[c] E-mail address: DHancock@email.uncc.edu. Telephone: (704)687-8863. Corresponding author: Dawson R. Hancock, Ph.D. Address for Correspondence: University of North Carolina at Charlotte, 9201 University City Boulevard, Charlotte, North Carolina, U.S.A. 28223

Obviously, test anxiety can be considered an important factor in relation to academic performance. It has been proposed that test anxiety is one of the most disruptive factors associated with underachievement of students. Sarason (1984) stated that test anxiety is a debilitating factor at all academic levels. Because of its strong influence on academic achievement, test anxiety has been identified as one of the variables in the motivation and learning strategies model proposed by Pintrich (Paulsen & Gentry, 1995).

Research Problem

Test anxiety is a serious problem for many students. It has been described as the most powerful impediment to learning in an educational setting (Matthew, Tracy & Scott, 2000). Test anxiety has been linked to fears of negative evaluation, dislike of testing, and less effective study skills (Hambree, 1988) and has been identified as one of the factors that impairs academic performance (Everson & Millsap, 1991 and Tobias, 1980; Gregory, 1999). Many educators are disturbed over the trauma experienced by students during test taking time. This study was conducted to examine this issue in college students with the goal of helping students seek appropriate strategies to overcome debilitative test anxiety.

Literature Review

The Definition of Anxiety

Anxiety is a complex concept and this complexity is illustrated by the various definitions of anxiety in the literature. Anxiety describes cognitive, affective, and behavioral responses that will result in poor performance and possibly failure in an evaluative situation (Ian & Owens, 1996). According to Spielberger (1966), anxiety stems from an individual's feeling of guilt from committing wrongful acts.

Anxiety can also be described as an unpleasant state of tension arising from disapproval in interpersonal relations (Eady, 1999). Anxiety actually arises due to direct threat to some value considered important to an individual's existence as a personality (Spielberger, 1966). Furthermore, anxiety can be considered as a sense or feeling of discomfort and worry about undefined threat. The threat can be physical or psychological in nature and may involve the anticipation of bodily injury, damage to self-esteem, or harm to personal welfare.

The Definition of Test Anxiety

Anxiety is also considered to have an important relation to academic performance, particularly in the form of test anxiety. In this context, test anxiety is viewed as a special part of general anxiety. Test anxiety is a universal phenomenon and has been studied in many different cultures (e.g., Morris, Davis & Hutchings, 1981, Spielberger, 1980 and Zeidner, 1992). Test anxiety is an extreme fear of performing poorly on examinations and it is a common form of anxiety among students. Such anxiety arises during evaluation situations or events. It can be explained as an affect or feeling of apprehension or fear and discomfort together with cognitive difficulties (Isaac & Orit, 1997).

Test anxiety is closely related to negative emotions. It is because when one's performances are being evaluated, an emotional reaction will appear. Therefore, during the evaluation, one may feel uneasiness, distress, or fear if one is not prepared and not confident with his or her abilities to perform well. However, if one is well prepared and very confident with himself or herself, the opposite feeling will arise (McDonald, 2001). On the other hand, Sarason and Stoops (1978) view that test anxiety is related to time whereby an individual may develop anxiety a long time prior to the examination. This implies that the preparation for the examination can also be affected. Therefore, such fear of tests may contribute to ineffective preparation for the test. Test anxiety also arises when the evaluative situation is interpreted as threatening (Mwamwenda, 1994).

Test Anxiety and Academic Performance

Test anxiety is a major educational problem affecting millions of students in schools and colleges (Everson & Millsap, 1991). It is also widely recognized as a significant contributor to academic performance (Gregory, 1999). Many empirical studies have shown that test anxiety is a major debilitating factor on all academic levels, from the elementary level to the university level (Sarason, 1984). This view is also supported by the finding of Tobias (1980), who reported that test anxiety is one of the variables that are most commonly related to poor performance among students. Test anxiety is found to be negatively related to college students' performance (Pintrich & Garcia, 1991 and Pintrich & De Groot, 1990). According to Ian and Owens (1996), approximately twenty percent of students consistently suffer from poor performance due to high test anxiety.

The effects of test anxiety on academic performance have been thoroughly investigated by many researchers. Generally, the study of the relationship between test anxiety and academic achievement began in the early 1900's (McDonald, 2001). The comprehensive reviews by Hambree (1988) on the Meta analysis of 562 studies showed that test anxiety caused poor performance. It implied that test anxiety had a negative relationship with the students' performance, where high test anxious students tended to score lower than the low test anxious students. This result was supported by the findings of various studies (McDonald, 2001).

High test anxiety students may view the testing situation differently compared to their low test anxiety counterparts. Such differing views may be expressed conceptually by variations in the features of the situation that students recognized as important and by the emphasis they replaced on those features (Schutz, Davis & Schwaneflugel, 2002). Studies conducted by Sarason in 1980 show that highly test anxious students perform relatively poor under an evaluative situation and that their performance is hindered by excessive self-preoccupation with concern about failures and its consequences. Sarason also reported that the influence of test anxiety is most pronounced in those situations when the testing situation is competitive.

The study of test anxiety was also conducted involving an Arab population. The results showed that Arab students experienced higher test anxiety compared to American students. It was interpreted that Arab students experienced higher levels of test anxiety due to consequences of extreme importance of the test to students in their society (El-Zahhar & Hocevar, 1991). Similarly, it has been reported that college students in Egypt, Turkey and Mexico scored higher on test anxiety than students in America. In addition, test anxiety may also benefit the students in relation to their performance. This is because without any fear of failure, the students may make inadequate preparation for an examination that may lead to poor performance. However, if the level of test anxiety is above optimum level, it may disrupt preparation and create distress during the test and will result in an impairment of students' performance. Even worse, there are students who resort to an avoidance approach to testing by not sitting for an examination due to extreme fear (McDonald, 2001).

Theoretical Framework

In the test anxiety literature, several theories or models measure the test anxiety construct and in explain the effects of test anxiety on academic performance. Among the models suggested are the two-factor model by Spielberger (1980) and the four-factor model proposed by Sarason (1984). In addition, the two most common models used in explaining the effect of test anxiety on academic performance are the Interference and Deficits models. Detailed explanations of the models are discussed in this section.

Dimensionality of Test Anxiety

It has been theorised that the construct of test anxiety is multidimensional. Among the various conceptualisations of test anxiety, Spielberger's (1980) two-factor model (i.e., Worry and Emotionality) and Sarason's (1984) four-factor model (i.e., Worry, Tension, Test Irrelevant Thinking and Bodily Symptoms) have been discussed widely in many empirical studies (e.g., Benson & Bandalos, 1992; David, et al., 2000; Hodapp & Benson, 1996; Hong, 1998 and Nasser, Takahashi & Benson, 1997).

Initially, Liebert and Morris (1967) proposed that test anxiety consisted of Worry (Cognitive) and Emotionality components. Then, Spielberger, Gonzales, Taylor, Algaze and Anton (1978) developed the Test Anxiety Inventory (TAI) that followed the lead of Liebert and Morris (1967) and sought to refine a two-dimensional measure of test anxiety (i.e., two-factor model). Cognitive components refer to the mental activity that revolve around during test situations and will give an impact to the individual. In this two-factor model, Worry is the cognitive activity that accompanies the test anxiety. In contrast, Emotionality components are the psychological components of test anxiety and refer to tension, high heart rate, sweating, feeling sick and shaking (McDonald, 2001).

On the other hand, Sarason (1984) and Wine (1982) suggested that test anxiety is consisted of cognitive, emotionality, behavioural and bodily reaction components. This occurs because test anxiety is a multidimensional constructs the separation of cognitive and emotionality should be addressed properly. Mainly due to this reason, Sarason (1984) subsequently categorised test anxiety construct into four components which are Tension, Worry, Bodily Symptoms and Test Irrelevant Thinking (i.e., four-factor model). Worry and Test Irrelevant Thinking are considered Cognitive components whereby Tension and Bodily Symptoms are grouped into Emotionality components. For the purpose of the present study, the Sarason (1984) four-factor model will be adopted in assessing test anxiety construct using the Revised Test Anxiety scale (RTA) developed by Benson and El-Zahhar (1994).

The Association between Cognitive Components with Academic Performance

Cognition is claimed to be the most consistently and strongly related (i.e., negatively) to academic performance (David et al., 2000). This result was supported by other studies such as Kin and Roklin, 1994; O'Neil and Abedi, 1992; Zeidner and Nevo, 1991 and Liebert and Morris, 1967 (as cited in Hong, 1999). The cognitive test anxiety is hypothesised to have a debilitating effect on academic achievement because it may produce self-depreciating thoughts that will distract a student from thinking about relevant academic problems and cause her to focus on irrelevant thought (Ho, 2000).

Worry is described as the unwanted and uncontrollable cognitive activity that relates with negative thoughts that result in emotional discomfort to the individual. Examples of negative thoughts include expecting to perform poorly on a test compared to other students, not being confident or feeling doubtful of one's ability and the consequences of failing the test. Between the two cognitive components, Worry has a strong inverse relationship with academic performance (Hong, 1998 & 1999; Morris et al., 1981 & Sarason, 1984).

The second element of Cognitive component is Test Irrelevant Thinking. This refers to intrusive, distracting and non-evaluative thoughts during the examination. For example, a student thinks of matters unrelated to the questions being asked in the examination. David et al (2000), who conducted a study involving Irish undergraduate students by using the RTA, found that Test Irrelevant Thinking is the strongest predictor of examination performance. This result is actually contradictory with those obtained by Hong (1998; 1999), Morris et al. (1981), and Sarason (1984).

The Association between Emotionality Components with Academic Performance

The Emotionality component of test anxiety is comprised of Bodily Symptoms and Tension. The Emotionality component of test anxiety is not too debilitating to students' performance (David et al. 2000). The above result is supported by Worth, Glazeski, Kirkland, Jones and Van Norman (1979) cited by David et al.(2000) which reported that the main difference between the low and high test anxious student is based on their cognitive reaction but not on physiological arousal (i.e., Emotionality) during the test. It is in line with the study conducted by David et al. (2000) who found that both Emotionality components are less negatively related to student performance as compared to the Cognitive component.

Bodily Symptoms refer to the student's physical reaction before and during test taking such as having a headache, tightening of the muscles and experiencing difficulty in breathing. David et al. (2000) found that Bodily Symptoms have less of a negative impact on performance. Tension is the second element of Emotionality in test anxiety model. It refers to the student feeling tense during testing and feeling uneasy just before getting test results. Study indicated that Tension has slightly more negative impact towards student performance as compared to Bodily Symptoms (David et al., 2000).

Academic Performance

This study uses students' marks from final examinations in three courses – Cost Accounting (ACCD 213), Company Accounts II (ACCD 313), and Business Accounting II (ACCF 063) – offered to undergraduates at the Universiti Tenaga Nasional (UNITEN). The maximum mark that a student may achieve is 100 while the lowest is 0.

Test Anxiety Models

Among the models that have been suggested for explaining the effect of test anxiety on academic performance are the Interference and Deficit models.

Interference Model. The Interference Model describes test anxious student who know or sufficiently understand the content of course material but who went blank during the examination. In such a situation, the particular student is unable to recall prior learning or course materials (Wine, 1980). This model also indicated that students with high levels of test anxiety tend to divide their attention between the task demand (i.e., examination) and personal concerns, particularly negative self-preoccupation. However, students with low levels of test anxiety may devote most of their attention to task demands (Wine, 1980). This implies that the Interference model stresses the detrimental effect of task irrelevant thought during the test taking situation. A study that was conducted by Morris et al. (1981) supported this model.

In addition, the high test anxious students may be involved in more negative thinking which perhaps interferes with the task demand (i.e., focusing on exam) when the students are under evaluative threat (Mwamwenda, 1994). The decline in academic performance caused by high test anxiety is a reflection of self doubt rather than lack of ability (Sarason & Stoops, 1978). The concept of the Interference model of test anxiety was supported by the majority of test anxiety researchers (David et al., 2000). For example, Hambree (1988) supporting the Interference model, concluded from a meta-analysis of 562 studies that test anxiety interferes with students' recall of prior learning.

Deficit Model. In the Deficit model two types of factors were taken into consideration which caused poor academic performance due to high test anxiety experienced by students: study skills and test taking skills. Study skills describe student's behaviours during meaningful learning that are intended to improve the acquisition, retention and retrieval of new knowledge (Tobias, 1985). This model assumes that student performance is reduced due to less initial acquisition or storage of the course materials contents rather than interference in retrieving course materials previously learned. According to Jochen and Arndt (1999) high test anxious students had less effective study skills than their low anxious counterparts. Therefore they have less knowledge of the relevant course materials.

The model also assumes that poor academic performance is caused by deficiencies in students' test taking skills. Elevation in test anxiety during testing presumably is caused by students' awareness of doing poorly. Tobias (1985) stated that test taking skills significantly affected performance on essay and multiple-choice examinations but had a less important effect on calculation (i.e., mathematics examinations).

In order to clarify the differences between the Interference and Deficit models in explaining the effect of test anxiety on academic performance, the diagram in Figure 1 is referred to. The diagram is composed of three components, which are input, processing and output. Input refers to the presentation of instructional material to student. Processing represents the operations performed by students to encode, organise and store the input (i.e., study skills) and output denotes the performance of students on evaluative measures. Test anxiety affects all three components (Tobias, 1985).

Test anxiety at the input stage refers to the apprehension that students experience when they are presented with new learning material. The level of test anxiety depends on the student's ability to attend to, concentrate on and encode information. Anxiety experienced at this stage may reduce the effectiveness of input by limiting the anxious student's ability to attend to material presented by the instructor and reducing the student's ability to represent input internally (Bailey, Ongwuegbuzie & Daley, 2000). Students with high levels of test anxiety at this stage may ask their lecturer to repeat sentences or explain more often than do their low anxious counterparts.

Anxiety at the processing stage refers to the apprehension students' experience when performing cognitive operation on new information. The amount of test anxiety during processing depends on the complexity of the information, the extent to which memory is realised, and the level of organisation of the presented material (Tobias, 1985). At this stage, anxiety can impede learning by reducing the efficiency with which memory processes are used to solve problems. Moreover, high levels of anxiety at the processing stage may reduce a student's ability to understand messages or to learn new material (Bailey et al., 2000).

Finally, anxiety at the output stage involved the apprehension students experienced when required to demonstrate their ability to use previously learned material. Particularly, anxiety at this stage involved interference that appears after processing had been completed, but before it had been reproduced effectively as output. High level of anxiety at this stage might hinder students' ability to reproduce the learned material when it is required. Bailey et al. (2000) noted that the three stages of test anxiety are interdependent. Each stage depends on the successful completion of the previous one.

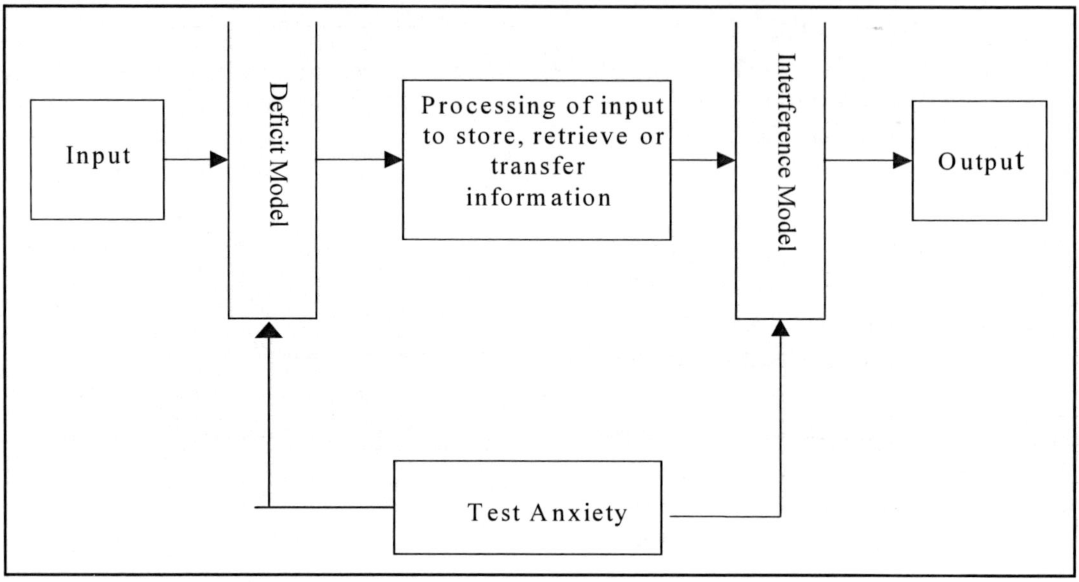

Figure 1. Theoretical Model of the Current Study [1].

The major difference between Interference and Deficit can be seen clearly in the post processing. At this point, the Interference model assumes that learning had occurred; however, the evaluative threat posed by the examination situation interferes with the students' ability to retrieve information. The students are said to "go blank" during examination and therefore are unable to recall prior knowledge. On the other hand, the Deficit model of test anxiety seems to affect the input and processing components. The inadequate initial preparation or poor test taking skills among the students may account for the reduced academic performance (Tobias, 1985). For the purpose of this study, the Interference model is the preferred test anxiety model in explaining its effects on students' performance. This model is adopted as the majority of researchers have supported this concept (e.g., Deffenbecher, 1980; Hambree, 1988; Morris et al., 1981; Mwamwenda, 1994 and Sarason & Stoops, 1978).

Schematic Diagram

The schematic diagram in Figure 2 summarizes the theoretical framework of the present study. There are four components of test anxiety (i.e., Worry, Test Irrelevant Thinking, Bodily Symptoms and Tension) that serve as independent variables. Performance is the dependent variable in the study, which refers to student's final examination marks of accounting courses.

---

[1] Source: Tobias S. (1985). "Test Anxiety: Interference, Defective Skills and Cognitive Capacity". *Educational Psychologist*, *20*(3), 135-142.

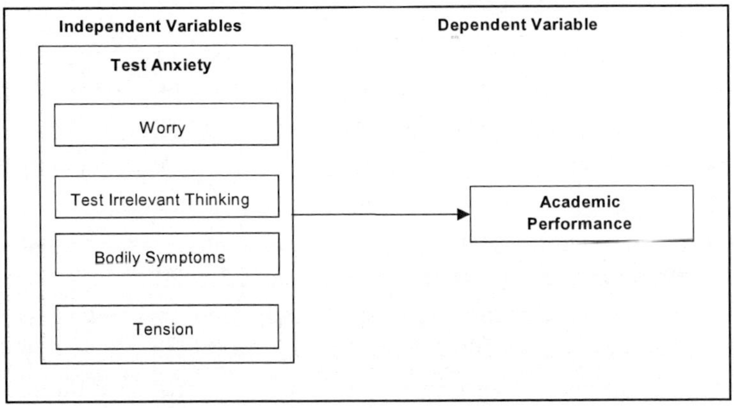

Figure 2. Schematic Diagram.

Research Design

This section discusses the research questions, type of study, data collection method, and the sample as well as the instrument and its validity. In addition, this chapter also discusses the data analyses, data types, and statistical analyses using Factor Analysis, K-S test, Correlation, One-way ANOVA, and Independent sample T-tests.

Research Questions

There are three main research questions that will be addressed in the present study.

- How do test anxiety variables relate to the academic performance of students?
- Does the level of test anxiety among students vary between three groups of students?
- Does the level of test anxiety among the students vary in different demographic and environmental situation?

Data Collection

In this study, data were collected using self-reported questionnaires at the end of the semester for each courses offered at UNITEN. The data collection was approximately one month before the final examination. The study involved all the population of students that enrolled in the three courses i.e., Cost Accounting (DBS), Company Accounts II (DIA) and Business Accounting II (Business Foundation). As data were gathered only once, this current study can be considered a cross-sectional study. However, the students' academic performances (i.e., final examination marks) were obtained from the academic records of the students.

Instrument

The students responded to a self-reported questionnaire called the Revised Test Anxiety (RTA) developed and verified by Benson and El-Zahhar (1994). The instrument was developed based on the combination of Test Anxiety Inventory (TAI), created by Spielberger, Gonzalez, Taylor, Algaze and Anton (1978) and Reaction To Test scale (RTT) proposed by Sarason (1984). From the combination of 60 items (20 items from TAI and 40 items from RTT), a process of item deletion resulted in 20 items of RTA consisting of the four dimensions of Worry, Test Irrelevant Thinking, Bodily Symptoms and Tension. The RTA is based on the theoretical four-factor dimensionality proposed by Sarason (1994). The goal of RTA is to incorporate the best qualities of each scale, to maintain multiple dimensions as theorised by Sarason, to provide a scale with acceptable precision and to develop valid measure of test anxiety for multinational samples.

The instrument consists of 20 questions or items based on a 4-point Likert scale. The scales are 1 = almost never, 2 = sometimes, 3 = often and 4 = almost always. Higher scores reflects higher test anxiety. RTA can be divided into two broad components; Cognitive and Emotionality. The Cognitive component comprises Worry and Test Irrelevant Thinking, while the Emotionality component comprises Tension and Bodily Symptoms. The twenty items in the RTA are distributed among the four components as follows: Worry (6 items), Test Irrelevant Thinking (4 items), Tension (5 items) and Bodily Symptoms (5 items).

Benson and El-Zahhar (1994) have demonstrated the stability of the dimensionality estimates of 20 items RTA scale by cross-validation among American and Egyptian samples. In addition, David et al (2000), who conducted a study to validate the RTA by using a sample of Irish students, found that the RTA is a useful cross cultural instrument to measure test anxiety. Therefore, the instrument used in this study is reliable and valid in measuring test anxiety among the UNITEN students in Malaysia.

Analysis

In conducting the statistical analysis, SPSS version 12 was used. This section explains the data analysis process.

Data Types

Initially, it is important to identify the types of data gathered whether they are ordinal, ratio, nominal or interval. In this study, the data were obtained through self-reported questionnaires received from the students using 4-point Likert scale.

According to Keller and Warrack (2000), if data can be ordered or ranked preferentially, those data are considered as ranked data and are said to have an ordinal scale. The responses using a 4-point Likert scale are considered non-quantitative data because the data are ranked based on preferences. In addition, Mason, Lind and Marchal (1999) suggested that we are not able to differentiate the magnitude of the differences between the ranks. For instance, is the difference between "almost never" and "sometimes" the same as the difference between "almost always" and "often?" We can only conclude that rating 1 is better than rating 2 or 3 or 4 but we cannot determine how much better. Thus, it is clear that the data obtained are ordinal data (Keller & Warrack, 2000; Mason et al., 1999).

Statistical Analysis

When the data are ranked, average is not the appropriate measure. Keller and Warrack (2000) proposed the use of non-parametric statistical tests for ranked data. However, this present study utilised factor scores for further analysis as it is considered as ratio data. Hair et al. (1992) recommended the use of factor scores if the instrument used to collect the original data is well constructed, valid and reliable. As the RTA is a reliable and valid instrument to measure test anxiety, factor scores are utilised for analysis involving test anxiety variables. In addition, we can use parametric test if the data are normally distributed. In this study the confidence level of statistical tests is 95%. All the statistical analysis with p-values of 0.05 or less are considered as significant to reject the null hypothesis.

Normality. Kolmogorov-Smirnov Test (K-S Test) was used to test the normality of data, which comprise the four test anxiety factors; Tension, Test Irrelevant Thinking, Bodily Symptoms and Worry. Parametric tests are appropriate for normally distributed data and non-parametric are appropriate for data that are not normally distributed.

Factor Analysis. The study utilised a well-established research instrument (RTA). However, because the data are collected from very different groups of students, factor analysis was performed. In order to determine the number of factors to be extracted from the variables, the common rule was the eigenvalue of more than 1.

Correlation. With regards to the first research question on the association between test anxiety and academic performance, the bivariate correlation was performed. Pearson correlation is an appropriate measure for normally distributed data and Spearman correlation for data that are not normally distributed.

One-way ANOVA. The second research question is to measure the differences in the level of test anxiety among students. ANOVA tests are performed for data that are normally distributed. ANOVA tests were also performed to answer the third research question regarding the effect of demographic factors which involved comparison between more than two groups (i.e., age, reasons for enrolment and study habit).

Independent Sample T-test. The study also investigated the effect of demographic factors on the test anxiety level which involved comparison between two groups. Demographic factors include student gender, hometown, secondary school profile and exposure to accounting subjects during SPM. For the test anxiety variables that are normally distributed, independent sample t-tests were performed.

Results, Interpretation, and Discussion

Factor Analysis

Factor Analysis is a data reduction technique used to reduce a large number of variables to a smaller set of underlying factors, which summarise the important information contained in the variables. The following are the results for the factor analysis test.

Kaiser-Meyer-Olkin (KMO) and Bartlett's Test. In performing factor analysis, the KMO and Bartlett's Tests were used. These tests measure sampling adequacy. The results of KMO is 0.820 and a good measure should be greater than 0.6. Thus, it indicated good sampling adequacy. In addition, the Bartlett's test of sphericity was significant with a p-value of 0.000. The anti-image correlation matrices revealed all the measure of sampling adequacy are well above acceptable level of 0.5.

The Rotated Factor Matrix. Based on the rotated factor matrix table (see Table 1), which employed the Varimax rotation method, the results indicate five factors from the total of 20 variables or items used to measure test anxiety. The results are quite inconsistent with the study conducted by Benson and El-Zahhar (1994). All the factors are named accordingly based on their items. The existing four factors are retained with the addition of one new factor.

The first factor known as **Bodily Symptoms** comprises 6 items with factor loading ranging from 0.349 to 0.597. These items assess how much students experienced Bodily Symptoms before taking tests. Such bodily symptoms include headache, trembling, muscle tightening and difficulty in breathing. An example of Bodily Symptoms would be getting a headache during an important test.

Table 1. Rotated Factor Matrix

	Factor				
	1	2	3	4	5
Item 16	.597				
Item 15	.569				
Item 18	.520	.313			
Item 17	.497				
item 10	.361				
item 6	.349				
item 9		.656			
item 14		.626			
item 7		.591			
item 13		.532			
item 5			.551		
item 4			.539		
item 20			.484		

Table 1. (Continued)

	Factor				
	1	2	3	4	5
item 12	.339		.360		
item 11			.336		
item 8					
item 3			.327	.589	
item 2				.447	
item 19					.498
item 1				.366	.449

Extraction Method: Principal Axis Factoring. Rotation Method: Varimax with Kaiser Normalization.

The second factor, **Test Irrelevant Thinking,** measures the students' judgement on how relevant an examination is to them. An example can be seen in the following statement: "During tests I find myself thinking of things unrelated to the material being tested." There are 4 items that were grouped into this factor with factor loadings ranging from 0.532 to 0.656. The result was consistent with Benson and El-Zahhar (1994).

The third factor, **Tension,** comprises 5 items and the results are slightly inconsistent with what was found by Benson and El-Zahhar (1994). The factor loadings of the 5 items ranged from 0.336 to 0.551. The factor assesses the level of tension experienced by the students before and during testing or examination. An example of this is the statement, "I start feeling very uneasy just before getting a test paper back."

The forth factors, termed as **self defeat**, measures students' negative perceptions during testing. The factor comprises two items and loadings range from 0.447 to 0.589. An example of this is the statement, "I seem to defeat myself while taking important tests".

The last factor in test anxiety construct is **Worry**. It has 2 items that are used to assess the level of worry among students. The factor load ranged from 0.449 to 0.498. An example of Worry can be seen in the statement, "Thinking about my grade in a program interferes with my work on tests." All of the five factors will be the basis to form further analysis in relation to test anxiety. Item 8 from the RTA was dropped due to a correlation of less than 0.30.

Normality Test

The study utilised K-S tests in order to test the normality of variables. There are five main variables in relation to the test anxiety construct; Bodily Symptoms, Test Irrelevant Thinking, Tension, Self-Defeat and Worry. The results illustrated in Table 2 indicated that all test anxiety variables were normally distributed. Bodily Symptoms (p-value = 0.130), Test Irrelevant Thinking, (p-value = 0.649), Tension (p-value = 0.320), Self-Defeat (p-value = 0.140) and Worry, (p-value = 0.846). With regards to academic performance (i.e., final examination marks for accounting courses) the results indicated a normal distribution.

Table 2. One-Sample Kolmogorov-Smirnov Test

	Factor 1	Factor 2	Factor 3	Factor 4	Factor 5	Exam Marks
N	308	308	308	308	308	345
Std. Deviation	.81260873	.83818322	.76977603	.72612033	.71086918	14.109
Kolmogorov-Smirnov Z	1.169	.737	.956	1.154	.614	1.003
Asymp. Sig. (2-tailed)	.130	.649	.320	.140	.846	.266

The Association between Test Anxiety and Academic Performance

The primary research objective is to measure and determine the associations between test anxiety and academic performance of the DIA, DBS and Business Foundation students. It was hypothesised that the test anxiety construct is inversely related to academic performance. Therefore, it is important to test such relationships as previous studies demonstrated inverse relationships between test anxiety and academic performance. For instance, Hambree (1988) found that test anxiety had negative relationships with academic performance where high test anxiety students tended to score lower than low test anxiety students. The above relationship was tested using the Pearson correlation.

The results indicate that Self-defeat was found to have a significant relationship with academic performance (p-value =0.039 and r = - 0.119) for all programs. In relation to individual programs, DIA and Business Foundation programs reported a significant relationship with academic performance. DBS programs showed no significant result. For DIA programs, the result revealed that only the Worry variable was found to be negatively associated with performance (p-value = 0.006 and r = - 0.363). For Business Foundation, Self-defeat (p-value = 0.019 and r = -0.365) and Worry (p-value = 0.006 and r = -0.418) results showed a negative association with academic performance. The other variables indicated no significant result.

Comparison of Test Anxiety Level between Groups

The second research objective has been divided into two parts which compare the test anxiety levels among the three cohorts of DBS students (i.e., students from semester 2, 2003/2004, semester 1, 2004/2005 and semester 2, 2004/2005) and compare the test anxiety levels among DIA, DBS and Business Foundation students. Both objectives were tested using one-way ANOVA. For the first objective, it was hypothesised that there was a significant difference in the level of test anxiety construct among the three cohorts of DBS students. The present study involved 117 students from semester 2, 2003/2004, 114 students from semester 1, 2004/2005 and 120 students from semester 2, 2004/2005.

Based on the results obtained, there is sufficient evidence to infer that there is a significant different in the level of Worry (p-value = 0.013) among these three groups. The students from semester 2, 2004/2005 experienced the highest level of Worry (mean 0.199) compared to their counterparts from semester 2, 2003/2004 and semester 1, 2004/2005. The other variables showed no significant differences.

For the second part of this objective, it was hypothesised that the level of test anxiety between DIA, DBS and Business Foundation students was significantly different. Based on analysis performed, three variables were found to have significant results as presented in Table 3.

Table 3. Differences in test anxiety level

Factor	B. Symptom	Tension	Self-defeat
P-value	0.000	0.012	0.048
DIA (mean)	-0.135	-0.192	-0.102
DBS (mean)	0.114	-0.003	0.065
B. Foundation (mean)	-0.410	0.276	-0.203

Table 3 shows that the Business Foundation students exhibit lower levels of Bodily symptoms (mean –0.410) while the DBS students exhibit the highest score (mean 0.114). In relation to the Self-defeat variable, the same result is applied. Surprisingly, the Business Foundation students were found to experience the highest level of Tension (mean 0.276) as compared to their counterparts.

The Effect of Demographic and Environmental Factors on Test Anxiety

The third research objective concerns the effect of demographic and environmental factors towards test anxiety level. Among the demographic factors are the students' gender, hometown, exposure to accounting subjects during SPM, age, reasons for enrollment and students' study behaviour (i.e., preferred study format, study time, study hours per week and study before test). The above demographic factors were hypothesised to have significant effects on test anxiety level.

The results indicated that only student's study behaviour such as preferred study hours per week and study before test showed the significant effect to the level of test anxiety. The other demographic factors exhibited no significant result. A preferred study hour refers to the amount of hours allocated for reviewing the course material. The three choices given were: more than 10 hours, 5 to 9 hours and less than 4 hours. It was found that only Test irrelevant thinking (p-value = 0.019) did support the hypothesis. The others showed no significant result. It revealed that the students who study less than 4 hours per week experienced high levels of Test irrelevant thinking (mean 1.160). The students who study more than 10 hours per week exhibited the opposite result (mean –0.336).

The respondents were asked about their study attitude before they sat for any tests. The three choices given were "consistent study", "when I feel like it" and "last minute study". The result reported that Bodily symptom (p-value = 0.023) and Worry (p-value = 0.042) variables have sufficient evidence to infer the hypothesis. It was found that the students who have a consistent study behavior exhibited the highest score (mean 0.094). Surprisingly, the students who studied last minute, indicated the lowest score (mean –0.107). Unlike the Bodily symptom variable, the students who had a consistent study pattern experienced the lowest level of Worry (mean –0.152) while the students who had a last minutes study pattern experienced the highest level of Worry (mean 0.094).

Discussion of the Results

This section discusses the association between test anxiety and academic performance as well as the comparison of test anxiety level among the DBS students from different cohorts and students from various programs. It also discusses the effect of demographic and environmental factors towards test anxiety.

The Association between Test Anxiety and Academic Performance

On the basis of research viewed earlier, it has been reported that there are negative relationships between the levels of test anxiety and academic performance. Those who score high in test anxiety generally performed less well academically than those who have a low level of test anxiety (Hambree, 1988). In the present study, the same pattern of results was replicated. From the findings, Self-defeat was found to have an inverse relationship with academic performance for all programs. Business Foundation students reported a similar pattern of results with the additional Worry variable. The DIA program also indicated a negative relationship between Worry and academic performance.

For the current study, Worry was found to have a strong association with academic performance particularly with the students enrolled in the Business Foundation program. Worry refers to uncontrollable cognitive activity that relates to negative thought that results in emotional discomfort to an individual. Examples of negative thought include expecting to perform poorly on test, not being confident or being doubtful of one's ability and thinking extensively about the consequences of failing the test. Therefore, the students who score high in level of Worry are more likely to have lower academic results. This result was consistent with the study found by Sarason (1984) indicating that Worry is more strongly related to poor performance. In addition, Wine (1980 and 1971) reported that the impairment of performance is due to the cognitive component and Worry is one element in the cognitive component.

The results of the present study indicated that Worry is strongly and negatively associated with performance. Thus, it supports the Interference model such as when high anxious students are under evaluative situations, they engage more on cognitive activity (i.e., Worry) that may interfere with their task accomplishment (i.e., answering the examination questions). This result is supported by Mwamwenda (1994). Clearly, the Interference model seems relevant in the present study. Thus, the accounting lecturers in particular have to implement the appropriate test anxiety treatments which focus on reducing the test anxiety that inhibits students from retrieving course contents during examinations.

Comparison of Test Anxiety Level among the Students between UiTM Campuses

The current study revealed that the Worry variable showed a significant difference in terms of level of test anxiety among the three cohorts of DBS students. The result suggests that the students from semester 2, 2004/2005 were more likely to be exposed to the negative thought which might have resulted in emotional discomfort as compared to their counterparts.

In comparing the level of test anxiety among the DIA, DBS and Business Foundation students, the present study reported that Bodily symptom, Tension and Self-defeat showed a significant difference in the level of test anxiety among these groups of student. The Business Foundation students were found to have the lowest level of Bodily symptoms and Self- defeat while DBS students exhibited the highest score for both variables. Therefore we can infer that DBS students were more anxious and more likely to experience headache, stomachache and shaking during test taking. However, Business Foundation students feel more tension during the test and feel uneasy just before they receive their test paper back.

The Effect of Demographic and Environmental Factors towards Test Anxiety

Some research suggests that test anxiety can be situationally specific and thus may vary depending on the environmental or demographic factors (Bruce, 1994). There are several environmental and demographic factors considered in this study in order to serve the third research objective. They include student's gender, hometown, exposure to accounting subjects during SPM, age, reasons for enrollment and student's study behaviour. This section highlights the significance of the results.

The students may relate test anxiety to the preparation done before exams or their study behaviour. Normally, less preparation would seem to lead to higher test anxiety due to the greater chance of poor performance. The result of the present study revealed the relationship between the level of test anxiety and level of preparation (i.e., student's study behavior). In relation to preferred study hours, the finding suggests that the students should engage in their study for more than 4 hours per week. It is proven that those who studied less than 4 hours per week were more likely to be less prepared, thus more anxious for the tests, particularly for the courses concerned.

Unexpectedly, the current findings reported that the students who studied consistently before their tests indicated the highest level of Bodily symptoms and the opposite result was found. However, the students who studied consistently exhibited the lowest score for level of Worry and those who studied last minute experienced high levels of Worry. This finding implies that students should engage in their studies consistently. It is proven that those who study consistently are more likely to be well prepared, thus less anxious for the test. The present study was inconsistent with the result obtained by David (2004) who reported no significant difference in the level of test anxiety and study behaviour.

Conclusions, Recommendations, and Future Research

The four-factor model of test anxiety in the RTA scale established by Benson and El Zahhar (1994) can be used as a basis for describing data in the present study. The factorial invariance across diverse population suggests that the RTA scale is potentially a useful cross-cultural instrument.

In line with previous research, the present study demonstrates an inverse relationship between test anxiety and academic performance. The Cognitive factor (i.e., Worry) has emerged as the strongest predictor of academic performance among the factors. This result suggests that students may be able to reduce test anxiety by addressing the problem of distracting thought during examinations. In examining levels of test anxiety among DIA, DBS and Business Foundation students from UNITEN, the DBS students reported the highest score in the most significant variables. Furthermore, the level of test anxiety varies depending on environmental and demographic factors. Most of the demographic factors exhibit no significant results.

From the theoretical standpoint, the effect of test anxiety on academic performance can be explained within the Interference and Deficit models. The current results support the Interference model which stresses the detrimental effect of negative thoughts during test taking situations.

The two models used in explaining the effect of test anxiety on academic performance have been conceptualised by some researchers as being mutually exclusive (Jochen & Arndt, 1999). However, some of the researchers proposed that both Interference and Deficit were complementary rather than contradictory (Naveh-Benjamin, McKeachie & Lin 1981). This implies that lower test score of anxious students can occur either by lack of study skills or interference in the retrieval of prior learning or by the combination of both. This assumption sets the stage for further investigation to test whether both models are contradictory or complementary. In addition, research is also encouraged to investigate the effect of test anxiety on performance with the inclusion of intervening variables such as self-efficacy, personality and learning strategies.

References

Ames, C. A., (1990). "Motivation: What teachers need to know", *Teachers College Record,* **91**(3), 409-422.

Austin, J. S. & Patridge, E. (1995). "Prevent School Failure: Treat Test Anxiety", *Preventing School Failure,* **40**(1), 10-14.

Bailey, P., Ongwuegbuzie, A. J. & Daley, C. E. (2000). "Correlates of Anxiety at Three stages of the Foreign Language Learning Process", *Journal of Language and Social Psychology,* **19**(4), 474-493.

Benson, J. & Bandalos, D. L. (1992). "Second-Order Confirmatory Factor Analysis of the Reactions to Tests Scale with Cross-Validation", *Multivariate Behavioral Research*, **27** (3), 459-487.

Benson, J. & El-Zahhar, N. (1994). "Further Refinement and Validation of the Revised Test Anxiety Scale", *Structural Equation Modeling*, **1**(3), 203-221.

Birenbaum, M. & Nasser, F. (1994). "On the Relationship between Test Anxiety and Test Performance", *Measurement and Evaluation in Counseling and Development*, **27**(1), 293-302.

Bruce, F. D. (1994). "The Effects of Motivational Orientation, Self-Efficacy and Feedback Condition on Test Anxiety", *Journal of Instructional Psychology*, **21**(2), 114-120.

Cattell, R. B. & Scheier, I. H. (1961). "The Meaning and measurement of Neuroticism and Anxiety", New York: Ronald Press.

Cheung, Chau-Kiu & Kwok, Siu-Tong (1998). "Activities and Academic Achievement among College Students", *Journal of Genetic Psychology*, **159**(2), 147-163.

Cokley, K. O., Bernard, N., Cunningham, D. & Motoike, J. (2001). "A Psychometric Investigation of the Academic Motivation Scale Using a United States Sample", *Measurement and Evaluation in Counselling and Development*, **34**(2), 109-120.

Crocker, L., Schmitt, A. & Tang, L., (1988). "Test Anxiety and standardised Achievement Test Performance in the Middle School Years", *Measurement and Evaluation in Counselling and Development*, **20**(4), 149-157.

David, M., Brendan, B. & Gary, A. (2000). "An Evaluation of the Factor Structure and Predictive Utility of a Test Anxiety Scale with Reference to Student's Past Performance and Personality Indices". *The British Journal of Educational Psychology*, **40**(1), 17-27.

Deffenbacher, J. L (1980). "Worry and Emotionality in Test Anxiety, In Sarason, I .G (Ed.), Test Anxiety: Theory, Research and Application". Hillsdale, NJ: Lawrence Erlbaum Associates, 111-124.

Eady, S. (1999). "An Investigation of Possible Correlation of General Anxiety with Performance in Eleven-Plus Scores in Year 6 Primary Pupils", *Educational Psychology*, **19**(3), 347-364.

El-Zahhar, N. & Hocevar, D. (1991). "Cultural and Sexual Differences in Test Anxiety, Traits Anxiety and Arousability, Egypt, Brazil and the United States", *Journal of Cross-Cultural Psychology*, **22**, 238-249.

Everson, H.T. & Millsap, R.E. (1991). "Isolating Gender Differences in Test Anxiety: A Confirmatory Factor Analysis of the Test Anxiety Inventory", *Educational and Psychological Measurement*, **51**(1), 243-251.

Geiger, M. A. & Cooper, E. A. (1995) "Predicting Academic Performance: The Impact of Expectancy and Needs Theory", *Journal of Experimental Education*, **63**(3), 251-263.

Gregory S. W. (1999). "Personality Variables in Levels of Predicted and Actual Test Anxiety among College Students", *Educational Research Quarterly*, **22**(3), 3-10.

Hair et al., (1992). "Multivariate Data Analysis", (3 rd Ed), New York: McMillan.

Halsted, J. W. (1994). "Some of My Best Friends are Books: Guiding Gifted Readers From Pre-school to High School", OH: *Ohio Psychology Press*.

Hambree, R. (1988). "Correlates, Causes, Effect and treatment of Test Anxiety", *Review of Educational Research*, **58**(1), 47-77.

Hill, K. T., Wigfield, A. & Plass, J. (1980). "Effects of Different Kind of Optimizing Instruction on Seventh and Eighth Grade Children's Achievement Test Performance", Paper Presented at the Annual Meeting of American Educational Research Association, Boston.

Ho, H. Z. (2000). "The Affective and Cognitive Dimension of Math Anxiety: A Cross-National Study", *Journal for Research in Mathematics Education,* **31**(3), 362-380.

Hodapp, V. & Benson, J. (1996). "The Multi Dimensionality of Test Anxiety: A Test of different Models", *Anxiety, Stress and Coping*, **10**, 219-244.

Holroyd, K. A & Appel, M. A (1980). In Sarason, I .G (Ed.), "Test Anxiety: Theory, Research and Application". Hillsdale, NJ: Lawrence Erlbaum Associates, 129-151.

Hong, E. (1998). "Differential Stability of Individual Differences in State and Trait Test Anxiety", *Learning and Individual Differences*, **10**(1), 51-70.

Hong, E. (1999). "Test Anxiety, Perceived Test Difficulty and Test Performance: Temporal Patterns of their Effects", *Learning and Individual Differences*, **11**(4), 431-448.

Ian, N. & Owens, A. (1996). "Self-Esteem and Anxiety in Secondary School Achievement", *Journal of Social Behavior and Personality*, **11**(3), 521-531.

Isaac, A. F. & Orit, B. J., (1997). "Measuring Perceived Test Anxiety in Adolescents: A Self-Report Scale", *Educational and Psychological Measurement*, **57**(6), 1035-1047.

Jiao, Q. G & Onwuegbuzie, A. J (1999). "Is Library Anxiety Important", *Library Review*, **48**(6), 278-282.

Jochen, M. & Arndt, B. (1999). "Test Anxiety versus Academic Scales: A Comparison of Two Alternative Models for Predicting Performance in a Statistic Exam", *The British Journal of Educational Psychology*, **69**(1), 105-113.

Keller, G. & Warrack, B., (2000). "Statistics for Management and Economics", (5th ed.), CA: Thompson Learning.

Liebert, R. M. & Morris, L. W. (1967). "Cognitive and Emotional Components of Test Anxiety: A Distinction and some Initial Data", *Psychological Reports,* **20**, 975-978.

Ma (1999). "A Meta-Analysis of the Relationship between Anxiety Towards mathematics and Achievement in Mathematics", *Journal for Research in mathematics Education,* **30** (5), 520-541.

Mason, R. D., Lind, D. A. & Marchal, W. G., (1999). "Statistical Techniques in Business and Economics", (10th ed.), US: McGraw-Hill

Matthew, E., Tracy, B. D. & Scott, W. D. (2000). "The Efficacy of Eye Movement Desensitization and Reprocessing Therapy Techniques in the Treatment of Test Anxiety of College Students", *Journal of College Counselling,* **3**(1), 36-49.

McDonald, A. S. (2001). "The Prevalence and Effects of Test Anxiety in School Children", *Educational Psychology*, **21**(1), 89-102.

Mealey, D. L. & Host, T. R. (1992). "Coping With Test Anxiety", *College Teaching,* **40**(4), 147-151.

Morris, L. W., Davis, M. A. & Hutchings, C. H. (1981). "Cognitive and Emotional Components of Anxiety: Literature Review and A Revised Worry–Emotionality Scale", *Journal of Educational Psychology,* **73**, 541-555.

Mwamwenda, T. S. (1994). "Gender Differences in Scores on Test Anxiety and Academic Achievement among South African university Graduate Students", *South African Journal of Psychology,* **24**(4), 228-231.

Nasser, F., Takahashi, T. & Benson, J. (1997). "The Structure of Test Anxiety in Israeli – Arab High School Students: An Application of Confirmatory Factor Analysis with Miniscales", *Anxiety, Stress and Coping,* **10**, 129-151.

Naveh-Benjamin, M., McKeachie, W. & Lin, Y. (1987). "Two Types of Test Anxious Students: Support For An Information Processing Model", *Journal of Educational Psychology,* **79**, 131-136.

Paulsen, M. B. & Gentry, J. A. (1995). "Motivation, Learning Strategies and Academic Performance: A Study of the College Finance Classroom", *Financial Practice and Education,* **5**(1), 78-90.

Pintrich, P. R. & De Groot, E. V. (1990). "Motivational and Self-Regulated Learning Components of Classroom academic performance", *Journal of Educational Psychology,* **82**(1), 33-40.

Pintrich, P. R. & Garcia, T., (1991). Student Goal Orientation and Self-Regulation in the College Classroom, In Advances in Motivation and achievement, Vol. 7, M. Maehr and Pintrich, P. R., Eds., Greenwich, CT, JAI Press, 371-402.

Ronald, A. B. (2000). "Does Humour in Course Tests Reduce Anxiety and Improve Performance", *College Teaching,* **48**(4), 151-159.

Ryan, A. M. (2001). "Explaining the Black-White Test Score Gap: The Role of Test Perceptions", *Human Performance,* **14**(1), 45-76.

Sandra, S. E. A. & Johnson, C. Y. (1998). "Is Journal Writing an Effective Method of Reducing Anxiety Towards Statistics", *Journal of Instructional Psychology,* **25**(1),49-58.

Sakaran, U., (1992). "Research Methods for Business: A Skill Building Approach", (2nd ed.) NY: John Wiley & Sons, Inc.

Sarason, I. G. & Stoops, R. (1978). "Test Anxiety and the Passage of Time", *Journal of Consulting and Clinical Psychology,* **46**(1), 102-109.

Sarason, I. G. (1978). "The Test Anxiety Scale: Concept and Research", In C. D. Spielberger and I. G. Sarason (Eds.), *Stress and Anxiety,* Vol. 5. Washington, D. C: Hemisphere Publishing Corporation, 193-216.

Sarason, I. G. (1984). "Stress, Anxiety and Cognitive Interference: Reaction To Tests", *Journal of Personality and Social Psychology,* **46**(4), 929-938.

Schutz, P. A., Davis, H. A. & Schwanenflugel, P. J. (2002). "Organisation of Concepts Relevant to Emotion and Their Regulation during Test Taking", *Journal of Experimental education,* **70**(4), 316-342.

Scuitto, M. J. (1995). "Student-Centered Methods For Decreasing Anxiety and Increasing Interest Level in Undergraduate Statistics Course", *Journal of Instructional Psychology,* **22**(8), 277-280.

Siti Rosmaini, Ariff & Normah Omar (2003). "The Effect of Test Anxiety Towards Performance of Accounting Students", SEMACC Proceedings.

Somuncuogle, Y. & Yildirim, A. (1999). "Relationship Between Achievement Goal Orientations and use of Learning Strategies", *Journal of Educational Research.* **92**(5), 267-278.

Spielberger, C. D. (1966). Anxiety and Behaviour, New York: Academic Press.

Spielberger, C. D. (1980). "Preliminary Professional Manual for Test Anxiety Inventory", *Palo Alto CA Consulting Psychologist Press.*

Spielberger, C. D., Gonzales, H., Taylor, C., Algaze, B. & Anton, W. (1978). "Examination, Stress and Test Anxiety", In Spielberger, C. & Sarason, I. G. (Eds.), *Stress and Anxiety,* Vol. 5, NY: Hemisphere/Wiley.

Spielberger, C. D., Anton, W., & Bedell, J. (1976). The Nature and Treatment of Test Anxiety, In M. Zuckerman, & C. D. Spielberger (Eds.), Emotion and Anxiety: New Concepts, Methods and Application. Hillsdale, NJ: Erlbaum, 317-345.

Thomas, R. H & Joseph, M. F. (1997). "Helping High Ability Students Overcome Math Anxiety Through Bibliotherapy", *Journal of Secondary Gifted Education,* **8**(4), 164-179.

Tobias, S. (1980). "Anxiety and Instruction", In Sarason, I. G. (Ed.), Test Anxiety: Theory, Research and Applications, Hillsdale, NJ: Erlbaum, 289-310.

Tobias, S. (1985). "Test Anxiety: Interference, Defective Skills and Cognitive Capacity", *Educational Psychologist,* **20** (3), 135-142.

Tyron, G. S. (1980). "The Measurement and treatment of Test Anxiety", *Review of Educational Research,* **50**(2), 343-372.

Wine, J. D. (1982). "Evaluation Anxiety: A Cognitive Attentional Construct", In H. W. Krohne & L. Laux (Eds.). *Achievement, Stress and Anxiety.* Washington D. C: Hemisphere, 207-219.

Zeidner, M. (1992). "Source of Academic Stress: The Case of 1st Year Jewish and Arab College Students in Israel", *Higher Education,* **24**, 25-40.

In: Anxiety in College Students
Editor: Benjamin Ayres and Michelle Bristow
ISBN: 978-1-60692-282-8

Chapter IV

Writing your Way to Health? The Effects of Disclosure of Past Stressful Events in German Students

Lisette Morris, Annedore Linkemann and Birgit Kröner-Herwig*
Clinical Psychology and Psychotherapy
University of Göttingen, Germany

Abstract

In 1986 Pennebaker and Beall published their renowned study on the long-term beneficial health effects of disclosing traumatic events in 4 brief sequential writing sessions. Their results have been confirmed in various studies, but conflicting results have also been reported. The intent of our study was to replicate the experiments from Pennebaker and Beall (1986), Pennebaker et al. (1988), and Greenberg and Stone (1992) using a German student sample. Additionally, essay variables that point to the emotional processing of events (e.g., depth of self-exploration, number of negative/positive emotions, intensity of emotional expression) were examined as potential mechanisms of action. Trait measures of personality which could moderate the personal consequences of disclosure (alexithymia, self-concealment, worrying, social support) were also assessed. In a second study the experimental condition (disclosure) was varied by implementing "coping" vs. "helping" instructions as variations of the original condition. Under the coping condition participants were asked to elaborate on what they used to do, continue to do, or could do in the future to better cope with the event. Under the helping condition participants were asked to imagine themselves in the role of a adviser and elaborate on what they would recommend to persons also dealing with the trauma in order to better cope with the event. The expected beneficial effects of disclosure on long-term health

* Prof. Dr. B. Kroener-Herwig; Georg-Elias-Mueller-Institut für Psychologie; Dep. Clinical Psychology and Psychotherapy; Gosslerstr. 14; D - 37073 Goettingen; Email: bkroene@uni-goettingen.de

(e.g., physician visits, physical symptoms, affectivity) could not be corroborated in either the first or the second study. None of the examined essay variables of emotional processing and only a single personality variable was able to explain significant variance in the health-related outcome variables influence. Nevertheless, substantial reductions in posttraumatic stress symptoms (e.g., intrusions, avoidance, arousal), were found in both experiments. These improvements were significantly related to essay variables of emotional expression and self-exploration and were particularly pronounced under the activation of a prosocial motivation (helping condition).

Repeated, albeit brief, expressive writing about personally upsetting or traumatic events resulted in an immediate increase in negative mood but did not lead to long-term positive health consequences in a German student sample. It did, however, promote better processing of stressful or traumatic events, as evidenced by reductions in posttraumatic stress symptoms. The instruction to formulate recommendations for persons dealing with the same trauma seems more helpful than standard disclosure or focusing on one's own past, present, and future coping endeavours. Overall, expressive writing seems to be a successful method of improving trauma processing. Determining the appropriate setting (e.g., self-help vs. therapeutic context) for disclore can be seen as an objective of future research.

Introduction

Pennebaker & Beall's (1986) study published under the title "Confronting a traumatic event: Towards an understanding of inhibition and disease" caused quite a sensation among clinical psychologists and incited numerous replication studies, primarily in the USA. In their original study, the authors asked students to write about personally upsetting or traumatic experiences from one of the following three perspectives: emphasising feelings without describing the actual experience (trauma-emotion condition), emphasising factual aspects of the experience without mentioning feelings (trauma-fact condition), or describing both the experience and the associated feelings (trauma-combination condition). In a control condition, students were instructed to write in an factual manner about different trivial topics (e.g., their living room, the shoes they were wearing). In all four conditions, writing took place on 4 consecutive days for a period of 15 minutes per day.

The physical symptoms and mood of the students were assessed directly prior to and following writing and a number of health-related variables were assessed at follow-up 4 to 6 months later. Short-term effects of writing were not found for physical symptoms, but significant effects were found, for mood. Ss in all three trauma conditions reported a deterioration of mood subsequent to writing, whereas controls reported improved mood.

The most important effect, however, was the significantly better health status found in the trauma-combination condition at follow-up. Ss in both the trauma-emotion and trauma-combination conditions reported significant reductions of health problems (4-month) relative to the other conditions, while significantly fewer days with illness-related restriction of activity (4-month) and fewer visits to the university health care centre (6-month follow-up) were found only in the trauma-combination condition.

The authors concluded that written disclosure of traumatic or stressful experiences in a manner that combines emotional expression and factual description is beneficial to health, at least in a sample of young students. Thus, it seemed that with the disclosure paradigm a simple intervention capable of enhancing physical, and perhaps even psychological, health had been found.

Numerous replication studies conducted by Pennebaker and associates as well as by independent researchers followed and various modifications were made to the original paradigm. In some studies Ss were asked to write about specific events like job loss (Spera et al, 1994), entering college (Pennebaker et al., 1990; Pennebaker & Francis, 1996) or suffering from rheumatic disease (Kelly et al, 1997). In some of the studies disclosure took place not through writing but by oral report (e.g., Pennebaker et al. 1987; Donnelly & Murray, 1991; Esterling et al, 1994) or bodily expression (Krantz & Pennebaker, 1996). Additionally, the length of writing sessions was varied (e.g., up to 45 minutes by Schoutrop et al, 1996), as was the number of sessions (1 session by Greenberg et al, 1996; 5 sessions by Spera et al, 1994).

Nearly all early studies corroborated the negative short-term effect of expressive writing on mood (e.g., Petrie et al, 1995; Francis & Pennebaker, 1992, Greenberg et al, 1996) and many further studies found the postulated short-term increase in physical symptoms (e.g., Pennebaker et al, 1988; Greenberg & Stone, 1992; Booth et al, 1997). The long-term beneficial effects on physical health were supported by numerous studies which documented improvements ranging from reductions in health care utilization (e.g., Pennebaker et al, 1990, Pennebaker & Francis, 1996, Pennebaker et al, 1988) to improved immunological parameters (e.g., Esterling et al, 1994; Pennebaker et al, 1988; Lutgendorf et al, 1994; Petrie et al, 1995). In other studies, however, expressive writing did not positively affect subjective health measures (e.g., Petrie et al, 1995; Spera et al, 1994; Murray & Segal, 1994). Results concerning the long-term effect of disclosure on psychological well-being were also contradictory. Pennebaker et al's (1988) results as well as the findings from Schoutrop et al (1996) pointed to long-term improvements of mood following writing. No effect, however, was seen by Greenberg and Stone (1992) and an unexpected long-term increase in negative affect was reported by Greenberg et al (1996).

Overall, the studies seemed to support the theoretical model formulated by Pennebaker (1988, 1989) on inhibition and confrontation. Based on the tenet that people have an innate desire to express their feelings and to communicate significant experiences, Pennebaker postulated that hindered interpersonal expression, due to feelings of guilt or shame or feared negative response of others, leads to negative physical and psychological consequences.

Inhibition was defined by Pennebaker (1989) as the process of consciously holding back or otherwise suppressing thoughts, feelings and behaviours. It entails physiological work and leads to an activation of the autonomic nervous system. In the long run, it places cumulative stress on the body, increasing the likelihood of stress-related physical and psychological symptoms or illness. Confrontation is seen as the opposite of inhibition. It is the process of actively facing significant personal experiences, while acknowledging and dealing with the associated feelings and thoughts. Confronting significant experiences makes the physiological work of suppressing associated thoughts and feelings obsolete and can, via reductions in overall stress level, negate the long-term effects of inhibition on physical health and psychological well-being.

Later the focus of attention was shifted more to the cognitive level (Francis & Pennebaker, 1992; Pennebaker et al., 1997). From this perspective, inhibition is seen as an impediment to the emotional processing of traumatic experiences, a hindrance to their assimilation and resolution. The inadequately processed experiences maintain their distressfulness as they resurface in the form of rumination or associated cognitive symptoms. Written or verbal confrontation, which entails the translation of traumatic memory into language, negates inhibition and works to promote the understanding and assimilation of the experiences, thereby facilitating their closure. The relevance of the reorganisation of traumatic memory and its integration into the autobiographical memory and self-concept echoes back to Horowitz (1976) and coincides with current models of the processes underlying confrontation therapy in posttraumatic stress disorder (Ehlers, 2000).

As the vast majority of the early studies were conducted in the USA and Canada, Petrie et al (1995), Paez et al. (1999), and Schoutrop et al (1996) are several exceptions, we were interested in the effect of disclosure on a German sample. The intent of our experiment was to replicate the studies from Pennebaker and Beall (1986), Pennebaker et al (1988) and Greenberg and Stone (1992) in order to find out whether we would achieve effects of disclosure comparable to those in the USA. Furthermore, we intended to study the disclosure process more closely by assessing relevant essay characteristics (e.g., frequency of positive and negative emotional expressions) and examining their influence on the short- and long-term effects of disclosure. A number of personality variables were also examined as potential moderators of the effects of disclosure.

Two studies were conducted, each on a different sample of students. In the first study, standard disclosure and control conditions were implemented. In the second study, two new variations of expressive writing were examined, one instructing the Ss to focus on coping endeavours and a second emphasising a “helping” perspective (see Methods: Study II).

Study I: Methods

The design was based on the studies from Pennebaker and Beall (1986), Pennebaker et al (1988), and Greenberg and Stone (1992) and employed analogous assessment instruments. A two factorial control group design with repeated measures was implemented in accordance with Pennebaker et al (1988). In the disclosure condition, Ss were instructed to write about a very upsetting or traumatic personal experience in their past and to emphasise revealing their deepest thoughts and feelings in their essays, while control Ss were asked to write about their daily routine and time management in an detailed and factual manner.

A total of 3 writing sessions were held, each lasting 20 minutes. Long-term effects of disclosure were assessed 6 weeks after writing in accordance with Pennebaker et al, (1988).

The sample consisted of 61 students, who were randomly assigned to one of the two conditions. Because of our focus on variables which could potentially moderate disclosure effects, a greater number of Ss were assigned to the experimental condition (40 vs. 21 in the control condition).

The following instruments, employed in disclosure research, were used (in the German translation) to assess *short-term* effects of expressive writing (pre - post comparison):

- Pennebaker Physical Symptom Scale (PPSS)
- Pennebaker Negative Mood Scale (PNMS)

Long-term effects (pre - 6-week follow-up comparison) were assessed using the following common instruments / measures:

- Pennebaker Inventory of Limbic Languidness (PILL)
- self-reported number of illness days
- self-reported number of days with illness-related activity restriction
- self-reported number of illness-related physician visits
- Positive and Negative Affect Schedule (PANAS, Watson, Clark & Telegen, 1988)
- subjective rating of the long-term effect of writing.

As an additional measure of long-term outcome, the self-report version of the PTSD Symptom Scale (PSS-SR, Foa et al, 1993) was administered to the Ss of the disclosure group.

The following essays characteristics, posited as potential mechanisms of action, were assessed in the disclosure condition:

- relative frequency of negative emotional expressions (Negative Affect Scale, Westbrook, 1976)
- relative frequency of positive emotional expressions (Positive Affect Scale)
- relative frequency of emotional expressions on the whole.

Additionally, the intensity of both positive and negative emotional expression in the essays was rated by independent judges on a 6-point scale (scale anchors taken from Schmidt-Atzert, 1981). The judges also rated the depth of self-exploration exhibited in the essays, yielding the variables average depth of self-exploration and change in self-exploration from day 1 to day 3. Self-exploration, which has proven its relevance for the course and efficacy of client-centred therapy (German Scale: Tausch, 1970), seemed a fitting construct for disclosure research. Finally, Ss in both conditions were asked to rate how emotionally revealing and personal their essays were.

Four personality variables were selected for examination as potential moderators of the short- and long-term effects of disclosure on the basis of their theoretical fit with Pennebaker's theory of inhibition and confrontation. The following instruments were employed for their assessment in the German version:

- Self-Concealment Scale (SCS, Larson & Chastain, 1990)
- Toronto Alexithymia Scale (TAS, Taylor et al, 1985)
- Penn State Worry Questionnaire (PSWQ, Meyer et al, 1990)
- Social Support Questionnaire (F-SozU, Fydrich et al, 1987)

Finally, Ss in the disclosure group were requested to rate the extent to which the experience was personally upsetting at the time of its occurrence and on the first day of writing. The participants were recruited via placards and handouts distributed in university facilities that provided information about the research project and its aim of tapping *"physiological responses to writing about personal experiences"* (Blood pressure and other physiological parameters were assessed during the experiment, but will not be reported here). Ss received a postpaid monetary incentive or partial course credit for participation in the study. Anonymity of personal data and essays was assured and enforced through strict adherence to data protection procedures. An offer of free counseling was made for any participants who felt emotionally shaken or upset after writing.

Study I: Results

A total of 39 female and 22 male Ss with a mean age of 23 years participated in the study (see tab. 1). Half of the Ss were psychology majors. Under the predetermined quota of 2:1 in favour of the experimental group, Ss were randomly assigned to the conditions. The Ss in the two conditions did not differ significantly with regard to sex or age.

Table 1. Characteristics of study I sample

Variable	Condition	
	Disclosure (n=40*)	**Control (n=21)**
Age (m,sd)	23.9 (4.1)	23.3 (4.0)
Sex (n, % female)	23 (57.5%)	16 (76%)
Major		
Psychology	47,5%	52%
Business/ Economics	32.5%	23.8%
Social sciences	5%	14.3%
Other	15.5%	9.9%

* 1 drop-out at follow-up

As a manipulation check subjects were asked to rate how personal and how emotionally revealing their essays were. Ss in the disclosure group gave significantly higher ratings with regard to both aspects (personal: $m_{disclosure} = 5.71$ (1.12), $m_{control} = 2.79$ (1.03), $p < .001$; emotionally revealing: $m_{disclosure} = 5.25$ (0.95), $m_{control} = 1.86$ (.85), $p < .001$). Analysis of the essay contents in the disclosure group corroborated the personal nature of the essays and revealed that Ss wrote about a broad spectrum of life events (tab. 2). The Ss rated the experiences described in their essays as quite upsetting at the time they occurred (m=5.8, sd=1.5, scale 1-7), though somewhat less so at the time of writing (m=4.0, sd=1.4). Nevertheless, the latter rating indicates that Ss wrote about experiences that continued to have a negative impact in their lives. Inspection of the essays of the control group revealed compliance with the writing instructions.

The first hypothesis tested relates to *short-term* effects of writing. The disclosure group was expected to show an increase in negative mood and physical symptoms following writing (see tab. 3, mean of all sessions). The hypothesis was statistically supported for negative mood, but not for physical symptoms.

Table 2. Contents of essays in study I disclosure group

Problems with boyfriend / girlfriend	15%
Severe illness or death of family member or close friend	15%
Own severe illness or deformity	12%
Problems with friends or peers	12%
Problems with family members	10%
Separation or divorce of parents	7%
Sexual or physical abuse	7%
Stressful events (not interpersonal)	7%
Major personal failure	5%
Other	10%

Table 3. Short-term effects of writing (study I): Item means (m), standard deviation (sd), and results from analysis of variance (interaction terms*)

Short-term effects			
Variables	Period	Condition	
		Disclosure	Control
1. PPSS	pre	1.63 (.40)	1.58 (.39)
(m,sd) $\alpha = 0.59^{+}$	post	1.65 (.43)	1.54 (.56)
2. PNMS	pre	1.87 (.64)	1.93 (.88)
(m,sd) $\alpha = 0.81$	post	2.05 (.74)	1.73 (.79)
VA(1)*: $F(1,59) = 0.62$, $p > .10$			
VA(2)*: $F(1,59) = 12.70$, $p = .001$			

$^{+}$ Cronbach's alpha
* period x condition

The second hypothesis related to *long-term* effects and postulated an improvement in physical health in the disclosure group. Results did not confirm the hypothesis. Ss in disclosure group failed to show a significant improvement relative to the control group in any of the health-related variables (see tab. 4). On the contrary, inspection of means revealed deteriorations in 2 of the 4 health-related variables, albeit in both the disclosure and control condition. The third set of hypotheses relates to the expected long-term improvement of psychological well-being in the disclosure group, predicting more positive and less negative affectivity relative to the controls, and also predicting a reduction of posttraumatic stress symptoms within the disclosure group. The hypothesis cannot be confirmed regarding affectivity. However, significant reductions in PSS-SR scales indicate a decreased presence of maladaptive processing 6 weeks after writing. Both re-experiencing and autonomic arousal are reduced (effect sizes $d = .72$ and $.54$, respectively), as are posttraumatic stress symptoms on the whole ($d = .56$)

Asked about long-term positive and negative effects of writing at follow-up, Ss in the disclosure group rate both effects to be stronger than the controls (positive: $m_{disclosure} = 2.43$ (1.32), $m_{control} = 1.57$ (.98), t-test: $p = 0.006$; negative $m_{disclosure} = 1.55$ (1.09), $m_{control} = 1.0$ (1.0); t-test: $p = 0.003$).

Table 4. Long-term effects of writing (study I): Item means (m), standard deviation (sd), and results from analysis of variance (interaction terms*) and t-tests

Health	Period	Condition	
		Disclosure	Control
1. PILL	pre	1.03 (0.46)	1.11 (0.37)
(m,sd) $\alpha = 0.91$	follow-up	0.99 (0.51)	1.07 (0.44)
2. Illness-related visits to physician[+]	pre	0.43 (0.90)	0.48 (1.25)
(m,sd)	follow-up	0.40 (1.08)	0.52 (0.98)
3. Days with illness-related restriction of	pre	2.63 (3.83)	2.55 (3.67)
activity[+] (m,sd)	follow-up	5.75 (17.27)	3.00 (6.60)
4. Illness days[+] (m,sd)	pre	2.30 (3.31)	1.93 (2.67)
	follow-up	4.03 (9.42)	3.86 (7.02)
Affectivity			
5. PANAS: negative	pre	2.05 (0.73)	1.78 (0.65)
(m,sd) $\alpha = 0.89$	follow-up	1.90 (0.66)	1.75 (0.67)
6. PANAS: positive	pre	3.37 (0.56)	3.17 (0.61)
(m,sd) $\alpha = 0.82$	follow-up	3.15 (0.56)	3.14 (0.71)
VA(1) *: $F(1,59) = .00$, $p > .10$ VA(2) *: $F(1,59) = .04$, $p > .10$ VA(3) *: $F(1,59) = .48$, $p > .10$ VA(4) *: $F(1,59) = .01$, $p > .10$ VA(5) *: $F(1,59) = .47$, $p > .10$ VA(6) *: $F(1,59) = 1.87$, $p > .10$			
PSS-SR [§]			Statistics
7. Re-experiencing (m, sd)	pre	0.92(0.64)	df=38 t=4.52
	follow-up	0.54 (0.45)	p=.000**
8. Avoidance (m, sd)	pre	0.81 (0.69)	t=1.16
	follow-up	0.70 (0.65)	p=.127
9. Arousal (m, sd)	pre	0.78 (0.58)	t=3.38
	follow-up	0.54 (0.56)	p=.001**
10. Total severity score	pre	0.83 (0.55)	t=3.50
	follow-up	0.61 (0.53)	p=.001**

* Period x condition

[+] Mean frequency

[§] Only assessed in disclosure group

All essay variables were examined for their influence on short- or long-term outcome. Only 4 of the 108 correlations examined reached significance ($p < .001$, see tab. 5). The results indicate that autonomic arousal is reduced to a larger extent when essays include more positive emotions and when the positive emotions are of greater intensity. Reductions in avoidance and total posttraumatic stress symptoms are greater, when self-exploration increases from day 1 to day 3.

The moderating effect of personality variables on short- and long-term outcome was also examined. Of the 48 correlation coefficients, only one reached significance (tab. 5): The long-term reduction of physical symptoms was more attenuated, the greater the extent of self-concealment.

In a last step of analysis, the influence of personality variables on the manner of writing, as assessed with the essay variables, was examined. The only personality variable that correlated significantly with the examined essay characteristics was "worrying". Essays written by habitual worriers contained relatively more emotional expressions on the whole ($r = .435$, $p = .005$) and more negative emotional expressions in particular ($r = .511$, $p = .001$) than non-worriers' essays. Also, the stronger the tendency to worry, the deeper the self-exploration exhibited in the essays ($r = .378$, $p = .016$)

Table 5. Significant correlations ($p \leq 0.01$) between moderator variables (essay or personality variables) and outcome variables (short- and long-term) in the disclosure group (study I)

Moderator variable	Outcome	Correlation: r
Frequency of positive emotions in essay	Reduced arousal (PSS-SR)	.452 (p = .002)
Intensity of positive emotions in essay	Reduced arousal (PSS-SR)	.421 (p = .004)
Increasing self-exploration day 1 to day 3	Reduced posttraumatic stress symptoms (PSS-SR)	.424 (p = .004)
Increasing self-exploration day 1 to day 3	Reduced avoidance (PSS-SR)	.376 (p = .009)
Self-Concealment	Physical symptoms (PILL)	-.366 (p = .01)

Study II: Method

Because of the unexpected negative outcome regarding the postulated long-term beneficial effect of expressive writing on physical health, a second study was conducted to examine whether disclosure instructions modified to promote self-efficacy and coping would produce more positive effects. Therefore, in addition to the standard disclosure condition, two further experimental conditions, "coping" and "helping", were implemented, in which modifications were made to the writing instructions given on day 3. In the "coping" condition, Ss were instructed on to reflect upon what they have done in the past, continue to do, or could do in future to better cope with the traumatic experience they wrote about during the first 2 sessions. This instruction aimed at increasing Ss' awareness of their past, present, and future coping behaviour and thereby at increasing their sense of self-efficacy in dealing with the traumatic experience. It was postulated that the instruction could elicit a constructive reappraisal of the experience which would, in turn, facilitate emotional resolution (see Murray et al, 1989). In the "helping" condition, Ss were asked to imagine themselves in the role of an adviser and to elaborate on what they would recommend to persons dealing with the same trauma they experienced in order to better cope with the event. Midlarsky & Kahana (1994) as well as Berking (1998) have presented data indicating that adopting a prosocial role can have positive cognitive and emotional consequences. A control condition analogous to study I was also implemented, in which Ss were asked to write about their daily routine and time management in a detailed and factual manner.

22 Ss were randomly assigned to each of the four conditions. This time a different set of instruments, selected based on the psychometric quality of the validated German versions, was used for the assessment of long-term effects. The circumstance that the study I instruments were, for the most part, translations of questionnaires originally developed for Anglo-American samples and not yet psychometrically evaluated for German samples was seen as a limitation worthy of amelioration in study II.

Physical symptoms (prior PILL) were assessed via the Complaints Schedule (Beschwerden-Liste, von Zerssen, 1976), affectivity (prior PANAS) through a validated German version of the Profile of Mood States (McNair et al, 1971), and PTSD symptoms via the tested German version of the Impact of Event Scale (Horowitz et al, 1979). The individual health-related items from study I (e.g., illness days) were implemented, as was a questionnaire scale tapping satisfaction with one's health (Fahrenberg et al, 1986). To assess the effect of writing on mood regulation, which is posited as one of the mechanisms underlying health improvement, the questionnaire "Generalized Expectancy for Negative Mood Regulation" (Catanzaro & Mearns, 1990, Catanzaro & Greenwod, 1994) was administered. Furthermore, an item assessing self-efficacy regarding coping with the critical event was added. The conductance of study II was similar to study I in all other aspects.

Study II: Results

The sample comprised a total of 84 Ss, the majority of which were female and whose average age varied in the four conditions between 21 and 24 years (see tab. 6). Four Ss dropped out of the study (i.e., did not return follow-up data). Like in study I, most of the participants were students majoring in psychology. No significant differences between groups were found with regard to sociodemographic variables. Analysis of the essay contents in the three experimental conditions (disclosure, coping, helping) indicates that Ss wrote about experiences similar to those in study I. Problems with boyfriend / girlfriend were, however, more frequently written about in study II, while problems with friends and peers, and own severe illness or deformity were less frequent than in study I.

Two two-factorial analyses of variance (condition x period) on the *short-term* effects of writing showed significant differences between groups regarding physical symptoms (PPSS) and negative mood (PNMS, see tab. 7). A post-hoc Scheffé test revealed that this effect can be attributed to differences between the disclosure and control conditions: The disclosure group reported more physical symptoms and greater negative mood directly after writing.

The postulated *long-term* effect of improvements in physical health could not be corroborated in this study. None of the analyses of variance on the health-related variables yielded significant interaction effects, reflecting the absence of health differences between the controls and the three experimental groups, in which the Ss had written in an emotionally expressive manner about traumatic experiences (see tab. 8).

Table 6. Characteristics of study II sample

Variable	Condition			
	Disclosure n = 20*	Coping n = 21	Helping n = 22	Control n = 21
Age (m,sd)	24.1 (5.7)	21.8 (2.4)	22.2 (3.2)	21.2 (2.6)
Sex (n, % female)	13 (65%)	14 (67%)	15 (64%)	14 (67%)
Major				
Psychology	50%	76.2%	45.5%	57.1%
Law	5%	4.8%	13.6%	19%
Other	35%	19.0%	40.9%	19.0%
Non-students	10%			4.8%

* deviation from n = 22: drop-outs at follow-up

Table 7. Short-term effects of writing in study II: Item means (m), standard deviations (sd), and results from analysis of variance (interaction terms) and post-hoc Scheffé-tests

Variables	Period	Condition			
		Disclosure	Coping	Helping	Control
1. PPSS (m,sd)	pre	1.41 (.40)	1.36 (.32)	1.49 (.39)	1.60 (.57)
	post	1.64 (.40)	1.35 (.37)	1.54 (.39)	1.42 (.33)
2. PNMS (m,sd)	pre	1.56 (.64)	1.67 (.97)	1.65 (.70)	1.51 (.58)
	post	1.98 (1.05)	1.79 (1.16)	1.72 (.78)	1.41 (.48)
VA (1)* F (3,80)= 3.75, p = .014 VA (2)* F (3,80) = 4.16, p = .009 Post-hoc Scheffé (1): control / disclosure, p = .016 Post-hoc Scheffé (2): control / disclosure, p = .010					

Analyses of variance conducted on the long-term effects of writing on affectivity and yielded significant differences between groups regarding depression, fatigue and vigour. A post-hoc Scheffé test revealed that this interaction reflects differences between the helping and coping conditions: Ss in the coping condition reported feeling less vigorous and more fatigued than Ss in the helping group.

Analysis of variance of PTSD symptoms (IES) revealed a significant interaction effect for intrusion and a marginally significant interaction effect for avoidance. These effects can be attributed to the expected lack of change in the control group and reductions in intrusions and avoidance found in the disclosure and helping conditions, respectively. The post-hoc Scheffé test supported this interpretation (see tab. 8). Overall, the highest average effect on symptoms of posttraumatic stress was found in the helping group (d = .71), while the other experimental conditions yielded somewhat attenuated effects (disclosure: d = .52, coping: d = .43) and no change occurred in controls (d = .07).

Table 8. Long-term effects of writing in study II: Means (m), standard deviations (sd), and results from analysis of variance (interaction terms) and post-hoc Scheffé-tests

Variable	Period	Condition			
		Disclosure	Coping	Helping	Control
Health					
1. Symptoms	pre follow-up	0.77 (.43) 0.80 (.36)	0.78 (.33) 0.77 (.49)	0.78 (.33) 0.65 (.39)	0.84 (.42) 0.76 (.35)
2. Satisfaction with health	pre follow-up	2.91 (1.12) 2.89 (1.01)	2.92 (1.23) 3.29 (1.29)	3.13 (.97) 3.24 (1.02)	3.02 (.96) 2.82 (.70)
3. Visits to physician+	pre follow-up	0.05 (.22) 0.40 (1.57)	0.05 (.22) 0.10 (.44)	0.14 (.35) 0.05 (.21)	0.33 (.73) 0.00 (.00)
4. Activity restriction+	pre follow-up	1.75 (3.16) 3.16 (6.83)	1.11 (1.70) 1.53 (2.32)	0.77 (2.19) 0.86 (1.49)	1.19 (2.32) 0.91 (1.76)
5. Illness days+	pre follow-up	2.05 (4.57) 2.65 (6.47)	1.43 (2.01) 1.95 (4.77)	1.45 (2.46) 0.77 (1.60)	2.19 (6.49) 0.71 (1.68)
Affectivity: POMS					
6. Depression α = 0.92*	pre follow-up	0.89 (.85) 0.81 (.63)	(.69) 1.23 (1.21)	0.86 (.69) 0.55 (.45)	1.10 (.65) 0.90 (.68)
7. Fatigue α = 0.89	pre follow-up	1.22 (.88) 1.36 (.80)	1.07 (.67) 1.68 (.65)	1.22 (.72) 1.10 (.70)	1.25 (.79) 1.37 (.58)
8. Anger α = 0.90	pre follow-up	(1.09) 1.10 (.96)	0.94 (.71) 1.05 (.87)	0.77 (.51) 0.72 (.57)	0.94 (.72) 1.20 (.85)
9. Vigor α = 0.90	prä follow-up	1.86 (.83) 1.47 (.79)	1.85 (.70) 1.24 (.71)	1.49 (.79) 1.70 (.81)	1.61 (.76) 1.63 (.90)
IES (scale 0 - 3)					
10. Intrusion α = 0.82	pre follow-up	1.36 (.76) .79 (.63)	1.24 (.82) 1.00 (.91)	1.22 (.73) 0.69 (.68)	0.99 (.60) 0.92 (.75)
11. Avoidance α = 0.75	pre follow-up	1.06 (.70) 0.89 (.61)	0.84 (.59) 0.63 (.50)	1.08 (.66) 0.65 (.61)	0.92 (.60) 0.93 (.63)
VA (1)* F (3, 80) = 1.22 p > .10 VA (2)* F (3, 80) = 2.56 p = .061 VA (3)* F (3, 80) = .58 p > .10 VA (4)* F (3, 80) = .65 p > .10 VA (5)* F (3, 80) = 2.02 p > .10 VA (6)* F (3, 80) = 2.91 p = .04 VA (7)* F (3, 80) = 5.40 p = .002 VA (8)* F (3, 80) = .51 p > .10 VA (9)* F (3, 80) = 5.56 p = .002 VA (10)* F (3, 80) = 3.23 p = .027 VA (11)* F (3, 80) = 2.29 p = .084					
Post-hoc Scheffé: (2) control / helping, p = .071 Post-hoc Scheffé: (6) helping / coping, p = .055 Post-hoc Scheffé: (7) control / coping, p=.083; helping / coping, p = .003 Post-hoc Scheffé: (9) control / coping, p=.060; disclosure / helping p=.082; helping / coping, p = .005 Post-hoc Scheffé: (10) control / disclosure, p = .076 Post-hoc Scheffé: (11) control / helping, p = .086					

* Cronbach's Alpha

+ Mean frequencies

While analysis of variance yielded no significant long-term effects of expressive writing on mood regulation (assessed with the NMR), a significant interaction effect (period x condition) was found for Ss' perceived coping self-efficacy. On the descriptive level, the increase in self-efficacy was most pronounced in the helping condition followed by the coping condition. Inquired as to the positive and negative long-term effects of writing, Ss in the helping group reported significantly more positive consequences than controls. No other differences were found.

Table 9. Mood regulation and coping competency in study II: Item means (m), standard deviation (sd), and results of analysis variance (interaction terms*)

Variables		Period	Condition			
			Disclosure	Coping	Helping	Control
1.	Mood regulation (m,sd) $\alpha = 0.85^{+}$	pre	3.40 (.40)	3.31 (.43)	3.41 (.42)	3.35 (.39)
		follow-up	3.52 (.40)	3.31 (.50)	3.59 (.48)	3.43 (.47)
2.	Coping competency (m,sd) $\alpha = 0.82^{+}$	pre	1.70 (.73)	1.74 (.87)	1.55 (1.06)	1.81 (1.08)
		post§	1.85 (.99)	2.16 (.96)	2.09 (.68)	1.76 (.83)
		follow-up	1.75 (1.07)	2.10 (1.02)	2.10 (1.07)	1.81 (.93)

VA (1)* $F(3,80) = 1.14$, $p > .10$
VA ($2_{pre-post}$)* $F(3,80) = 1.79$, $p > .10$
VA ($2_{pre-follow-up}$)* $F(3,80) = 2.71$, $p = .05$

+ Cronbachs Alpha
§ After 3rd writing session
*period x condition

Study I: Discussion

In many studies a relative increase in negative mood directly after writing about upsetting events has been observed, an effect which Pennebaker (1993) has postulated as being a prerequisite for the long-term positive effects of disclosure. This negative effect on mood was corroborated in our study, though inspection of means revealed the effect to be attributable to an improvement of mood in the control group and a comparable deterioration of mood in the disclosure group. It is important to emphasise that the disclosure Ss wrote about truly upsetting and traumatic events, as shown by the analysis of essay contents and the self-rating of the extent to which the experience was troubling at occurrence and now.

The expected short-term increase in physical symptoms due to the emotional impact of expressive writing, which has been observed at least in some prior studies, was not shown in our data. This may be due to inadequacies of the German version of the PPSS, an interpretation supported by the relatively low internal consistency of the scale ($\alpha = .59$ vs. $\alpha = .75$ reported by Pennebaker, 1982). Data of the second study should decide on this interpretation.

The positive long-term effect of expressive writing on physical health could not be found at 6-week follow-up for any of the health-related variables assessed in the study. Thus, the beneficial effects of disclosure on physical health reported by Pennebaker and colleagues (1986, 1988) could not be replicated in our German sample. In fact, increases in both illness days and days with illness-related restriction of activity were found in the disclosure condition at follow-up. Such increases, however, were also observed in the control group and seem quite likely due to the seasonal influence of follow-up taking place during winter. The very high variance within Ss (see e.g. "illness-related restriction of activities") indicates the presence of heterogeneous health trajectories, especially in the disclosure group.

It should be pointed out that all health-related variables in our study were of a subjective nature. Unlike American universities, Germany universities do not operate student health care centres, a source from which objective health data was obtained in prior studies. Though possible that health improvement not apparent in subjective measures might be found in objective health data, the likelihood of such a divergence of health measures is small. Furthermore, it bears attention that our study was not unique in being unable to corroborate health improvement: Significant health-related differences between conditions were also absent in other studies (Greenberg & Stone, 1992; Murray et al, 1989; Murray & Segal, 1994; Gidron et al, 1996).

The results concerning long-term effects of expressive writing on psychological well-being are contradictory. Though no improvement relative to controls was found for positive or negative affectivity, significant reductions were found in maladaptive processing 6 weeks after writing: Re-experiencing, autonomic arousal and posttraumatic stress symptoms on the whole occurred less frequently.

The study also focussed on potential mechanisms of written disclosure by examining the relationship between a number of essay variables and the postulated short- and long-term effects of disclosure. The essay characteristics were assessed by self-report (e.g., rating of extent to which the essay was emotionally revealing) as well as by independent judges' rating (e.g., depth of self-exploration). Despite the overall lack of significant long-term effects of disclosure on health status and affectivity, meaningful correlations between essay characteristics and outcome variables could have been found that would lend support to Pennebaker's theory of inhibition and confrontation. However, only 4 out of 108 calculated correlations reached significant and the few significant correlations were all related to the domain of posttraumatic stress symptoms, the only outcome variables for which significant effects were found. Interestingly, the significant correlations were not exclusive to the scales for which long-term effects were found: Re-experiencing, though significantly reduced at follow-up, was not associated with any of the examined essay characteristics, while avoidance, though not significantly changed following disclosure, was. Associations were found between the more frequent and intense expression of positive emotions in essays and a higher the reduction in arousal. This effect, though not predicted by inhibition theory, seems quite plausible in light of Lazarus' stress coping model, in which positive reappraisal reduces the stress response. Associations were also found between increasing self-exploration (day 1 to day 3) and reductions in avoidance as well as posttraumatic stress symptoms on the whole.

Surprisingly, the assessed personality variables were of little to no relevance for short- and long-term consequences of disclosure. The constructs of personality variables like alexithymia (lack of ability to perceive and express emotions) and self-concealment (conscious inhibition of expressing emotions to others) made the hypothesis of their influence on the disclosure process and its outcome highly probable. Nevertheless, only one significant correlation was found regarding self-concealment and *long-term* change of physical symptoms. The unexpected absence of these theoretically highly plausible associations may be indicative of a weakness in the theory of inhibition and confrontation.

Study II: Discussion

The second study was conducted to determine whether the negative results of study I might be due, in part, to inadequacies in the German versions of the selected assessment instruments. More importantly, however, was the study's aim of examining whether modified disclosure instructions promoting self-efficacy and coping would be more successful in producing the postulated positive effects on physical health and psychological well-being.

Negative short-term effects of expressive writing were found in study II for both mood and physical symptoms. Interestingly, the increases in both were most pronounced in the disclosure condition, which differed significantly from the control condition. The coping and helping conditions, on the other hand, evidenced only slight, if any, increases in physical symptoms and negative mood.

As in study I, positive long-term effects of writing on physical health were conspicuously absent. Not only were there no effects with regard to the Complaints Schedule, an instrument specifically validated for German samples, none of the subjective health measures indicated a beneficial effect of expressive writing on physical health.

The observed long-term effects on mood were unexpectedly attributable to differences between the helping and coping conditions, controls were not involved. Nevertheless, the deterioration of mood in the coping Ss, relative to the helping Ss, merits comment. The only predicted long-term improvements of psychological well-being were found with the Impact of Event Scale. A marginally significant interaction effect was revealed for "avoidance" and a significant interaction effect for "intrusion". Altogether the helping group showed the largest reduction in posttraumatic stress symptoms,

The newly explored variable "expectancy of negative mood regulation" did not respond to expressive writing, either in its standard or modified form. Self-rated coping competency did, however, as evidenced by the significant interaction effect in the analysis of variance on follow-up data. Though the post-hoc Scheffé-test did not reveal any significant pairwise differences, inspection of means showed that the largest increase in perceived coping competency was found in the helping condition, marginal increases were found in the other experimental groups, while the controls evidenced no change.

Regarding global estimate of positive effects of writing by the Ss, the helping group gives the highest rating and the control the lowest.

Summary

In both of our studies, the main assumption made by Pennebaker that confronting personally upsetting experiences via a brief writing intervention, can lead to positive long-term health consequences could not be corroborated. The vision of being able to achieve improvements in physical health and psychological well-being by writing in an emotionally expressive way about negative experiences does not seem to be warranted by the results of the present study. Thus, our findings contradict not only the early disclosure studies but also the results of a metaanalysis from Smyth (1998), in which medium effect sizes were reported for both physical health (d = .42) and psychological well-being (d = .66).

We want to point, however, that the effects reported in some studies did not reflect improvement in the disclosure condition, but rather a deterioration of health in the control group (Pennebaker & Beall, 1986; Pennebaker & Francis, 1996; Greenberg et al, 1996). Taken together with our negative results on health improvement and the lack of substantial correlations between theoretically fitting personality constructs and outcome variables, a more sceptical view of disclosure seems warranted.

On the other hand, however, we found substantial changes in symptoms of post traumatic stress. In the first experiment re-experiencing and autonomic arousal were reduced after disclosure and a decrease in posttraumatic stress symptoms on the whole was found. In the second experiment, the positive effect of disclosure on these symptoms could be replicated using an instrument that was psychometrically validated for German samples. A significant reduction in intrusions was found as well as a marginally significant reduction of avoidance. These effects (reduction of symptoms) were most pronounced in the helping group. It seems that taking on the role of an adviser and recommending coping strategies to others dealing with the same experience can increase perceived coping competency and thereby facilitate improved emotional processing. Contrary to our expectations, the coping instruction was not as effective. It is plausible that the coping instruction may have reactivated the memory of unsuccessful coping endeavours in some of the Ss. On the other hand Cameron & Nicholls (1998) found positive effects in their somewhat different coping intervention.

Thus, disclosure had a positive long-term effect on the processing of traumatic experiences but not on physical health or mood. Perhaps the effects on trauma processing, which are of medium size in the helping and disclosure group were not strong enough to have consequences for general health.

Conclusions from our studies are that writing about upsetting or traumatic events can be useful as a self-help strategy to improve coping with the trauma but it can not replace more comprehensive professional interventions when the negative impact of the stressful event on the individual is strong.

Is there any explanation for the discrepancy between our results and the beneficial health effects reported in the early studies from Pennebaker and Beall (1986) and others? Our samples do not differ from the others with regard to Ss' status and age. The marginal gender difference between conditions in study I cannot explain the discrepancies, as gender had no moderating effect on outcome. The experiences the Ss wrote about are similar to the essay contents reported by Pennebaker and Beall (1986) or Pennebaker et al (1988). The health-related assessment measures and instruments were analogous, with the exception of a lack of objective health data. It seems highly unlikely, however, that self-report measures of health should be less sensitive to change than objective parameters. It could be argued that our follow-up assessment was premature, the time span of 6 weeks being too short for the beneficial effects on health to occur. This argument, however, loses its strength in view of health improvements reported by Pennebaker et al, (1988), who implemented a follow-up of the same length, and found reductions in health centre visits and increased immunocompetence 6 weeks after writing. Improvements in health have been reported for as short a time span as 4 weeks after writing (Greenberg et al, 1996). It cannot be ruled out that sociocultural factors may play a role in the discrepant results as nearly all supporting findings originate from the USA and Canada. What factors these might be, however, is far from clear.

Interest in the theory of inhibition and confrontation has not waned over the years: Since the first wave of research in the late eighties and the nineties, numerous new studies using the disclosure paradigm have been conducted. The study samples have grown more diverse ranging from prisoners (Tromp, 1998; Richards et al, 2000), individuals in mourning (Eddins, 1999, Ströbe et al, 2002), persons afflicted with cervical dysplasia (Cook, 2001) and prostate cancer (Rosenberg et al, 2002[prostate cancer]), to patients presenting with somatisation (Schilte et al, 2001), fibromyalgia (Gillis, 2002) and major depression (Hitt, 2001). College students were examined by Marlo & Wagner (1999) and Kloss & Lisman (2002), school children (8-13 years) by Reynolds et al (2000), and Klapow et al (2001) tested the disclosure hypothesis on a sample of primary care patients of an older age (66 years or older).

Beneficial effects of disclosure are reported in some of the studies, e.g. by Gillis et al (2002), who found functional improvement in patients with fibromyalgia as well as better sleep quality. Rosenberg et al (2002) reported reductions of physical symptoms and health care utilisation in prostate cancer patients, though no effect was found on psychological variables or disease-related parameters of immunocompetence. Richards et al's (2000) psychiatric prisoners showed a reduction in postwriting infirmary visits. Reduced health care utilisation was also found in older primary health care patients, though somatic symptoms and distress remained unchanged (Klapow et al, 2001). Whether Tromp's report (1998) of increased mental health care utilization in prisoners points to a positive effect (more sensitivity to psychological symptoms) or a negative effect (more symptoms) remains unclear.

In other studies, however, disclosure was less successful in promoting psychological or physical health (Wilson, 2000; Marlo & Wagner, 1999; Schilte et al, 2001; Ströbe et al, 2002; Reynolds et al, 2000; Kloss & Lisman, 2002). Thus, evidence seems to be accumulating that the effects of disclosure are less positive and less dramatic than assumed after the first studies. Unfortunately, outcome variables indicative of the dysfunctional processing of traumatic events were rarely assessed, so that further support for the results of our studies is lacking.

Furthermore, the variables mediating and moderating the effect of disclosure are far from clear. Additional research is needed to systematically analyse relevant variables and elucidate the mechanisms of action. The current focus of disclosure research on health-related variables and the neglect of psychological processing seems adversarial to the clarification of the potential utility of written disclosure as a means of self-help or in conjunction with psychotherapy.

References

Berking, M. (1998). Vom hilflosen Patienten zum hilfreichen Experten? Empirische Studie über Möglichkeiten therapeutischen Arbeitens mit altruistischen Wirkfaktoren bei chronischen Schmerzpatienten. (From the helpless patient to a helpful expert? Empirical study of the chance to work with altruistic motivation in the treatment of chronic pain). Unpublished master thesis, Georg-August-University of Göttingen.

Booth, R.J., Petrie, K.J. & Pennebaker, J.W. (1997). Changes in circulation lymphocyte numbers following emotional disclosure: Evidence of buffering? *Stress Medicine,* 13, 23-29.

Cameron, L.D. & Nicholls, G. (1998). Expression of stressful experiences through writing: Effects of a self-regulation manipulation for pessimists and optimists. *Health Psychology,* 17, 84-92.

Catanzaro, S.J. & Greenwood, G. (1994). Expectancies for negative mood regulation, coping, and dysphoria among college students. *Journal of Counseling Psychology,* 41, 34-44.

Catanzaro, S.J. & Mearns, J. (1990). Measuring generalized expectancies for negative mood regulation: initial scale development and implications. *Journal of Personality Assessment,* 54, 546-563.

Cook, B.L. (2001). Relationships between cognitive-affective processing of past trauma and psychophysiological and immune parameters in women at risk for cervical cancer. Dissertation Abstracts International: Section B: *The Sciences & Engineering,* 61, 5556.

Donnelly, D.A. & Murray, E.L. (1991). Cognitive and emotional changes in written essaya and therapy interviews. *Journal of Social and Clinical Psychology,* 10, 334-350.

Eddins, C. (1999). Self-disclosure and the course of midlife conjugal bereavement. (coping strategies, mourning). Dissertation Abstracts International: Section B: *The Sciences & Engineering,* 60, 1849.

Ehlers, A. (2000). Posttraumatische Belastungsstörungen. (Posttraumatic anxiety disorders). *Göttingen,* Hogrefe.

Esterling, B.A., Antoni, M.H., Fletcher, M.A., Margulies, S. & Schneidermann, N. (1994). Emotional disclosure through writing or speaking modulates latent Eppstein-Barr-virus antibody titers. *Journal of Consulting and Clinical Psychology,* 62, 130-140.

Fahrenberg, J., Myrtek, D., Wilk, D. & Kreutel, K. (1986). Multimodale Erfassung der Lebenszufriedenheit: eine Untersuchung an Herz-Kreislauf-Patienten. (Multimodal assessment of life satisfaction: a study on CHD patients). *Psychotherapie, Psychosomatik, Medizinische Psychologie,* 36, 347-354.

Foa, D.B., Riggs, D.S., Dancu, C.V. & Rothbaum, B.O. (1993). Reliability and validity of a brieg instrument for assessing post-traumatic stress disorder. *Journal of Traumatic Stress,* 6, 459-473.

Francis, M.E. & Pennebaker, J.W. (1992). Putting stress into words: The impact of writing on physiological, absentee, and self-reported emotional well-being measures. American *Journal of Health Promotion,* 6, 280-287.

Fydrich, T., Sommer, G., Menzel, G. & Höll, B. (1987). Fragebogen zur sozialen Unterstützung (Kurzform, Sozu-K-22). (Questionnaire of social support). *Zeitschrift für Klinische Psychologie,* 16, 434-436.

Gidron, Y., Peri, T., Connolly, J.F. & Shalev, A.Y. (1996). Written disclosure in posttraumatic stress disorder: Is it benificial for the patient? *Journal of Nervous and Mental Disease,* 184, 505-507.

Gillis, M.E. (2002). The effects of written emotional disclosure on adjustment in fibromyalgia syndrome. Dissertation Abstracts International: Section B: *The Sciences & Engineering,* 63, 1562.

Greenberg, M.A., & Stone, A. (1992). Emotional disclosure about traumas and its relation to health: Effects of previous disclosure and trauma severity. *Journal of Personality and Social Psychology,* 63, 75-84.

Greenberg, M.A., Wortman, C.B. & Stone, A.A. (1996). Emotional expression and physical health: Revising traumatic memories or fostering self-regulation? *Journal of Personality and Social Psychology,* 71, 588-602.

Henderson, B.N., Davison, K.P., Pennebaker, J.W. & James, W. (2002). Disease disclosure patterns among breast cancer patients. *Psychology & Health,* 17 (1), 51-62.

Hitt, S. K. (2001). Disclosure, psychophysiology, and major depression. Dissertation Abstracts International: Section B: *The Sciences & Engineering,* 61, 5566.

Horowitz, M.J. (1976). Stress response syndromes. (2nd ed.) Northvale, NJ: Jakob Aronson.

Horowitz, M.J., Wilner, N. & Alvarez, W. (1979). Impact of event scale: a measure of subjective stress. *Psychosomatic Medicine,* 41, 209-218.

Klapow, J.C., Schmidt, S.M., Taylor, L.A., Roller, P. & Li, Q. (2001). Symptom management in older primary care patients: feasibility of an experimental, written self-disclosure protocol. *Annals of Internal Medicine,* 134, 905-11.

Kloss, J.D. & Lisman, S.A. (2002). An exposure-based examination of the effects of written emotional disclosure. *British Journal of Health Psychology,* 7 (1), 31.46.

Kelley, J.E., Lumley, M.A. & Leisen, J.C.C. (1997). Health effects of emotional disclosure in rhematoid arthritis patients. *Health Psychology,* 16, 331-340.

Klapow, J.C., Schmidt, S.M., Taylor, L.A., Roller, P., Li, Q., Calhoun, J.W., Wallander, J. & Pennebaker, J.W. (2001). Symptom management in older primary care patients: feasibility of an experiment, written self-disclosure protocol. *Annals of Internal Medicine,* 134, 905-911.

Kloss, J.D. & Lisman, S.A. (2002). An exposure-based examination of the effects of written emotional disclosure. *British Journal of Health Psychology,* 7(1), 31-46.

Krantz, A., & Pennebaker, J.W. (1996). Bodily versus written expression of traumatic experience. Manuscript submitted for publication [Zit. nach Pennebaker, 1997, S. 164].

Larson, D.G. & Chastain, R.L. (1990). Self-concealment: Conceptualization, measurement, and health implications. *Journal of Social and Clinical Psychology,* 9, 439-455.

Linkemann, A. (2001). Schreiben über belastende Lebensereignisse und dessen Einfluss auf körperliches und psychisches Wohlbefinden. (Writing about threatful life events and its influence on physical and psychological well-being). Unpublished PhD, University of Göttingen.

Lutgendorf, S.K., Antoni, M.H., Kumar, M. & Schneidermann, N. (1994). Changes in cognitive coping strategies predict EBV-antibody titer change following a stressor disclosure induction. *Journal of Psychosomatic Research*, 38, 63-78.

Marlo, H. & Wagner, M.K. (1999). Expression of negative and positive events through writing: Implications for psychotherapy and health. *Psychology & Health,* 14,193-215.

McNair, D.M., Lorr, M. & Droppleman, L.F. (1971). ETIS manual for the Profile of Mood States. San Diego, California: Educational and Industrial Testing Service.

Meyer, T.J., Miller, M.L., Metzger, R.L. & Borkovec, T.D. (1990). Development and validation of the Penn State Worry Questionnaire. *Behavior Research and Therapy*, 28, 487-495.

Midlarsky, E. & Kahana, E. (1994). Altruism in later life. Thousand Oaks, California: Sage.

Murray, E.J., Lamnin, A.D. & Carver, C.S. (1989). Emotional expression in written essays and psychotherapy. *Journal of Social and Clinical Psychology,* 8, 414-429.

Murray, E.J. & Segal, D.L. (1994). Emotional processing in vocal and written expression of feelings about traumatic experiences. *Journal of Traumatic Stress,* 7, 391-405.

Paez, D., Velasco, C. & Gonzalez, J.L. (1999). Expressive writing and the role of alexithymia as a dispositional deficit in self-disclosure and psychological health. *Journal of Personality & Social Psychology,* 77, 630-641.

Pennebaker, J.W. & Beall, S.K. (1986). Confronting a traumatic event: Toward an understanding of inhibition and disease. *Journal of Abnormal Psychology,* 95, 274-281.

Pennebaker, J.W., Hughes, C.F. & O'Heeron, R.C. (1987). The psychophysiology of confession: Linking inhibitory and psychosomatic processes. *Journal of Personality and Social Psychology,* 52. 781-793.

Pennebaker, J.W., Kiecolt-Glaser, J.K. & Glaser, R. (1988). Disclosure of traumas and immune function: Health implications for psychotherapy. *Journal of Consulting and Clinical Psychology,* 56, 239-244.

Pennebaker, J.W. (1988). Confiding traumatic experiences and health. In S. Fisher & J. Reason (Eds.), *Handbook of life stress, cognition and health*. Chichester: John Wiley & Sons.

Pennebaker, J.W. (1989). Confession, inhibition, and disease. In L. Berkowitz (Ed.), *Advances in Experimental and Social Psychology*, 22, 211-244. New York: Academic Press.

Pennebaker, J.W., Colder, M. & Sharp, L.K. (1990). Accelerating the coping process. *Journal of Personality and Social Psychology,* 58, 528-537.

Pennebaker, J.W. & Francis, M.E. (1996). Cognitive, emotional, and language processes in disclosure. *Cognition and Emotion,* 10, 601-626.

Pennebaker, J.W., Mayne, T. & Francis, M. (1997). Linguistic predictors of adaptive bereavement. *Journal of Personality and Social Psychology,* 52, 863-871.

Petrie, K.J., Booth, R.J., Pennebaker, J.W., Davison, K.P. & Thomas, M.G. (1995). Disclosure of trauma and immune response to a hepatitis B vaccination program. *Journal of Consulting and Clinical Psychology,* 63, 787-792.

Reynolds, M., Brewin, C. R. & Saxton, M. (2000). Emotional disclosure in school children. *Journal of Child Psychology and Psychiatry and Allied Disciplines,* 41, 151-9.

Richards, J.M., Beal, W.E. & Seagal, J.D. (2000). Effects of disclosure of traumatic events on illness behavior among psychiatric prison inmates. *Journal of Abnormal Psychology,* 109, 156-160.

Rosenberg, H.J., Rosenberg, S.D. & Ernstoff, M.S. (2002). Expressive disclosure and health outcomes in a prostate cancer population. International *Journal of Psychiatry in Medicine,* 32, 37-53.

Schilte, A. F., Portegijs, P., Blankenstein, A.H., van der Horst, H.E. & Latour, M. B. (2001). Randomised controlled trial of disclosure of emotionally important events in somatisation in primary care. *British Medical Journal,* 323, 86-89.

Schmidt-Atzert, L. (1981). Die verbale Kommunikation von Emotionen: Eine Bedingungsanalyse unter besonderer Berücksichtigung physiologischer Prozesse. (Verbal communication of emotions: an analysis with regard to physiological processing). Unpublished PhD thesis. Justus-Liebig-University, Giessen.

Schoutrop, M.J.A., Lange, A., Davidovich, U. & Salomon, H.B. (1996). The effects of writing assignments in traumatised individuals: An experimental study. *Psychosomatic Medicine,* 58, 64.

Smyth, J.M. (1998). Written emotional expression: Effect sizes, outcome types, and moderating variables. *Journal of Consulting and Clinical Psychology,* 66, 174-184.

Spera , S.P., Burhfeind, E.D. & Pennebaker, J.W. (1994). Expressive writing and coping with job loss. *Academy of Management Journal,* 37, 722-733.

Ströbe, M.; Ströbe, W., Schut, H., Zech, E. & van-den Bout, J. (2002). Does disclosure of emotions facilitate recovery from bereavement? Evidence from two prospective studies. *Journal of Consulting and Clinical Psychology,* 70, 169-78.

Tausch, R. (1970). *Gesprächspsychotherapie (Client-centered therapy)* (4. ergänzte Aufl.). Göttingen: Hogrefe.

Taylor, J.T., Ryan, D. & Bagby, R.M. (1985). Toward the development of a new self-report alexithymia scale. *Psychotherapy and Psychosomatics,* 44, 191-199.

Traue, H. C. (1998). Emotion und Gesundheit. (Emotion and health). Heidelberg: Spektrum Akademischer Verlag.

Tromp, S.N. (1998). Use of self-guided writing therapy as an intervention for trauma: A sample of incarcerated women. Dissertation Abstracts International: Section B: *The Sciences & Engineering,* 58, 3936.

Westbrook, M.T. (1976). Positive affect: A method of content analysis for verbal samples. *Journal of Consulting and Clinical Psychology,* 44, 715-719.

Wilson, L. (2000). The health and psychological effects of sequenced and unsequenced emotional expression regarding college adjustment experiences. Dissertation Abstracts International Section A: *Humanities & Social Sciences,* 60, 3274.

Zerssen, D. von, (1976). *Die Beschwerden-Liste. (Symptom list).* Weinheim: Beltz.

In: Anxiety in College Students
Editor: Benjamin Ayres and Michelle Bristow
ISBN: 978-1-60692-282-8

Chapter V

Stress Among Students in Developing Countries- An Overview

Shashidhar Acharya
Manipal College of Dental Sciences, Manipal, India

Abstract

Mankind since the dawn of history has been afflicted with various forms of diseases. Communicable diseases that took a heavy toll of human life in medieval and prehistoric times, have been replaced by non- communicable diseases and conditions in the recent times. Among the six factors which are responsible for the major share of these diseases, Stress occupies an important place (Rose, G.A. and Blackburn H. 1968). The Oxford English dictionary defines stress as pressure, tension or worry resulting from the problems in one's life. It is thus a condition of the mind, in which a person loses his calm tranquility and equanimity and experiences extreme discomfiture.

A Brief History

With advances in preventive medicine and the practice of public health, the pattern of disease began to change in the developed world; many of the acute illnesses were brought under control. However as old problems were solved, new health problems in the form of chronic non communicable diseases began to emerge, e.g., cancer, diabetes, cardiovascular diseases, alcoholism and drug addiction especially in the affluent societies. These diseases that required the understanding of their social and behavioral aspects led to a new phase of public health in the 1960's called the "Social Engineering Phase" (Anderson, C.L. et al, 1978). As our understanding of the dimensions of health grew, so did the list of dimensions. In addition to the physical dimension, other dimensions have gained importance. These dimensions have a direct or indirect effect on stress and stress induced illnesses. They are:

- **Mental Dimension**: Research has shown that psychological factors can induce conditions like hypertension, peptic ulcer and bronchial asthma. (WHO 1964).
- **Social Dimension**: It implies harmony and integration within the individual, between each individuals and the world in which they live (Cmich, D.E., 1984).
- **Spiritual Dimension**: Spiritual health refers to that part of the individual that reaches out and strives for meaning and purpose in life. It includes integrity , principals and ethics, the purposes in life ,commitment to some higher being and belief in concepts that are not subject to 'state of the art' explanation.(Eberst, R.M., 1984)
- **Emotional Dimension**: Historically the mental and emotional dimensions have been seen as one element or as two closely related elements. However new research has shown them to be distinct entities (Eberst, R.M., 1984).
- **Vocational Dimension**: It is a part of human existence. When work is fully adapted to human goals, capabilities and limitations, it often plays a role in promoting physical and mental health. Physical work is associated with improvement in physical capacity, while goal achievement and self-realization in work are a source of satisfaction and enhanced self-esteem (WHO, 1985).

Students as a Risk Group

Among all groups in the population, students especially college students are a group who are particularly prone and susceptible to stress. As a college student, the life can be stressful. In moderate doses, stress challenges students to do their best and keeps them learning and growing. For example, finals are an especially stressful time. Since the final exam has a high percentage in the total score and the outcome is uncertain, there will be high level of stress. This stress can prompt students to study harder, longer, and learn more from the extra effort. So positive stress was defined as functional stress when it enhances our individual or group performance.

On the other hand, the body does not distinguish between negative and positive stress: both excitement and anxiety strain the body's resources and depress the immune system. Stress varies in intensity and duration. Stress that lasts a short period of time can rapidly motivate us. However, stressor that lasts too long, happens too often, or is too strong may bring us physical, behavioral, and psychological problems. Then it becomes the negative stress or dysfunctional stress.

Negative stress can affect a person physically. A person under stress may suffer reduced physical coordination and control, sleeplessness, reduction in the ability to concentrate, store information in memory. And it may be even worse. Research has revealed that at least 50% of all diseases, including peptic ulcer, colitis, hypertension, enuresis, migraine headache, insomnia, and other illnesses, can be attributed to constant stress-related origins. Stress also can affect the individual mentally such as reducing self-esteem, decreasing interpersonal and academic effectiveness and creating a cycle of self-blame and self-doubt. Without adequate coping skills, people often adopt irrational behaviors such as disruptive eating patterns, increased smoking or alcohol consumption, isolation, irritability, harsh treatment of others, compulsive shopping to escape from the over- stressed situation temporarily.

Being over-stressed can be harmful to students. Goldman has reported that being over-stressed can be harmful to students (Goldman et al, 1997). 167 college students participated the survey. The results were concluded from their Self-Perception Profiles, including intellectual ability, scholastic competence, job competence, appearance, social acceptance, close friendships, finding humor in one's life, and global self worth. From the survey data, the authors arrived the conclusion that stress did bring negative effects on college students' self-perception.

Many other authors expatiated that high pressure of college study, the conflicting role demands, and the fast-changing environment, all lead to the relative high level of stress in college students. Undoubtedly, a high level of stress is found to be harmful to the health of students both psychologically and physically.

This may be due to the transitional nature of college life (Towbes and Cohen, 1996).This transition creates a situation where regular contacts with traditional supports like old friends and family may be reduced.The ability of such social supports to mediate the effect of exposure to stress is wellknown (Ensel and Lin, 1991; Moss,1973; Schutt et al, 1994; Thoits, 1995).They must adjust to being away from home for the first time, maintain a high level of academic achievement and adjust to a new social environment. College students must learn to balance the competing demands of academics, developing new social contacts, and being responsible for their own daily needs. While these stressors do not cause anxiety or tension by themselves, they may do so by the interaction with the individual's perceptions and reaction to these stressors. (Romano, 1992) The amount of stress experienced may be influenced by the individual's ability to cope with stressful situations. If stress is not dealt with effectively, feelings of loneliness, sleeplessness, nervousness and excessive worrying may result. (Wright, 1967).

The dynamic relationship between the person and his environment in stress perception and reaction is especially magnified in college students. The problems and situations encountered by college students may differ from those faced by others.(Hirsh and Ellis, 1996).Unlike other vocations, the college student is continuously exposed to stressful situations like periodic tests , examinations, projects etc.(Wright, 1964).Earning high grades is not the only source of stress for college students. Other sources of stress include excessive homework, unclear assignments, uncomfortable class rooms (Kohn and Frazer, 1986), and relations with faculty members, time pressures (Sgan-Cohen and Lowental, 1988), relationships with family and friends, eating, sleeping habits, and loneliness (Wright, 1967).

College marks the period where new systems of support are being created. This process itself can cause stress. It has been shown that peer events and other social gatherings designed to reduce stress end up doing the opposite (Dill and Henley, 1998). Stress has been associated with a variety of negative fallouts like suicide ideation (Hirsch and Ellis, 1996), smoking, (Naquin and Gilbert, 1996) and drinking (Morgan, 1997; McCormack, 1996). It has been seen that females tend to perceive higher levels of stress than males (Megel et.al, 1994)

In short, it can be said that the reasons for student stress are: 1) Societal Pressure 2) Low self esteem 3) Exam stress 4) Educational System and 5) Pressure from parents and teachers.

Stress Among Students in the Health Care Professions

Students from health care professions like medicine, dentistry, nursing and other fields suffer from various degrees of stress like all the other students of various disciplines. However the challenges a medical or a dental student has to face are very much different than that of students of other disciplines. Since the health care profession is a healing profession, the students have to develop traits like empathy, patience, special communication skills, ethical values, an aptitude for social service in addition to didactic learning. It is for these traits that the society respects the health care profession and its practitioners and rates it so highly. In their quest to live up to the society's expectations medical students suffer tremendous stress. Stress in medical training has been the subject of numerous investigations (e.g. Special issue of Medical Education, Volume 28, 1994).

Medical school may be particularly stressful as students come into close contact with serious illness and death, in addition to meeting the demands of the curriculum. (http://www.gmc-uk.org/n_hance/med/student.htm). It could be argued that a certain amount of stress is necessary for students to perform well. An over relaxed attitude could lead to complacency and a failure to do sufficient work. Stress however leads to psychological ill health in medical students. Several studies have examined the relationship between the causes of stress and psychological morbidity. Depression and anxiety are associated with concerns about mastering knowledge, personal endurance and ability and lack of time for other activities (Vitaliano PP et al 1984; Stewart SM et al 1997). Anxiety is also associated with feelings of anonymity, peer competition, long hours and loss of social time (Vitaliano PP et al 1984; Stewart SM et al 1997). Studies that have tried to identify the sources of stress among medical students generally point to three main areas: academic pressures, social issues and financial problems. (Vitaliano PP et al 1984).

Academic Pressures

The majority of stressful incidents in traditional curricula are related to medical training rather than to personal problems (Coles C, 1994; Guthrie EA et al, 1995). Workload and feeling overwhelmed by the amount of information to be mastered are major sources of stress. Fears of failing or falling behind are particular preoccupations. Other significant academic sources of stress include disillusionment with medicine and the realities of medical school (Guthrie EA et al, 1995), perception of hurdle jumping (Coles C, 1994), relationship with teachers (Guthrie EA et al, 1995; Firth J, 1986) and dealing with death and suffering (Firth J, 1986).

During the undergraduate course, medical students are damagingly overloaded with content and the relevance of much of what they are taught often eludes them. Vast amounts of information are commited to memory for dubious reasons and doubtful benefit.In the clinical years students find themselves unable to apply in a professional setting what they know well enough for examinations. This situation is especially acute in non English speaking countries and those countries where English is not widely spoken. Since all the textbooks and literature are in English, many students who are not well versed with the language find it very difficult to understand the basic concepts.Even the examinations are sometimes not defensible educationally and to students appear as hurdles to be surmounted rather than opportunities for assessing progress. The situation is similar if not more pronounced in developing countries (Acharya S 2003, Rajab 2001). In studies done in India, academic factors were greater perceived than all other factors as a cause of stress (Supe 1998), however there was no differences among students at different levels of the medical course regarding academic factors. (Supe, 1998; Indrayan A et al 1985).

Generalized stressors which differentiate the basic science from the clinical years as well as stressors which are unique to each year have been identified (Keniston, 1967; Gaensbauer and Mizner, 1980; Coombs and St John 1981; Knight 1981; Bok 1984). A number of studies have been conducted on the perceived stressors, problems and concerns of medical students (Coburn and Joviasas 1975; Edwards and Zimet 1976; Bjorksten et al 1983; Lloyd and Gartrell 1983; Heins et al 1984; Levin and Franklin 1984; Linn and Zeppa 1984; Firth 1986; Rosenthal et al 1986; Carmel and Bernstein 1987; Wolf et al 1987, 1988). Common themes may be identified from these studies although they were conducted over a 15 year interval with students from different years, different schools and different cultures. Generally the academic demands were most problematic. Personal-interpersonal issues were also of concern perhaps stemming the magnitude of the academic demands. Regarding the academic demands, during the basic sciences the major themes dealt with the massive amount of material to be mastered in preparations for the stressful examinations, while in the clinical years , the major themes dealt with caring for the sick patients and dealing with medical personnel. Financial responsibilities were also a major concern to many students who graduate with loans to pay off. It is clear that many students forego their personal interests and interpersonal ties and experience feelings of emotional isolation and alienation (Gaensbauer and Mizner, 1980; Coombs and Fawzy, 1986) by tipping the balance in favour of academic superiority at the expense of personal growth and development.

Although the focus of much of the research has been on stress and its adverse effects on medical students, there are also some data about the positive aspects and uplifting experiences of medical students. In a retrospective study of graduating seniors, the most uplifting experiences were about recreation and relationships (Wolf et al 1988). The one exception was good examination performance which was rated as the second highest uplift. The fact that it was also rated as the most stressful item shows how the lives of medical students often revolve around examination schedules. With first year students, the most frequently endorsed uplifting items were related to hedonistic concerns (e.g. Having fun, laughing,). A common theme for the senior and first year students was the importance of maintaining contact with friends and family. The sense of belonging and social support are certainly preferable to possible feelings of social isolation and alieation that can arise from unmet psychologic needs.

Social issues that can cause stress include the effects of being a student on personal life, in particular managing leisure activities and social relationships. (Firth J, 1986; Stewart SM et al 1997,)The factors causing stress vary with the stage of the course. Concern about workload, performance, and personal competence seem particularly marked in first year.(Guthrie EA et al, 1995; Stewart SM et al 1997).In studies of medical students in later years factors inherent in medical training such as dealing with patients, disease and death, relationships with consultants and effects on personal life are important.(Firth J, 1986).

Attitudes Values and Personality Change During the Study Period

Medical training has traditionally been a long and arduous process. Despite this, admission into medical schools remains fiercely competitive. Silver described enthusiastic freshman medical students soon becoming cynical, depressed, dejected, frightened or frustrated (Silver H.K., 1982). Stress in medical students is common (Supe, 1994; Stewart S.M et al 1997), even in the early stages of training. There is evidence to suggest that there is a shift in personality, attitudes, and values during the course of medical education. It has been shown in both cross sectional and longitudinal studies that cynical attitudes increased and expressions of humanitarion feelings decreased as students progressed through medical school(Eron 1955,1958).Graduating medical students perceived that they became more cynical over the course of their medical education(Wolf et al 1989a). It has been shown that there is a shift to more hedonistic personality characteristics in two longitudinal studies (Burstein et al 1980; Whittmore et al 1985).In a longitudinal study on depressed mood in which assessments were conducted six times from first year to the last year, at least 12 % of the class showed depressive symptoms at any assessment during the first three years ,the highest being 25% during the end of the first year (Clark and Zeldov 1988). In a second longitudinal study with first and second year students, the incidence of major depression or probable major depression was 12 % (Zoccodillo et al 1986). The lifetime prevalence was 25 % or three times the rate in the general population.With first year medical students, the anxiety levels were one standard deviation above the mean relative to non-patient levels and the depression doubled over the course of the first year (Vitaliano et al 1989b).In another study ,self esteem and positive mood decreased while negative mood(Depression and hostility) increased over the course of the first year (Wolf et al 1991a). In a study of first and second year medical students, symptoms of anxiety were reported above the median of the population of psychiatric patients (Vitaliano et al 1984). In one study, 62 out of 172 first year students (36%) in the north of England had probable psychological disturbance according to a well recognized psychological questionnaire (Guthrie E.A et al, 1995). On entering medical school, students experience a rise in depression scores that persisted over time (Henning K et al , 1998). Trainees (students, interns, and residents) suffer high levels of stress, which lead to alcohol and drug abuse(Johnson N et al,1990) interpersonal relationship difficulties (Gallegos K et al ,1990) depression and anxiety(Pitts FN et al 1961;Salt P. et al 1984) and even suicide (Richings J.C 1986) Medical students have mean anxiety scores one standard deviation above those of non-patients, and their depression levels increase significantly throughout the first year of medical school(Vitaliano P et al 1989). Stress may also harm trainees' professional effectiveness: it decreases attention (Smith K, 1990) reduces concentration (Askenasy J, Lewin I,1996), impinges on decision-making skills(Lehner P et al,1997:Klein G et al, 1996) and reduces trainees' abilities to establish strong physician-patient relationships(Pastore FR et al, 1995). There are many causes for psychological distress in medical students. Training is long and hard, and character traits such as perfectionism have been associated with depression and anxiety both in medical students (Helmers K.F et al, 1997) and doctors (Schreier AR, and Abramovitch H, 1997). Medical students with low A level grades, an anxious personality, and reliance on avoidance coping strategies are also at risk (Stewart S.M et al 1997). Students commonly worry about the curriculum, personal competence, endurance, and finding time to have a life outside medical school (Stewart S.M et al 1997). These results suggest that there is a shift to a more cynical and hedonistic orientation during medical school as well as significant elevations and increases in symptoms of depression and anxiety. These shifts may in part be attributable to coping with a stressful learning environment.

School Environment

Very considerable attention is now being given to medical school as a social environment. The interface between the teaching staff and the medical students has long been a focus of research. Three decades ago investigations at Cornell University found sufficient respect and courtesy on the part of the teaching staff and the institution to consider that students were explicitly considered as collegues (Merton et al 1957). In contrast, investigations from Chicago found that at Kansas, medical students were disparaged and isolated as a student body, distanced from their teachers(Becker et al 1961).A similar situation can still be seen in developing countries like India (Acharya S 2003). Some clinicians deploy a style of teaching by humiliation. The climate of medical education is often unsupportive and threatening where it should be collaborative. This situation is especially prevalent in countries like India where most of medical schools do not provide adequate support services for students and trainees to harmful effects of stress.In a study of 581 students at 10 medical schools across the United States, 96.5% of respondents reported at least one type of perceived mistreatment or harassment during their training (Baldwin W.C et al, 1991). The most frequently type reported was public humiliation. Someone else taking the credit for one's work or being threatened with unfair grades or physical harm was also reported. Sexual harassment was a common complaint (55%). Mistreatment was most frequently attributed to residents and attending physicians. Mistreatment has been found to be widespread and pervasive during medical education (Silver 1982; Rosenberg and Silver 1984;Wolf et al 1989b; Sheehan et al 1990; Baldwin et al 1991; Silver and Glicken 1990; Richman et al 1992). Percieved psychological mistreatment by interns / residents and clinical teachers were found to be most widespread and there was also evidence found for sexual harassment. Increased perceived mistreatment was found to be positively associated with a perceived increase in cynicism (Wolf et al 1991b). It is possible that psychological harm and injury can have a lasting effect on the students(Sheehan et al 1990;Silver and Glicken 1990; Richman et al 1992). For example in one study students who reported experiencing atleast one abusive experience were significantly more likely to experience depressive symptoms and drink for escape purposes(Richman et al 192). The harmful consequences of the assault and insults reflected in the term 'traumatic deidealisation ' refer to an undercutting of self esteem and lowering of ideals about teachers and the medical profession by medical students (Kay 1990). These assaults and insults make it particularly problematic for emotionally vulnerable medical students whose identities as doctors are largely established during medical school (Knight 1981; Sheehan et al 1990; Silver and Glicken 1990). This perceived mistreatment can be detrimental to the psychological development of the students and potentially interfere with developing a positive doctor – patient relationship.

Demographic Characteristics

It is also important to consider the demographic differences in the way students may respond to the stress of medical education. Regarding the sex differences during the first year, women students developed more psychiatric symptoms and tended to report less satisfaction with life by mid year and remained more symptomatic by the end of the year but to a lesser extent(Lloyd and Gartrell 1981).Women also reported more role conflict and described their families as less supportive of their career choice. In a second study women students reported more negative effect and physical symptoms during the first term of medical schools as well as reporting a greater decrease in positive emotions and perceived peer friendliness than men (Alagna and Morkoff 1986). In an Indian study on dental students ,it was found that males tended to have greater stress than females.(Acharya S,2003). Although minority students (Black and Hispanic) reported greater social supports, higher self esteem ,lower anxiety and more internal locus of control, upon entering medical school, after one year the black students manifested slightly lower self esteem and higher levels of hostility and external locus of control. The Hispanic students continued to report higher self esteem and greater social supports but showed increased external locus of control and higher alcohol consumption. In a second study , black students perceived more stressors than white medical students in the same environment during the first year (Strayhorn 1980). Regarding marital status , the stressors of medical school were more severe for the single students; moreover, stress levels of formerly single students declined after marriage (Coombs and Fawzy 1982). It is important to take these demographic variables into account in designing future studies and intervention programs. In an Indian study, no difference in stress was observed in perceived stress on the basis of sex, place of stay, Mother tongue or on the basis of place of school or junior college education (Supe et al 1998).

Coping in Medical School

The ways in which medical students cope with stress in medical education, rather than the stressors per se may be the primary determinant of their health (Lazaraus and Folkman 1984). Coping and perceived social support are important mediating variables between stress and health outcomes(Lazaraus and Folkman 1984).Three adaptive styles for coping with stressors seem prominent among medical students: 1) Vigorous efforts to master ,overcome or counteract them instead of trying to live with or escape them.2) Changing the environment rather than themselves. And 3) Translating their feelings into ideas , manipulating these ideas , and sometimes forgetting the original feelings (Keniston 1967). Problem focused coping directed at altering or managing the problem causing the distress and emotion – focused coping directed at regulating the emotional response to the problem are two strategies which have been identified for dealing with stress (Lazaraus and Folkman 1984). Problem focused coping was used most frequently in a 4 year retrospective study with graduating medical students (Wolf et al 1988). These students also reported using a diversity of coping strategies (Wolf et al 1988), which is common in dealing with stressful encounters (Lazaraus and Folkman 1984). In a longitudinal study with first year medical students , problem focused and seeking social support coping decreased while emotion focused strategies increased (Vitaliano et al 1989b). Satisfaction with social supports decreased over the course of the first year and did not exert a protective role against psychological distress (Vitaliano et al 1989b). In another study, social support and psychiatric symptomatology were positively associated by mid year for first year students (Foorman and Lloyd 1986).It is conceivable that in a medical school environment , social ties may place competing demands on the student's time and energy and have potentially detrimental effects on health.

Effect of Coping Styles on Stress

Research shows that students with active coping styles (those who can tackle problems in a positive and straightforward manner) have lower levels of psychological distress (Stewart S.M et al 1997). However in an Indian study , it was found that stress was more common in medical students who have a dominant strategy of coping as positive reappraisal ,accepting responsibility, and planful solving. Those with the dominant strategy of escaping and distancing from difficult situation reported less stress. (Supe 1998). Preliminary evidence suggests that teaching medical students more effective coping strategies reduces distress in the short term (Mosley TH, and Perrin SG, 1994), and provides long-term protective effects (Michie S and Sandhu S, 1994). Helping students develop better ways of dealing with stress at an early stage of their medical undergraduate training needs to be considered, as students who suffer from distress in the first year of the course are at the highest risk of developing symptoms of stress later on (Guthrie E and Black D, 1998) In view of the potential long term benefits of managing stress in a more effective way, it may be important for students to develop such skills early on in their medical career.

Stress, Coping and Health Outcome

There are considerable data supporting the relationship between stress and health outcome (Notman et al 1984; Vitaliano et al. 1984; Carmel and Berbstein 1987; Strayhorn 1989;Wolf et al 1989b;1999a;Bramness et al 1991).In these studies ,stress was measured in diverse ways with different instruments and related to a variety of psychological and physical outcome measures , for example, 6 medical school pressures including intangible phenomena such as threat and anonymity and more practical problems such as limited personal time and long hours were related to anxiety(Vitaliano et al 1984),while in a second study the perceived stressfulness of patient contact and medical practice demands were correlated with trait anxiety (Cornell and Bernstein 1987). In a nine month longitudinal study ,with first year medical students , hassles (Wide range of personal and professional irritating and annoying experiences) predicted concurrent and subsequent mood(Wolf et al 1989b), while with another sample of first year students, hassles at the beginning of first year were related to psychological symptoms at the beginning and the end of the year(Wolf et al 1991a). Percieved mistreatment has also been related to a variety of mental health status , outcome measures including depressive and anxiety symptoms, hostility problem and escapist drinking,alchohol consumption leves and gender role orientation(Richman et al 1992), with Norwegian students, stress was a good predictor of mental health and consistent with the findings of U.S schools(Bramness et al 1991).

Two studies merit highlighting because of the unique methodology employed of grouping stydents by perceived stress (Vitaliano et al 1989) and psychological symptoms(Miller and Surtees 1991). Four groups were identified in the first study: 1) Resistors – Stress scores began and ended low; 2) Persistors – Scores began and remained high 3) Adaptors – Scores decreased from high to low; and 4) Maladaptors - Scores increased from low to high. These four groups were distinguishable by a variety of psychosocial variables including type A personality, anger expression and coping (Vitaliano 1989a). For example, resistors and maladopters began the year with similar levels of suppressed anger, external locus of control and wishful thinking, while at the end of the year, the maladaptors had significant increases in these variables whereas the resistors did not. In the second study , a subgroup of students who were continuosly symptomatic were distinguished from other groups by the following factors: 1) They were slow to make friends 2) Had inappropriate support from relatives 3) Had a tendency to have rows 4) Had steady girl or boyfriends and 5) Had vulnerable personalities(Miller and Surtees 1991). Differentiating students on stress, psychological symptoms and relevant dimensions and relating these factors to psychosocial and health/disease variables is a valuable approach for gaining a better understanding of stress,coping and health during medical education.

In the Precursors Study , medical student reactions to stress as self reported on a checklist of habits of nervous tension reflected individual psychobiological differences that are linked with future health or disease (Thomas 1971,1976; Thomas and McCabe 1980). The differing behavioral and affective reactions to stress appear to precede the initial clinical manifestations of major disease states by upto 20 to 30 years (Thomas and McCabe 1980). In a recent report from the Precursors Study (Graves and Thomas 1991),two of the 25 items from the Habits of Nervous Tension Questionnaire which were the strongest predictors of suicide were irritability and urinary frequency. Both these irems suggest that the proposed psychological sensitivities may relate to physiologic reactivity(Graves and Thomas 1991).These findings certainly have important implications for a preventive approach to health for medical students.

Coping was related to psychological distress in a longitudinal study of medical students (Vitaliano 1989b).Problem-focused coping was negatively related to distress while emotion-focused coping was positively focused to distress. This finding is consistent with the previous study of 12 diverse samples (Vitaliano et al 1986), in which problem focused coping was significantly and negatively related with psychological distress in 11 of the 12 samples while wishful thinking was positively related to distress in 10 of the 12 samples (Vitaliano et al 1986). Therefore, how medical students cope with stress during medical education can relate to health outcome which has important implications for intervention programmes designed to enhance adaptive coping strategies.

Cultural and Social Factors in Developing Countries

A lot of research has gone into the factors affecting stress and the coping systems in western countries. The support systems in the developed countries are very advanced and refined with the latest in science to back them up. However the Asian situation is very different. Owing to the difference in culture, there are some differences when it comes to factors affecting stress and the support systems in Asian countries.

There are huge differences between the education systems of Asian countries and the west. The American system is very flexible in the sense that students can choose among a host of classes and courses in high school and college. This means that they can change their major midway through college. This usually means that students in U.S receive more exposure to a variety of subjects and hence are more aware of their career options and opportunities. The American education system is designed in such a way so as not to hurt or reduce the self esteem of a student and most of the students pass the high school level. Also the education system is geared towards satisfying the needs of the industry. Student expression is encouraged and the teacher plays more of a supportive role than that of an instructor.

The Indian education system is one of the toughest and most competitive in the world. This education system is very rigid in the sense that the students upon enrolling for a graduate course can under no circumstances change their majors midway. Numerous subjects are heaped on the students at the school level. This undue thrust ends up blunting the student's sensitivity. Secondly the stiff competition that is rampant nowadays at all levels of education is also responsible for the discomfiture. Competition is akin to gambling and there is resultant stress. The student is forced to go through the drudgery of carrying on with the course, which he or she doesn't like. This can affect their academic performance. The whole graduate program is exam oriented and does not focus on the all round development of the individual. The fear of examinations begins almost as early as the IIIrd grade and persists upto even postgraduate levels. A number of social and psychological factors such as parental pressure, lack of career opportunities, uncertain future and so forth may trigger them off.This fear of examination is very much evident in medical and dental students also(Acharya S ,2003).

The syllabus is strictly written. One has to know the textbooks very well and if possible understand the content or other wise just learn the answers with out understanding it. This is because there is a lot of stress on theory and not on practical work. Some of the textbooks are never updated. Students continue to study the textbooks that were written 10 years ago. In short, students lose interest in their studies, as it is very boring, monotonous and tedious. The purpose of the educational system is not specified. In spite of spending lots of money for a good education and finishing graduation, many students still don't get jobs. The high school education system is very tough and harsh on the students who are burdened with a huge curriculum which is sometimes equivalent to that of American majors programs. Many students find it difficult to cope with the stress and resort to suicide, drug abuse, delinquency etc. The' corporal' mentality of the teaching faculty, a legacy of the British rule is still rampant, resulting in the near dictatorial attitude of the faculty. The students are not encouraged to form their own opinions, and open discussions are clearly discouraged. Not agreeing with the faculty's orders may lead to punitive action ranging from being ridiculed publicly in front of other students to failure in the examinations. In spite of being officially banned, corporal punishment is still rampant in schools especially in the rural areas.. Because of the relative absence of support and counseling centers, the student has nowhere to turn to other than his family. In many cases, the family too is found wanting in giving support during this crucial period. It is the parents who constantly dump their own pent up or unfulfilled ambitions on their children. In the process the dreams and ambitions of the children get thwarted. Most parents want their off springs to be doctors or engineers, even if the children may not have inclinations or capabilities for the same. In fact, a child's academic record and performance becomes a prestige issue for the parents and even families.

Sometimes parents feel a big blow is given to their self-esteem if their child fails or gets very bad marks in the exams. So they emotionally torture their child, which, is also one of the reasons why the student is driven to extreme measures like suicides. This phenomenon is common to all the Asian families where emphasis on hard work, discipline and respect for authority is inherent. (Suzuki, 1980).

The families in their anxiety about their ward's future ride roughshod over any concerns that their child might have , and encourage them to just "Take it on the Chin". Children are many a time forced to join an educational graduate program by their parents against their wishes. Such students have been found to suffer from more stress than those who joined of their accord (Acharya, 2003). Students joining courses that do not guarantee gainful employment suffer from more stress than the others (Acharya, 2003). Sometimes students lose faith in themselves if they are constantly failing or because they only hear criticism from their teachers and parents. Due to this they feel that they are hopeless and cannot do anything in life. These factors lead to the student losing his or her self esteem and confidence. There are fights between friends or peers, on who is more intelligent than the other this also causes emotional stress and frustration on the student.

Medical students in developing countries like their counterparts in the west face a tremendous amount of stress during their period of education. But in addition to the common factors, students from developing countries have to face some special circumstances caused by the difference in socioeconomic and cultural factors. In the western countries the medical profession is always under public scrutiny and because of high awareness among the public, malpractice suits are common. This often leads to the doctor patient relationship deteriorating into a customer client relationship. Hence more emphasis is placed on collecting evidence from the patient like lab reports, special investigations, having witnesses etc, to prevent future career ruining lawsuits than on actual treatment. In their efforts to have an evidence-based practice, the basic ethos of the medical profession may get diluted. In developing countries, the amount of respect the doctors command in the society is phenomenal and sometimes intimidating. This is even more so in the rural areas where the concept of '*Vaidya Narayano Hari* " the Sanskrit phrase meaning " Doctor is equivalent to God " still prevails. Any treatment given or suggested by the doctor is considered sacrosanct. This may be one of the reasons why the number of malpractice litigations is negligible and almost non-existent in the rural areas. Since any treatment the doctor advises is followed with no questions asked, the doctor is under tremendous moral pressure to deliver. Evidence based practice is very much limited to some select urban areas. It is virtually non-existent in rural and semi urban areas because of the lack of basic laboratory facilities. The facilities though available in the big cities, are not affordable to a majority of the population. This creates a difficult situation where a doctor has to rely solely on the clinical signs and symptoms and his clinical training and experience when prescribing treatment. The students may find it very stressful to fit into the society's image of the medical profession. The development of the 'Imposter Phenomenon' because of these factors cannot be ruled out.

Studies have shown that cultural factors can affect the symptom expression of stress. Reports have shown that depression and anxiety are expressed in somatic terms in non western cultures in comparison to western cultures (Gureje et al 1997;Simon et al 1996). Kleinmann noted that in non western cultures, feelings of sadness, worthlessness and guilt were less common while somatic complaints such as feeling tired ,stomach aches ,headaches were more common. These somatic complaints have also been reported to include dizziness , fatigue and abdominal pain(Cheung1985; Kleinmann1988; Youngmann et al 1999).

Dental Students

Dentistry has been widely acknowledged as being associated with high levels of stress.(Atkinson et al 1991; Gorter R.C 1999). Stressors associated with dentistry include time and scheduling pressures, managing uncooperative patients, commercial issues and the highly technical and intensive nature of work.(Atkinson et al 1991; Gorter R.C et al 1999). The origins of this stress may lie in the process of dental education (Westerman G.H et al 1993; Heath J.R., et al 1999;Lamis D.R, 2001). In recent years, the injurious effects of stress experienced by dental students have received much attention. Stress has been shown to manifest as fatigue, tension, dizziness, sleeplessness, tachycardia, gastro intestinal symptoms and also irritability, anxiety and cynicism(Martinez N.P 1977;Knudsen W,1978;Wexler M,1978; Grandy T.G et al 1988;Cecchini J.J et al 1987;Tedesco L.A, 1986) In addition to this, a negative association has been reported between stress and academic performance of dental students(Cecchini J.J et al 1987;Tedesco L.A, 1986).Studies on dental students have shown that they are not much different from medical students when it comes to sources of stress, and coping mechanisms.

Recommendations

Some recommendations evolving from this overview of stress , coping , and health among students of medicine and its allied branches are advanced for enhancing the well being of the students.

- It is advantageous to obtain a clear understanding and have realistic expectation about what it takes to become a doctor and road that has to be traveled prior even to entering medical school (Coombs et al 1990).
- It is important to place a greater emphasis on qualitative variables in the admission process(Walton 1987;World Federation for Medical Education 1988; McGaghie 1990;Coombs 1991)
- The undergraduate medical school curriculum should include a didactic grounding and clinical experience in health promotion and disease prevention(Newfeld and Barrows 1974; Coles 1985;Kaufman et al 1989; Tayloret al 1989; Altekruse et al 1991)
- Health promotion programs (e.g Dickstein and Elks 1986; Wolf et al 1990;Basmuke et al 1992) are helpful in developing and maintaining a balanced lifestyle and can enhance the personal well-being of medical students.
- Medical, psychiatric and academic counseling should be made available to all medical students.
- Additional research is needed regarding all aspects of medical education with an emphasis on longitudinal research designs tapping into the complex interplay of environmental, personality, coping, academic and health outcome variables.
- It would be desirable to foster an international collaboration on well being issues among medical schools to work on improving all aspects of medical education such as periodic conferences of World Federation for Medical Education
- Periodic interaction of the faculty with trained educational psychologists who can train the faculty in the latest educational methodologies to maximize student performance and minimize stress (Acharya S 2003).
- Parents should be counseled during their children's pre-university period about the ill effects of pressurizing them to join an educational program against their wishes. This can be done by drafting the help of the high school authorities in conducting workshops involving parents and teachers on a regular basis. Career fairs can also be used as a forum for parent counseling (Acharya S 2003).
- Since it has been shown that students from predominantly non western cultures most of which are in developing countries express symptoms of stress through somatisation rather than psychologically, more attention should be paid by the educators to identify these symptoms to effectively deal with student stress.
- Students should also be taught to identify these symptoms among themselves and their friends, so that they can seek help at the appropriate forum.

References

Acharya S. Factors affecting stress among Indian dental students. *J Dent Educ*. 2003 Oct;67(10):1140-8.

Altekruse J.,Goldenberg K.,Rabin D.,Riegelman R.K., & Wiese W.H.Implementing the Association of Teachers of Preventive Medicine's recommendations into the undergraduate medical school curriculum.*Academic Medicine* 1991. ,6,312-316.

Anderson ,C.L. et al.*Community Health*, 1978. C.V.Mosby.

Askenasy J, Lewin I. The impact of missile warfare on self-reported sleep quality. *Sleep*.1996; 19:47 –51

Atkinson T.M., Millar K., Kay E.J., Blinkhorn A.S. Stress in dental practice. *Dent Update*. 1991; 18: 60-4.

Baldwin WC, Daugherty RS, Eckenfels EJ. Students perceptions of mistreatment and harassment during Medical School. A survey of ten United States Schools. *The Western Journal of Medicine* 1991;**155**(2):140-5.

Bramneess JG, Fixdal TC, Vaglun P. Effect of Medical School Stress on the Mental Health of Medical Students in early and later clinical curriculum. *Acta Psychiatrica Scandinavia* 1991;**84**(4):340-5.

Cecchini J.J., Friedman V. First year dental students: relationship between stress and performance. *Int J Psychosom*. 1987; 34: 17-19.

Cheung F.M. (1985). An overview of psychopathology in Hong Kong with special reference to somatic presentation. In W. Tseng and D.Wu (Eds).*Chinese culture and mental health.* (pp 287-304). Orlando: Academic Press Inc.

Cmich,D.E *Jr. School Health* 1984.54,(1)30-32

Coles C.Differences between conventional and problem – based curricula in their students' approaches to studying.*Medical Education* 1985.19,308-309.

Coles C.Medicine and Stress. *Med Educ* 1994;28: 3-4

Coombs R.H. Non cognitive components in the selection and training of medical students.*Med Educ* 1991.25,539-541.

Coombs RH, Perell K, Ruckh JM. Primary prevention of emotional impairment among medical trainees. *Academic Medicine* 1990;**65**(9):576-81.

Dickstein L.J. & Elkes J.,(1986).A health awareness workshop: Enhancing Coping skills in medical students.In:*Heal Thyself: The Health of health care professionals*(ed. by C.Scott & J. Hawk). Brunner/Mazel, New York.

Dill, Patricia L. and Tracey B. Henley. "Stressors of College: A Comparison of Traditional and Nontraditional Students." *Journal of Psychology* 1998. 132(1): 25-32.

Dismuke S.E., McCleary A.M., McCall J., & Runyan J.W.Integrating an educational program and health promotion ,disease prevention into a medical school: University of Tennessee. *American Journal of Health Promotion* 1992.6,363,372-379.

Eberst,R.M. *Jr.School Health* 1984.54(3)99-104

Ensel, Walter M., and Nan Lin. "The life stress paradigm and psychological distress." *Journal of Health and Social Behavior* 1991. 32: 321-341.

Firth J.Levels and sources of stress in medical students. *Br Med J* 1986; 292:1177-80

Firth-Cozens J. Predicting stress in general practitioners: 10 year follow up postal survey. *Br Med J* 1997;313:34-5.

Gallegos K, Bettinardi-Angres K, Talbott G. The effect of physician impairment on the family. *Maryland Med J*.1990; 39:1001 -7.

Gaughran F, Dineen S, Dineen M, Cole M, Daly RJ. Stress in medical students. *Ir Med J* 1997;90:184-5.

Goldrnan, Cristin S, and Wong, Eugene H. "Stress And The College Student." *Education*, Summer 97, Vol. 117 Issue 4, p604, 7p, 1 chart

Gorter R.C., Albrecht G., Hoogstraten J., Eijkman M.A.J. Professional burnout among Dutch dentists. *Community Dent Oral Epidemiol*. 1999; 27; 109-16.

Grandy T.G., Westerman G.H., Lupo J.V., Comb C.G. Stress symptoms among third year dental students. *J Dent Educ*. 1988; 52: 245-9.

Gurege. O, Simon.G, Ustus. T,Goldberg D.Somatization in a cross cultural perspective: A WHO study in primary care. *American Journal of Psychiatry* ,1997; 154(7); 989-995

Guthrie E, Black D, Bagalkote H, Shaw C, Campbell M, Creed F. Psychological stress and burnout in medical students: a five year prospective longitudinal study. *J R Soc Med* 1998;91:237-43.

Guthrie EA, Black D, Shaw CM, Hamilton J, Creed FH, Tomenson B. Embarking upon a medical career: psychological morbidity in first year medical students. *Med Educ* 1995;29:337-41.

Heath J.R., MacFarlane T.V., Umar M.S. Perceived sources of stress in dental students. *Dent Update*. 1999; 26: 94-100.

Helmers KF, Danoff D, Steinert Y, Leyton M, Young SN. Stress and depressed mood in medical students, law students, and graduate students at McGill University. *Acad Med* 1997;72:708-14.

Hirsch, J. K., & Ellis, J. B. Differences in life stress and reasons for living among college suicide ideators and non-Ideators. *College Student Journal* 1996. 30, 377-384.

Indrayan A, Rao S,Grover V,Agrawal K,Gupta A."Freshers perception of problems in medical education"*Indian J Med Educ* 1985;24:85-94

Johnson N, Michels P, Thomas J. Screening tests identify the prevalence of alcohol use among freshman medical students and among students' family of origin. *J South Carolina Med Assoc*.1990; 86:13 –4

Kaufmann A., Mennin S., Waterman R., Duban S., Hansbarger C., Silverblat H.,Obenshain S.C., Cantrowitz M.,Becker T.,Sammmet J., & Wiese W. The New Mexico Experiment: Education Innovation and Institutional Change.*Academic Medicine* 1989.64,285-294.

Klein G. The effect of acute stressors on decision making. In: Driskell J, Salas E (eds). *Stress and Human Performance*. Mahwah, NJ: Lawrence Erlbaum, 1996:48 -88.

Kleinmann A. *Rethinking Psychiatry: From Cultural Category to personal experience*. 1988; New York; Free Press

Kohn, J. P., & Frazer, G. H. An academic stress scale: Identification and rated importance of academic stressors. *Psychological Reports* 1986. 59, 415-426.

Lamis D.R. Perceived sources of stress among dental students at the University of Jordan. *J Dent Educ*. 2001; 65: 232-241.

Lehner P, Seyed-Solorforough M, O'Connor M, Sak S, Mullin T. Cognitive biases and time stress in team decision making. *Trans Systems, Man & Cybernetics*.1997; 27:698 -703.

Martinez N.P. Assessment of negative effects in dental students. *J Dent Educ.* 1977; 41: 31-36.

McCormack, Arlene Smith. Drinking in stressful situations: college men under pressure." *College Student Journal* 1996. 30 (1): 65-77.

McGaghie W.C. Qualitative variables in medical school admission. *Academic Medicine* 1990. 65,154-149.

Megel, Mary Erickson, Peggy Hawkins, Susie Sandstrom, Mary Ann Hoefler, and Kathleen Willrett "Health Promotion, Self-Esteem and Weight Among Female College Freshman." *Health Values*, 18 (4): 10- 19. 1994.

Michie S, Sandhu S. Stress management for clinical medical students. *Med Educ* 1994;28:528-33.

Miller P McC. The first year at medical school: some findings and student perceptions. *Med Educ* 1994;28:5-7.

Morgan, Sue. "Cheap drinks, heavy costs: students and alcohol." *Youth and Policy* 1997. 56: 42-54.

Mosley TH, Perrin SG, Neral SM, Dubbert PM, Grothues CA, Pinto BM. Stress, coping and well-being among third-year medical students. *Acad Med* 1994;69:765-7.

Moss, Gordon E. *Illness Immunity and Social Interaction*.1973. New York: John Wiley.

Naquin, M.R. and Glen G. Glibert. "College students' smoking behavior, perceived stress and coping styles." *Journal of Drug Education* 1996. 26 (4): 367-76.

Neufeld V.R, Barrows H.S, The 'McMaster Philosophy': An approach to medical education.*Joural of Medical Education* 1974.49,1040-50.

Pastore FR, Gambert SR, Plutchik A, Plutchik R. Empathy training for medical students. Unpublished manuscript, New York Medical College, 1995.

Pitts FN, Winokur G, Stewart MA. Psychiatric syndromes, anxiety symptoms and responses to stress in medical students. *Am J Psychiatry*. 1961;118:333 -40.

Richings JC, Khara GS, McDowell. Suicide in young doctors.*Br J Psychiatry*. 1986;149:475 –8

Richman JA, Flaherty JA, Rospenda KM, Christensen ML. Mental Health Consequences and correlates of reported medical student abuse. *JAMA* 1992; 267(5): 692-4.

Romano, J. L. (1992). Psychoeducational interventions for stress management and well-being. *Journal of Counseling and Development*, 71, 199-202.

Rose ,G.A.and Blackburn H.(1968)Cardiovascular Survey Methods, Geneva,WHO.

Salt P, Nadelson C, Notman M. Depression and anxiety among medical students. Paper presented at APA Annual Meeting, Los Angeles, CA, 1984.

Schreier AR, Abramovitch H. American medical students in Israel: stress and coping. *Br J Psych* 1997;171:519-23.

Schutt, Russell K., Tatjana Meschede and Jill Riordan. "Distress, suicidal thoughts and social support among homeless adults." *Journal of Health and Social Behavior,*1994. 35: 134-42

Sgan-Cohen, H. D., & Lowental, U. Sources of stress among Israeli dental students. *The Journal of the American College Health Association*,1988. 36, 317-321.

Sheehan KH, Sheehan DV, White K, Leibowitz A, Baldwin DC. A pilot study of medical student abuse and student perception of mistreatment and misconduct in Medical School. *JAMA* 1990;**263**:533-7.

Silver HK, Glicken AD, Medical Students abuse - incidence, severity and significance. *JAMA* 1990;**263**(4):527-32.

Silver HK. Medical Students and Medical School. *JAMA* 1982;**247**:309-310.

Simon.G, Gater.R, Kiseli.S,Piccinelli.M. Somatic symptoms of distress: An international primary care study. *Psychomatic Medicine* ,1996;58;481 – 488.

Smith A. Stress and information processing. In: Johnston M, Wallace L, et al (eds). *Stress and Medical Procedures*. Oxford Medical Publications. Oxford, England: Oxford University Press, 1990:184.

Stewart SM, Betson C, Lam TH, Marshall IB, Lee PW, Wong CM. Predicting stress in first year medical students: a longitudinal study. *Med Educ* 1997;31:163-8.

Suzuki, B. (1980). Education and the socialization of Asian Americans: A revisionist analysis of the "model minority" theses. In R. Endo, S. Sue, & N. Wagner (Eds.), *Asian-Americans: Social and psychological perspectives* (pp. 155-178). Palo Alto, CA: Science and Behavioral Books.

Taylor W.C.,Pels R.J.,& Lawrence R.S. A First year problem based curriculum in health promotion and disease prevention. *Academic Medicine*,1989.673-677.

Tedesco L.A. A psychosocial perspective on dental education experience and student performance. *J Dent Educ*. 1986; 50: 601-5.

Thoits, Peggy A. "Stress, coping and social support processes: Where are we? What Next?" *Journal of Health and Social Behavior*,1995. extra issue: 53-79.

Towbes, L. C., & Cohen, L. H. Chronic stress in the lives of college students: Scale development and prospective prediction of distress. *Journal of Youth and Adolescence*,1996. 25, 199-217.

Vitaliano P, Maiuro R, Russo J, Mitchell E. Medical student distress: a longitudinal study. *J Nerv Ment Dis*.1989; 177:70 –6

Vitaliano PP,Russo J,Carr JE,Heerwagen JH.Medical school pressures and their relationship to anxiety.*J Nervous Mental Dis* 1984;172:730-6.

Walton,H.J. Personality assessment of future doctors. *Journal of the Royal Society of Medicine*.1987.80,27-30.

Westerman G.H., Grandy T.G., Ocanto R.A., Eriksine C.G. Perceived sources of stress in the dental school environment. *J Dent Educ*. 1993; 57: 225-31.

Wexler M. Mental health and dental education. *J Dent Educ*. 1978; 42: 74-7.

WHO (1964).Techn.Rep.Ser.,275

WHO(1985)Techn Rep Ser., No.714

Wolf T.M., Randall H.,& Faucett J.A health promotion program for medical student: Louisiana State University Medical Center.American *Journal of Health Promotion*.1990 4,193-282.

Wolf TM, Randall HM, Von Almen K, Tynes LL. Perceived mistreatment and attitude change by graduating medical students: a retrospective study. *Medical Education* 1991;**25**:192-90.

World Federation for medical education. The Edinburgh Declaration. *Lancet*,1988. 8608,464.

Wright, J. J. Environmental stress evaluation in a student community. The *Journal of the American College Health Association*.1964, 12(5), 325-336.

Wright, J. J. Reported personal stress sources and adjustment of entering freshmen. *Journal of Counseling Psychology*.1967. 14(4), 371-373.

Youngmann.R, Minuchin-Itsigsolin.S, Miriam ,B. Manifestations of emotional distress among Ethiopian immigrants in Israel: Patent and Clinician Perspectives.*Transcultural Psychiatry*.1999;36(1), 45-63.

In: Anxiety in College Students
Editor: Benjamin Ayres and Michelle Bristow
ISBN: 978-1-60692-282-8

Chapter VI

Coping, Mental Health Status, and Current Life Regret in College Women Who Differ in their Lifetime Pregnancy Status: A Resilience Perspective*

Jennifer Langhinrichsen-Rohling*†, *Theresa Rehm*, *Michelle Breland and Alexis Inabinet
University of South Alabama, Mobile, Alabama USA

Abstract

This study examined the current mental health status, coping strategies, and perceived life regret of three types of female college students (n = 277): those who had never been pregnant (67.9%, n= 188); those who became pregnant at or before age 18 who were a priori considered to be resilient (14.8%, n = 41); and those who had experienced a pregnancy after age 18 (17.3%, n = 48). Data were collected at a diverse urban public university in the Southeast. This university has a significant number of commuter and non-traditional students. Results indicated that college women who had experienced an adult pregnancy reported significantly fewer maladaptive coping strategies than never-pregnant college women and those who had experienced a teenage pregnancy. Surprisingly, both groups of ever pregnant college women expressed

---

* This project was supported by Grant No. 2001-SI-FX-0006 awarded by the Office of Juvenile Justice and Delinquency Prevention, Office of Justice Programs, U.S. Department of Justice. Points of view or opinions in this document are those of the author and do not necessarily represent the official position or policies of the U.S. Department of Justice.

† Correspondence concerning this article should be addressed to Jennifer Langhinrichsen-Rohling, 385 Life Sciences Building, Psychology Department, University of South Alabama, Mobile, AL., 36688-0002, or the author can be reached via email at jlr@usouthal.edu.

significantly more life regret than never pregnant college women. Among the college women who had experienced a teenage pregnancy, two groups were delineated: those who were "thriving" versus those who were "at-risk" with regards to their current symptoms of depression, hostility, and hopelessness. Women in the "at-risk" group were significantly *less* likely to be simultaneously parenting and attending college than those in the "thriving" group. One potential implication is that identifying and intervening with these potentially at-risk college women may help improve retention rates and student morale at universities with a diverse student body.

Introduction

Individual differences in successful adaptation to stressful life events have prompted investigations of a construct termed resilience. Many different definitions of resilience have been used across studies (Luthar, Cicchetti, & Becker, 2000). Resilience requires an individual both to experience a precipitating adversity and subsequently to exhibit successful adaptation to the event. It is necessary to clearly operationally define both of these components in order to study the construct of resilience. For example, definitions of what constitutes a precipitating adversity have ranged from a single stressful experience to exposure to various levels of cumulative negative events (Luthar et al., 2000).

Methods of identifying individuals who have successfully adapted, or who are exhibiting resilience in response to adversity, have also varied. Carver (1998) suggested that resilient individuals are those who return to their prior level of functioning after experiencing adversity. Others have required that resilient individuals excel in one category, while maintaining at least average performance in other areas (Luthar, Doernberger, & Zigler, 1993). Still others have divided resilient individuals into distinct categories. For example, Masten (1994) specified three resilient outcomes: (1) the individual experiences a better-than-expected outcome, (2) positive adaptation is maintained despite the continued occurrence of stress, or (3) there is good recovery from trauma. Carver (1998) also argued that benefits could occur through adversity. He describes this as "thriving", and argues that thriving is a conceptually distinct construct from resilience.

The psychological components or mechanisms underlying resilience have also been delineated in diverse ways. According to Luthar and colleagues (2000), early explorations of resilience were centered on identifying children's pre-existing character traits, such as high self-esteem or resourcefulness (Masten & Garmezy, 1985; Moran & Eckenrode, 1992). More recently, researchers have argued the importance of conceptualizing resilience as a dynamic and multi-faceted process (Luther et al., 2000). This led to the inclusion of external in addition to internal factors when studying resilience. In 1992, Werner and Smith delineated three disparate factors that influence the development of resilience. They are: (1) attributes of the individual, (2) aspects of the person's families, and (3) characteristics of the individual's wider social environment. Bickart and Wolin (1997) have expanded this conceptualization by articulating seven essential attributes of the individual (i.e., insight, independence, relationships, initiative, creativity, humor, and morality). They also noted that the expression of these attributes interacts with environmental factors, which may or may not be related to the precipitating stressor, and may be expressed unevenly across time.

Consistent with this line of reasoning, in the current study, it is assumed that individuals who display resilience to one significant life event (i.e., teenage pregnancy) are more likely to demonstrate certain adaptive coping strategies and to possess particular individual attributes. These characteristics, such as high levels of personal competence and/or hopefulness, are likely to have contributed to their resilience. However, it is still plausible that some of these resilient individuals might simultaneously display some characteristics that would place them at risk for continued life difficulties; perhaps because of on-going mental health concerns or stress related to the life event, trauma related symptoms, and/or continued life regret over the initial adversity. Thus, resilient individuals may differ in the degree to which they can be considered to be "thriving", particularly if they are exposed to additional stressors over time.

Within the resilience literature, researchers have focused on a number of different adversities from which successful adaptation is difficult. For example, studies have examined resilience from family adversity (Fergusson & Lynskey, 1996), childhood sexual abuse (Himelein & McElrath, 1996; Wilcox, Richards, & O'Keeffe, 2004), growing up with alcoholic parents (Carle & Chassin, 2004; Statham, 2004), being exposed to the battering of their mothers (Humphreys, 2001), coping with a mentally ill parent (Polkki, Ervast, & Huupponen, 2004), and triumphing over a generally high level of stress and numerous life events (Burton, 2004; Carver & Scheier, 1989; Charney, 2004; Compas, 1987; Fergusson & Lynskey, 1996; Lazarus, 1993). In many of these studies, resilience has been studied by observing positively adjusted individuals who have already experienced the specific stressor or the general adversity. These individuals, termed resilient, are then compared to similar groups of individuals who did not experience the stressor to determine which factors of resilience contributed to the successful adaptation of the resilient individuals.

Relevant to the current study, and an important event to which relatively large numbers of young women must cope, is teenage pregnancy. It is well established that teenage pregnancy and childbearing is a significant problem in the United States (for reviews, see Adams, Adams-Taylor, & Pittman, 1989; Clemmens, 2002; Furstenberg, 1991; Hudson, Elek, & Campbell-Grossman, 2000; and Kivisto, 2001). Pregnancy is a unique adverse event in which to study resilience in that it often impacts individuals for the rest of their lives, particularly if they make the transition from pregnancy to parenthood. Furthermore, although pregnancy and childbearing are not typically viewed as negative events, the early timing, the emotional and physical requirements it places on an adolescent, and the increased likelihood that the event was unplanned for and/or unwanted, make it a significant stressor in a teenager's life (Adams et al, 1989). Even for older moms, pregnancy, childbearing, and subsequent parenting can be stressful, limiting women's available educational and career opportunities.

The consequences of teenage pregnancy have been shown to be even more detrimental. According to Adams et al. (1989) more than half of teenage mothers and a third of teenage fathers drop out of high school. This is significant because without a high school diploma, these adolescents are almost certain to live in poverty. The added expenses of raising a child, including large daycare costs, exacerbate this problem. In addition, adolescent mothers have been shown to have higher rates of depression and experience more stress in the parenting role than older mothers (Hudson et al., 2000). Being forced to take on the adult role of parenting before completing their own adult developmental tasks can make things especially difficult. At a time when their peers are enjoying social outings and other egocentric activities, becoming a teenage parent can compromise the development of self-identity and limit mate-selection (Leitch, 1998). Finally, concern over body image and the need for peer acceptance can cause self-esteem problems for teenage mothers (Hudson et al., 2000).

In spite of these circumstances, researchers have noted that pregnancy and parenting do not affect all individuals in the same way. Just as some abused children find the strength to succeed in spite of all odds, some adolescent mothers continue their education in spite of parenting demands begun during their teenage years. In the current study, we are defining these college women as resilient. Consistent with the literature, we assert that it is likely that both internal factors, or personality traits, and external factors, or situational conditions, contributed to their resilient status. The degree to which a subset of these women can be considered to be thriving versus being at continued risk in the college environment is the primary focus of the current study.

To date, the literature has been largely silent about whether there are current mental health characteristics or coping factors that differentiate college women who differ in terms of whether they experienced a teenage pregnancy, never experienced a pregnancy, or experienced a pregnancy after they were teenagers. Therefore, the present study was designed to investigate three areas of particular importance to understanding resilience and subsequent thriving: current mental health status (levels of hostility, hopelessness, and depression), perceived life regret, and continued use of adaptive versus maladaptive coping skills.

A priori, the following hypotheses were developed. First, because of the resilience demonstrated by matriculation, college women who experienced a teenage pregnancy were expected to demonstrate thriving in the academic environment as evidenced by fewer feelings of hopelessness and hostility, less current depression and perceived life regret, and increased use of adaptive coping strategies in comparison to both other groups of college women (never pregnant and adult pregnant). However, we expected considerable variability among these women such that a subset of college women who had experienced a teenage pregnancy could still be identified as "at-risk" with regards to their mental health functioning and coping skills.

Second, it was hypothesized that college women who experienced an unwed pregnancy will differ significantly from those who experienced a pregnancy while married, regardless of their age at the time of the pregnancy. To our knowledge, no preexisting research has compared these two groups of college women. However, exploratory hypotheses were generated such that college women who were unmarried when they became pregnant will exhibit more current hopelessness, hostility, depression, and life regret, as well as fewer adaptive coping strategies than college women who were married when they became pregnant. This is expected because of the greater stressors and reduced social support associated with unwed motherhood.

Finally, it is hypothesized that current college women who had a teenage pregnancy, but who are not currently parenting (because of abortion, adoption, miscarriage), will differ significantly from college women who experienced a teenage pregnancy and are simultaneously parenting a child while pursuing their education. These final analyses were exploratory in nature, and no a priori hypotheses were offered.

Method

Participants

Participants included 277 female college students who were enrolled in Introductory Psychology classes at an urban university located in the Southeastern part of the United States. The races of the participants were as follows: Caucasian (61%), African American (26%), Asian American (2.2%), Hispanic (1.8%), and Native American (0.4%). Twenty-three participants (8.3%) reported their race to be "other" and one participant (0.4%) did not report her race. The ages of the participants ranged from 19 to 54 years old, with a mean age of 23 years. The majority of the participants indicated that they were freshmen (59.2%). The sample also included sophomores (25.6%), juniors (9.4%), and seniors (4.7%). The grade point average (GPA) reported by the participants varied from 1.4 to 4.0, with a mean GPA of 3.1. These demographics are consistent with the demographics of the university's college women, excluding the high proportion of freshmen in the sample. However, this was to be expected given that these data were collected from female students taking an introductory class in Psychology.

Instruments

Participants were administered a 252-item questionnaire composed of several different scales. Questions on the survey were used to determine participant status according to the independent variables of teenage pregnancy status, marital status at time of pregnancy, and current motherhood status. Teenage pregnancy status was defined as the experience of a pregnancy at or before the age of 18. This was determined by participant answers on two questionnaire questions. The first question determined whether or not the college woman had ever experienced a pregnancy. A follow-up question determined the participant's age at the time of pregnancy, if a pregnancy had occurred. Marital status at the time of pregnancy was defined as being married at the time of conception, and was determined by one question. Finally, current motherhood status was defined as completing the pregnancy and currently parenting one or more children while attending college.

The dependent variables of interest were mental health status (current depression, hostility, and hopelessness), use of adaptive versus maladaptive coping strategies, and perceptions of current life regret. These three categories, within which the following scales were utilized, are described below.

Mental Health Status

Depressive Symptoms. Symptoms of depression were assessed with 10 items from the Center for Epidemiological Studies-Depression Scale (CES-D; Radloff, 1977). On this scale, participants rate how frequently they have experienced each of 10 symptoms related to depression over the past seven days. Each items is rated on a four-point scale (rarely or never = 0, some or little of the time = 1, occasionally or a moderate amount of time = 2, most or all of the time = 3). Higher scores represent greater levels of depression by indicating a higher number of symptoms and/or symptoms that are more frequent. This scale has been used successfully in college samples, showing good reliability and internal consistency (e.g., Langhinrichsen-Rohling, Arata, Bowers, O'Brien, & Morgan, 2004). The current sample had a coefficient alpha of 0.82 for this scale.

Hostility. Hostility was measured with six items adopted from the Symptom Checklist-90 (SLC-90; Derogatis, 1994). These six items were used to gauge respondents' current level of anger and irritation by asking them to rate how well each item pertains to them. Responses range from "not at all" to "extremely". Higher scores represent greater levels of hostility. In the current sample, these six items had a coefficient alpha of 0.84.

Hopelessness. Hoplesness was evaluated by six items designed to assess participants' negative expectations about themselves and their future. Five of the items were adopted from Kazdin's Hopelessness Scale for Children (HSC; Kazdin, French, Unis, Esveldt-Dawson, & Sherick, 1983). These five items, along with another item ("I don't expect to live a very long life"), were utilized successfully in previous research with both adolescents and college students by the primary author (Langhinrichsen-Rohling et al., 2004). Respondents are asked to rate how well they agree with each statement, with responses ranging from "strongly agree" to "strongly disagree". The coefficient alpha for the current sample was 0.72 for these six items, with higher scores indicating greater levels of hopelessness.

Adaptive Verses Maladaptive Coping Strategies

Coping. Coping was assessed with thirty items derived from the Adolescent Coping Orientation for Problem Experiences (A-COPE; Patterson & McCubbin, 1987). The A-COPE is a 54-item self-report questionnaire designed to measure adolescents' coping behaviors. Respondents are asked to rate how often they engage in each behavior when facing difficulties. Responses are based on a five-point scale ranging from "never" to "most of the time". The current study had a coefficient alpha of 0.83 for the thirty items taken from the A-COPE.

Several researchers, including the authors of this instrument, have performed factor analysis on the A-COPE scale (e.g., Patterson & McCubbin, 1987; Copeland & Hess, 1995; Langhinrichsen-Rohling, O'Brien, Klibert, Arata, & Bowers, 2006). The numbers of factors contained within the scale have varied and differing amounts of subscales have been used, ranging from 6 to 13 different subgroups of coping strategies. Likewise, researchers have utilized a variety of different names for the subscales, which, in turn have included different items. Thus, the current study chose to investigate coping more broadly, by only separating the items into two subscales.

Specifically, the thirty items from the A-COPE were divided into adaptive and maladaptive coping strategies for the current study; these two subscales were confirmed via factor analysis. The first subscale included 20 items and was labeled Adaptive Coping (alpha=0.88). Items on this subscale included activities such as apologizing, getting more involved in school and extracurricular activities, compromising, engaging in self improvement, optimistic thinking, joking, or organizing your life, seeking help from others, and/or talking with friends/ family about the problem. The second subscale contained 10 items and was labeled Maladaptive Coping (alpha=0.60). Items on this subscale included activities such as staying away from home, using drugs or alcohol, swearing, becoming aggressive, blaming others, and avoiding the problem.

Perceptions of Current Life Regret

Current life regret. Current life regret was assessed by one question on the questionnaire. Respondents were asked to indicate how much they agreed with the statement: "As I look back on my life, I am fairly well satisfied". Scores on this scale ranged from one to seven, with higher scores indicating more life regret.

Procedures

After obtaining IRB approval, participants were obtained from the Introductory Psychology Course Human Subject Pool. Participants volunteered for the study in order to fulfill a research requirement. Data were collected over three consecutive semesters. During the first two semesters, data were collected in person. To be eligible for participation, the student had to be female and over the age of 18. Eligible participants were given an appointment time, and were then given the anonymous, self-report survey in a small group setting. However, during the third semester the survey was put on-line on the Psychology Department research participation website. Participants remained anonymous via the web-based procedure.

All ethical procedures were followed, such as obtaining informed consent and providing appropriate debriefing procedures. At the conclusion of the survey, participants were also given the opportunity to indicate whether they were willing to participate in a follow-up interview if eligible. The results presented in this chapter represent only the data gathered from the self-report packets.

Results

The majority of the sample of college women had never experienced a pregnancy (n = 188; 67.9%). Of the 89 participants who had experienced a pregnancy, 41 were at or below the age of 18 at the time of conception (teenage pregnancy) and 48 were over the age of 18 when they became pregnant (adult pregnancy). The majority of participants reporting a pregnancy were also unmarried at the time of conception (n = 60; 68.2%). Of the 41 college women who experienced a teenage pregnancy, 25 (61.0%) were parenting at least one child while they were attending school. Fifteen of the women (36.6%) were not living with a child or parenting a child from their teenage pregnancy. Data for one of the teenage pregnant women were missing. Of the 48 college women who experienced a pregnancy as an adult, 35 (72.9%) completed the pregnancy and were currently parenting. Thirteen of the women (27.1%) were not currently parenting.

To test the first hypothesis, a three group (Never Pregnant, Teenage Pregnancy, and Adult Pregnancy) MANOVA was conducted with the three mental health measures as the dependent variables. Contrary to expectation, this analysis failed to reveal a significant main effect for group, *Roy's Largest Root* (3, 271) = .012, $p = .36$. As shown in Table 1, there were no significant between-group differences for current levels of hostility, depression, or hopelessness. However, on all three variables, the largest standard deviations were obtained for the teenage pregnancy group, indicating that, as anticipated, there may be considerable heterogeneity within this group of college women.

Table 1. Differences in Current Mental Health, Coping, and Perceived Life Regret among Never Pregnant, Teenage Pregnant, and Adult Pregnant College Women

Measure	Never Pregnant (n=188)	Teenage Pregnancy (n=41)	Adult Pregnancy (n=48)	*F*	*p*	ETA^2
Hostility						
M	3.01	3.66	3.17			
SD	3.52	3.95	3.46	<1	0.58	.00
Depression						
M	7.99	8.29	7.78			
SD	5.97	6.02	4.66	<1	0.92	.00
Hopelessness						
M	0.34	0.56	0.28	1.25	0.29	.01
SD	0.85	1.28	0.74			
Adaptive Coping						
M	66.64	62.34	63.62			
SD	13.06	13.95	11.42	2.43	0.09	.02
Maladaptive Coping						
M	22.67[a]	23.11[a]	20.61[b]			
SD	5.10	5.07	4.76	3.70	<.05	.03
Life Regret						
M	2.22[a]	2.59[b]	2.65[b]			
SD	0.98	0.89	1.06	5.04	<.01	.04

Female College Students (n = 277)

Note: N's vary slightly across analyses due to missing data. Post Hoc comparisons were conducted with Least Significant Differences tests. Means with different superscripts are significantly different from one another.

A three group (Never Pregnant, Teenage Pregnancy, and Adult Pregnancy) MANOVA with the adaptive and maladaptive coping subscales as the dependent variables was then conducted. As expected, this analysis did reveal an overall significant main effect for group, *Roy's Largest Root* (2, 271) = .030, $p < .05$. As shown in Table 1, follow-up univariate ANOVA's revealed significant between-group differences for reports of engagement in maladaptive coping strategies and a trend for group differences in reports of engagement in adaptive coping strategies. Follow-up LSD comparisons of the significant main effect for maladaptive coping strategies indicated that college women who reported experiencing an adult pregnancy engaged in significantly fewer maladaptive coping strategies than college women who had experienced a teenage pregnancy or college women who had never been pregnant. Significant between-group differences were also obtained for perceptions of life regret, F (2, 274) = 5.04, $p < .01$, $ETA^2 = .04$. Post-hoc analyses of the means indicated that both groups of college women who reported a pregnancy, regardless of their age at the time of conception, expressed significantly more life regret than college women who reported never being pregnant.

To test the degree to which marital status at the time of the pregnancy was associated with improved mental health functioning, greater adaptive and less maladaptive coping, and reduced life regret, a similar series of analyses were conducted comparing three groups of college women: Never Pregnant (n = 188), Unwed Pregnancy (n = 60), and Wed Pregnancy (n = 28). Because older women were more likely to be in the wed pregnancy group, age was included as a covariate in all of these analyses. Contrary to expectation, and according to a three group MANOVA with the three mental health scores as the dependent variables, there were no significant differences among the three groups in their reports of current symptoms of mental distress, *Roy's Largest Root* (3, 270) = .021, p = .14. Age did emerge as a significant co-variate in this analysis. Follow-up univariate analyses of the age effect revealed that college women's reports of feelings of hostility diminished with age, F (1, 271) = 5.96, $p < .05$, $ETA^2 = .02$.

A second three group (Never pregnant, Unwed Pregnant, and Wed Pregnant) MANOVA with the adaptive and maladaptive coping subscales as the dependent variables also failed to reveal a main effect for group, *Roy's Largest Root* (2, 272) = .012, p = .21. Moreover, age did not emerge as a significant co-variate in this analysis, *Roy's Largest Root* (2, 271) = .016, p = .12. Finally, an ANOVA did reveal a significant main effect for group in terms of their reports of life regret, F (2, 274) = 5.18, $p < .01$, $ETA^2 = .04$. However, LSD post-hoc comparisons indicated that this effect was due to the reduced life regret reported by the never pregnant college women (M = 2.22, SD = .98) in comparison to the two groups of ever pregnant college women. Contrary to expectation, the mean life regret scores of the unwed pregnant college women (M = 2.62, SD = .98) did not significantly differ from the mean life regret scores of the college women who were married at the time of their pregnancy (M = 2.62, SD = 1.03).

To consider the degree to which current parenting status impacted the mental health, coping behaviors, and life regret perceptions of college women who had experienced a teenage pregnancy, a third series of analyses were conducted. As shown in Table 2, a three group (Never Pregnant, Teenage Pregnancy Not Parenting, Teenage Pregnancy and Parenting) MANOVA with three mental health scores as the dependent variables revealed a significant overall main effect for group, *Roy's Largest Root* (3, 223) = .079, p = .001. Follow-up univariate ANOVA's revealed that the significant group effect held for symptoms of depression, F (2, 224) = 3.44, $p < .05$, $ETA^2 = .03$; hopelessness, F (2, 224) = 6.55, $p < .05$, $ETA^2 = .04$; and hostility, F (2, 224) = 3.45, $p < .05$, $ETA^2 = .03$. As shown in Table 3, the same pattern of mean differences were obtained for all three variables such that college women who had experienced a teenage pregnancy yet were not parenting were currently reporting higher levels of depression, greater feelings of hostility, and more hopelessness about the future than were either never pregnant college women or college women who had a teenage pregnancy but who were currently parenting.

Similarly, a three group MANOVA with the two coping subscales as dependent variables revealed a main effect for group, *Roy's Largest Root* (2, 224) = .041, p = .01. Follow-up univariate ANOVA's revealed that there were significant group differences in reports of maladaptive coping strategies utilized, F (2, 224) = 3.31, $p < .05$, ETA^2 = .03. There was also a trend for group differences in terms of reports of the utilization of adaptive coping strategies, F (2, 224) = 2.44, p = .09, ETA^2 = .02. LSD comparisons revealed the same pattern of mean differences such that college women reporting a teen pregnancy but no current parenting indicated that they were engaging in significantly more maladaptive coping strategies than either the never pregnant college women or the teenage pregnant college women who were parenting while attending college.

Table 2. Differences in Current Mental Health, Coping, and Perceived Life Regret among Never Pregnant, Teenage Pregnant and Parenting, and Teenage Pregnant and Not Parenting Women

Measure	Never Pregnant (n=188)	Teenage Pregnant and Not Parenting	Teenage Pregnant and Parenting (n=25)	*F*	*p*	*ETA²*
Hostility						
M	3.01[a]	5.40[b]	2.56[a]			
SD	3.52	4.55	3.27	3.45	<.05	.03
Depression						
M	7.99[a]	11.40[b]	6.36[a]	3.44	<.05	.03
SD	5.97	6.53	5.05			
Hopelessness						
M	0.34[a]	1.20[b]	0.20[a]	6.55	<.01	.06
SD	0.85	1.90	0.50			
Adaptive Coping						
M	66.64	59.90	62.97			
SD	13.06	13.81	13.75	2.44	0.09	.02
Maladaptive Coping						
M	22.67[a]	25.67[b]	21.47[a]			
SD	5.10	5.75	4.05	3.31	<.05	.03
Life Regret						
M	2.22[a]	2.47[ab]	2.68[b]			
SD	0.98	0.74	0.99	2.79	=.06	.02

Note: N's vary slightly across analyses due to missing data. Post Hoc comparisons were conducted with Least Significant Differences tests. Means with different superscripts are significantly different from one another.

A trend was found of group differences on reports of perceptions of life regret, F (2, 225) = 2.79, p = .06, ETA^2 = .02. In this analysis, significantly higher life regret scores were obtained by the teenage pregnant college women who were parenting (M = 2.68, SD = .99) than by never pregnant college women (M = 2.22, SD = .98). The mean life regret scores of the college women who had experienced a teenage pregnancy but were not parenting (M = 2.47, SD = .74) was in-between the means of the two other groups, and not significantly different from either one.

Table 3. Differences in Adaptive and Maladaptive Coping, and Perceived Life Regret among Thriving versus At-risk College Women who had experienced a teenage pregnancy

Measure	Teenage Pregnancy in Thriving Cluster (n=29)	Teenage Pregnancy in At-risk Cluster (n=11)	*F*	*p*	*ETA*^{2}
Adaptive Coping					
M	62.45	60.09			
SD	13.52	14.57	<1	0.63	.01
Maladaptive Coping					
M	21.91[b]	26.06[a]			
SD	4.01	6.57	5.81	<.05	.14
Life Regret					
M	2.45	3.00			
SD	0.95	0.63	3.16	=.08	.08

Note: N's vary slightly across analyses due to missing data.

Lastly, due to the greater variability obtained in the mental health scores of college women who reported experiencing a teenage pregnancy in comparison to the never pregnant and adult pregnant college women, a set of post-hoc analyses were conducted. Specifically, we sought to distinguish among the teenage pregnancy group, those who were "thriving" from those who were "at risk". To determine this, a K-means cluster analysis was conducted with the 40 women in the teenage pregnancy group who had complete scores on the hostility, depression, and hopelessness measures. Clusters were derived in three iterations. The final distance between cluster centers was 12.75.

Twenty-nine women were placed in cluster one and 11 women were placed in cluster two. Women in cluster one had lower scores on hostility (cluster center = 2), depression (cluster center = 5), and hopelessness (cluster center = 0) than did women in cluster two. Women in cluster two had higher scores on hostility (cluster center = 8), depression (cluster center = 16), and hopelessness (cluster center = 1). In keeping with Carver's (1998) theory, college women who had experienced a teenage pregnancy who were classified into cluster one could be considered to be "thriving", while those placed into cluster two might be considered to be still "at-risk" in spite of their resilience in continuing their education.

Not unexpectedly, there was a significant association between cluster membership and current parenting status, X^2 (1) = 4.42, $p < .05$. Only four of the 25 college women (16%) who had experienced a teenage pregnancy and were currently parenting were placed into the "at-risk" cluster, whereas seven of the 15 college women (47%) who had experienced a teenage pregnancy but who were not parenting a child were placed into the "at-risk" cluster. As shown in Table 3, in spite of relatively low power, additional analyses indicated that college women in the "at-risk" cluster also reported engaging in more maladaptive coping behaviors in response to stressors than did college women in the "thriving" cluster, F (1, 39) = 5.81, $p < .05$, ETA^2 = .14. Group membership accounted for 14 percent of the variance in scores on the maladaptive coping subscale. No significant differences in reports of engaging in adaptive coping strategies were obtained between the two clusters ($F < 1$). However, there was a trend for the two groups to differ in terms of their expression of life regret, F (1, 38) =

3.16, p = .08, ETA^2 = .08, with less life regret reported by those women in the "thriving" cluster (M = 2.45, SD = .95) than in the "at-risk" cluster (M = 3.00, SD = .63).

Discussion

In the current study, college women who had experienced a teenage pregnancy and yet were continuing to advance their education were operationally defined to be displaying resilience. About one-third of our sample of college women indicated that they had been pregnant at some time in the past; with approximately 45% of these women indicating the pregnancy occurred when they were 18 years old or younger. These women represent a sizable minority of the sample, suggesting that this is an important subgroup of students to consider when planning activities within a large diverse urban university.

Analyses were then conducted to determine if resilient teenage pregnant college women could be differentiated from never pregnant college women or from adult pregnant college women in terms of their current mental health status, utilization of coping strategies, or perceptions of life regret. Results suggested few, if any, group differences that were specific to the college women who had experienced a teenage pregnancy, making these findings consistent with definitions of resilience which have focused on individuals' return to their prior level of functioning after experiencing adversity as a central concept (Carver, 1998).

Unlike similar studies which have considered resilience in relation to a number of other life events primarily by studying individuals who have achieved a relatively unlikely positive outcome in relation to the stressor they have withstood (e.g., Carle & Chassin, 2004; Himelein & McElrath, 1996; Humphreys, 2001; Milgram & Palti, 1993; Statham, 2004; Wilcox et al., 2004), no particular adaptive coping strategies or lack of maladaptive coping strategies were identified in the current study that could be considered to be potential mechanisms underlying these teenage pregnant college women's educational resilience. This may be because of the diversity of outcomes associated with teenage pregnancy (i.e., abortion, miscarriage, adoption, delivery of a premature baby, single parenthood, continued involvement of grandparents during the mother's individuation process, early marriage, divorce or abuse, and subsequent children). As a result, resilient women in this group may have quite heterogeneous on-going experiences impacting them as they attend college. Or it may be that the variables included in the current study did not capture the key components of these women's mechanisms for resilience.

Therefore, additional research will be needed to understand the mechanisms of resilience utilized by college women who experienced a teenage pregnancy, perhaps by utilizing an in-depth qualitative interview as was done by Himelein and McElrath, 1996. Potential mechanisms to consider might include higher IQ and lower affiliation with delinquent peers post-pregnancy (Fergusson & Lynskey, 1996), as well as higher pre-existing educational aspirations (Tiet et al., 1998). The field is also likely to be advanced if a large enough sample of college women with a teenage pregnancy history is studied so that researchers can consider the associations between current functioning and particular choices, existing environmental factors, and/or outcomes associated with the stressful or traumatic event.

One between-group finding did emerge when comparing teenage pregnant, adult pregnant, and never pregnant college women. Specifically, both groups of college women who had experienced a pregnancy, regardless of their age at the time of conception, expressed greater life regret than the never pregnant group of college women. Qualitative research is necessary to determine definitive reasons; however, it is possible that these results could be explained by the greater demands placed on college students who are simultaneously parenting. These findings might also be driven by the nonparenting women within the pregnant groups whose greater life regret might be related to pregnancy loss (for reviews, see Brier, 2004; Neugebauer, 2003).

Furthermore, an unexpected finding emerged among the three groups such that the fewest maladaptive coping strategies were endorsed by college women who had become pregnant as adults. There are several possible explanations for this result including pre-existing factors associated with adult pregnancy prior to attending college (e.g., these women might have been more family oriented, more relationship oriented, or less sensation seeking than never pregnant or teenage pregnant college women). These findings might also relate to current situational or environmental factors that are more likely to occur for the adult pregnant college women (e.g., these women may be older, more financial stable, and/or have more role responsibilities as mother, student, wife, wage earner that serve as protective factors from engaging in some types of maladaptive coping strategies). Additional research is needed to confirm these results.

Theoretically, we expected one group of college women who had experienced a teenage pregnancy to be "thriving" while a second group could continue to be considered "at-risk" in spite of their initial resilience to the teenage pregnancy (Carver, 1998). A priori, we also chose to consider two potential situational factors that may impact the ever pregnant college woman's ability to thrive differently. They were: marital status at the time of conception and whether the previously pregnant woman is concurrently parenting while she is attending college. Results indicated that there were few findings associated with marital status at the time of conception; however, teenage pregnant college women who were not concurrently parenting differed significantly from teenage pregnant college women who were parenting and educating themselves simultaneously. Specifically, the non-parenting teenage pregnant women were more depressed, hostile, and hopeless. They also utilized more maladaptive coping strategies than never pregnant or teenage pregnant and parenting college women.

There are numerous possible explanations for these findings. One possibility is that raising a baby, even when it is conceived during adolescence, may be protective for college women. Another possibility is that pre-existing characteristics are associated both with a teenage pregnancy that doesn't lead to parenting and with increased symptoms of mental distress and increased use of maladaptive coping strategies during college. Unfortunately, the cross-sectional nature of these findings precludes a determination of when and how these relationships might have developed. Another limitation of the current study is that the survey we utilized did not directly assess the outcome of the teenage pregnancy (i.e., keeping the baby, abortion, miscarriage, adoption); making it impossible to consider whether particular choices were more or less associated with particular outcomes during college. It is possible, however, that the increased mental health symptoms expressed by this subgroup of pregnant women are differentially associated with choices made by the woman with regards to her adolescent pregnancy. Future research will be needed to determine this directly.

Finally, in a series of exploratory analyses, the mental health variables were used to create two clusters of women who had experienced a teenage pregnancy. Results garnered from cluster analysis indicated that 72.5% of the teenage pregnant college women could be considered to be "thriving" as they reported fewer symptoms of depression, and low hostility and hopelessness. In contrast, 27.5% of the teenage pregnant women could be considered "at-risk" because of their elevated reports of depressive symptoms, and higher levels of hopelessness and hostility. While there were a significantly higher proportion of non-parenting teenage pregnant women in the "at-risk" group than in the "thriving" group; there was not complete agreement between these two constructs. These findings suggest that a significant subgroup of college women who have experienced a teenage pregnancy may require additional services to facilitate their educational advancement and retention in the college environment. These women could be identified by mental health screening procedures.

References

Adams, G., Adams-Taylor, S., & Pittman, K. (1989). Adolescent pregnancy and parenthood: A review of the problems, solutions, and resources. *Family Relations, 38(2),* 223-229.

Bickart, T. S., & Wolin, S. (1997). Practicing resilience in the elementary classroom. *Principal Magazine*, November 1997, 1-3.

Brier, N. (2004). Anxiety after miscarriage: A review of the empirical literature and implications for clinical practice. *Birth, 31 (2),* 138-142.

Burton, K. B. (2004). Resilience in the face of psychological trauma. *Psychiatry, 67(3),* 231-234.

Carle, A. C., & Chassin, L. (2004). Resilience in a community sample of children of alcoholics: Its prevalence and relation to internalizing symptomatology and positive affect. *Applied Developmental Psychology, 25,* 577-595.

Carver, C. S. (1998). Resilience and thriving: Issues, models, and linkages. *Journal of Social Issues*, *54(2)*, 245-266.

Carver, C. S., & Scheier, M. F. (1989). Assessing coping strategies: A theoretically based approach. *Journal of Personality and Social Psychology, 56(2),* 267-283.

Charney, D. S. (2004). Psychobiological mechanisms of resilience and vulnerability: Implications for successful adaptation to extreme stress. *American Journal of Psychiatry, 161(2),* 195-216.

Clemmens, D. A. (2002). Adolescent mothers' depression after the birth of their babies: Weathering the storm. *Adolescence, 37(147),* 551-565.

Compas, B. E. (1987). Stress and life events during childhood and adolescence. *Clinical Psychology Review, 7,* 275-302.

Copeland, E. P., & Hess, R. S. (1995). Differences in young adolescents' coping strategies based on gender and ethnicity. *Journal of Early Adolescence, 15(2),* 203-219.

Derogatis, L. R. (1994). *Symptom Checklist-90-R: Administration, scoring, and procedures manual.* Minneapolis, MN: National Computer Systems, Inc.

Fergusson, D. M., & Lynskey, M. T. (1996). Adolescent resiliency to family adversity. *Journal of Child Psychology and Psychiatry, 37(3),* 281-292.

Furstenberg, F. F. Jr. (1991). As the pendulum swings: Teenage childbearing and social concern. *Family Relations, 40(2),* 127-138.

Himelein, M. J., & McElrath, J. V. (1996). Resilient child sexual abuse survivors: Cognitive coping and illusion. *Child Abuse and Neglect, 20(8),* 747-758.

Hudson, D., Elek, S., & Campbell-Grossman, C. (2000). Depression, self-esteem, loneliness, and social support among adolescent mothers participating in the New Parents Project. *Adolescence, 35(139),* 445-453.

Humphreys, J. C. (2001). Turnings and adaptations in resilient daughters of battered women. *Journal of Nursing Scholarship, 33(3),* 245-251.

Kazdin, A. E., French, N. H., Unis, A. S., Esveldt-Dawson, K. & Sherick, R. B. (1983). Hopelessness, depression, and suicidal intent among psychiatrically disturbed children. *Journal of Consulting and Clinical Psychology, 51,* 504-510.

Kivisto, P. (2001). Teenagers, pregnancy, and childbearing in a risk society: How do high-risk teens differ from their age peers? *Journal of Family Issues, 22(8),* 1044-1065.

Langhinrichsen-Rohling, J., Arata, C., Bowers, D., O'Brien, N., & Morgan, A. (2004). Suicidal behavior, negative affect, gender, and self-reported delinquency in college students. *Suicide and Life-Threatening Behavior, 34 (3),* 255-266.

Langhinrichsen-Rohling, J., O'Brien, N., Klibert, J., Arata, C., & Bowers, D. (2006). Gender specific associations among suicide proneness and coping strategies in college men and women. *College Students: Stress, Depression, and Mental Health* (pp. 12.1 – 12.14). Nova Science Publishers, Inc.

Lazarus, R. S. (1993). From psychological stress to the emotions: A history of changing outlooks. *Annual Review Psychology, 44,* 1-21.

Leitch, M. L. (1998). Contextual issues in teen pregnancy and parenting: Refining our scope of inquiry. *Family Relations, 47(2),* 145-148.

Luthar, S. S., Cicchetti, D., & Becker, B. (2000). The construct of resilience: A critical evaluation and guidelines for future work. *Child Development, 71(3),* 543-562.

Luthar, S. S., Doernberger, C. H., & Zigler, E. (1993). Resilience is not a unidimensional construct: Insights from a prospective study on inner-city adolescents. *Development and Psychopathology, 5,* 703-717.

Masten, A. S. (1994). Resilience in individual development: Successful adaptation despite risk and adversity. In M. C. Wang & E. W. Gordon (Eds.), *Educational resilience in inner- city America: Challenges and prospects* (pp. 3-25). Hillsdale, NJ: Erlbaum.

Masten, A. S., & Garmezy, N. (1985). Risk, vulnerability, and protective factors in developmental psychopathology. In B. Lahey & A. Kazdin (Eds.), *Advances in Clinical Child Psychology* (Vol. 8, pp. 1-52). New York: Plenum Press.

Milgram, N. A., & Palti, G. (1993). Psychosocial characteristics of resilient children. *Journal of Research in Personality, 27,* 207-221.

Moran, P. B., & Eckenrode, J. (1992). Protective personality characteristics among adolescent victims of maltreatment. *Child Abuse and Neglect, 16,* 743-754.

Neugebaur, R. (2003). Depressive symptoms at two months after miscarriage: Interpreting study findings from an epidemiological versus clinical perspective. *Depression and Anxiety, 17,* 152-161.

Patterson, J.M., & McCubbin, H.I. (1987). Adolescent coping styles and behaviors: Conceptualization and measurement. *Journal of Adolescence, 10*, 163.186.

Polkki, P. Ervast, S., & Huupponen, M. (2004). Coping and resilience of children of a mentally ill parent. *Social Work Visions from around the Globe: Citizens, Methods, and Approaches*, *39,* 151-163.

Radloff, L. S. (1977). The CES-D Scale: A self-report depression scale for research in the general population. *Applied Psychological Measurement, 1*, 385-401.

Statham, J. (2004). Effective services to support children in special circumstances. *Child: Care, Health & Development, 30(6),* 589-598.

Tiet, Q. Q., Bird, H. R., Davies, M., Hoven, C., Cohen, P., Jensen, P., & Goodman, S. (1998). Adverse life events and resilience. *Journal of the American Journal of Child and Adolescent Psychiatry, 37(11),* 1191-1201.

Werner, E. E., & Smith, R. S. (Eds.). (1992). *Overcoming the odds: High risk children from birth to adulthood.* Ithaca, NY: Cornell University Press.

Wilcox, D. T., Richards, F., & O'Keeffe, Z. C. (2004). Resilience and risk factors associated with experiencing childhood sexual abuse. *Child Abuse Review*, *13*, 338-352.

In: Anxiety in College Students
Editor: Benjamin Ayres and Michelle Bristow
ISBN: 978-1-60692-282-8

Chapter VII

Gender Differences in Proneness to Depression among Hungarian College Students

Ferenc Margitics and Zsuzsa Pauwlik
Department of Psychology at College of Nyíregyháza, Hungary

Abstract

Aims: Our research aimed to find out what role the risk mechanisms, as described in Goodman and Gotlib's (1999) model (genetic-biological, interpersonal, social learning related cognitive and stress related factors), play in the development of increased risk for depression in the case of men and women.

Methods: The genetic-biological factors were examined with certain temperament characteristics, the interpersonal factors with parental educational purpose, educational attitudes, educational style and parental treatment. In the case of factors related to social learning we looked at the dysfunctional attitudes and the attributional style. As far as the stressors are concerned, we observed the quality of family atmosphere, and the number of the positive and negative life events of the preceding six months and their subjective evaluation. Six hundred and eighty-one students took part in the research (465 female and 216 male).

Results: Our research results show that all of the increased risk mechanisms, namely the genetic-biological, interpersonal, social learning related cognitive, and stress related factors are connected with the development of vulnerability to depression, explaining 41.4% of the depression symptoms' variance in the case of women, and 36.5% in the case of men. Harm avoidance, a genetic-biological factor, proved to be the most significant risk mechanism, irrespective of the sexes. From among the environmental factors – irrespective of the sexes – one stress-related factor, the subjective evaluation of negative life experiences, which implies an increased sensitivity to stress, proved to be the strongest risk mechanism. While the above factors played an important role in the development of vulnerability to depression in both sexes, the social learning related cognitive and interpersonal risk mechanisms differed in their degree in women and men.

In the case of women, the social learning-related mechanisms proved to be stronger and higher impact risk factors than in the case of men. The effect of interpersonal factors seemed to be relatively the weakest in the development of increased risk for depression.

Limitations: The results of our research cannot be generalised to represent present day 18- to 23-year-old Hungarian youth due to the limitations of our sample.

Conclusion: The mental hygienic interpretation of our research findings is that in the future there should be more emphasis put on the personality development of college and university students, especially on the development of such competencies which aid them in effectively coping in their struggle with the depressive mood.

Keywords: depression symptoms, risk transmitting mechanisms, gender differences.

1. Introduction

The results of psychiatric epidemiological research show that depression has become one of the most common illnesses of our time. Based on Hungarian and international data, nearly 20 percent of adults have, at least once in their life, experienced a depressive episode and the prevalence of chronic depression is over 10 percent.

According to the results of research using self-rating scales, depressive syndrome is also very frequent in samples taken from the Hungarian population. Thirty-four percent of women and 19% of men interviewed reported symptoms of depression, which in the case of women reached 11.8% whereas in the case of men 5.5% of the serious clinical level [2,3]. A study carried out by Margitics [4] among college students showed mild, subclinical level of depression in 36.6% of the samples (40% of women, 29.3% of men) and moderate depression in 6.7% (8.4% of women, 3.4% of men).

Several well-documented studies carried out in the field of psychiatric epidemiology have proved a higher prevalence of depression among women. A great number of studies have dealt with the differences between the genders in the cases of chronic minor depression and dysthymia [5]. These studies consistently found that the proportion of prevalence is 2:1. Kessler et al [6], in minor depression, Angst and Merikangas [5] in short repetitive depression, found a consistently higher prevalence among women than among men. On the other hand, they did not find major differences between the genders in the prevalence of mania, neither in epidemiological research [7], nor in clinical studies [8].

The question arises of whether the proportion of prevalence is the same between the genders if the age of the study population is examined as well. Kessler at al [9] compared retrospective age-of-onset reports in a representative cross-sectional research with reports across subsamples of different age respondents. Group scales gained after the study of data distribution showed that differences between the genders relating to depression surfaced at the age of 11-15 and remained consistently higher later on.

Over the years several theories have been made to explain these differences between the genders. For instance, the female role theories argue that chronic stress connected to traditional female roles may cause higher prevalence of depression among women [10]. According to the rumination theory, women are more likely to deal with a problem longer than men and, as a result, the temporary symptoms of disphory turn to major parts of depression [11]. Both perspectives assume that the higher prevalence of clinically more significant depression among women is, at least partly, the result of their higher persistence.

Goodman and Gotlib [12] suggest the separation four mechanisms within an integrative model with the help of which the increased risk for depression can be explained. Two of these mechanisms are primarily genetical-biological while the other two are cognitive-interpersonal: the first mechanism focuses on the genetic factors, on the heritability of depression, the second is connected to innate dysfunctional neuroregulatory mechanisms, the third mechanism focuses on the confused interpersonal relations and dysfunctional cognitions related to social learning, the fourth mechanism includes the stressful context of a child's life; thus it can be connected to the stress load of a child

According to Goodman and Gotlib [12], all four above mentioned mechanisms are possible mechanisms of the increased risk for depression, but it is not quite clear to what extent they are responsible for the development of risk, or furthermore how they interact with each other. It is possible that one or more are present at the same time.

A substantial amount of literature discusses the consistent genetic transmission of depressive disturbance in the case of adults. According to the studies, which examined twins, families and adopted people, the risk for depression in the case of first grade relatives of those suffering from affective disturbance is 20-25%, in contrast to the 7% of risk level among the average population [13]. The genetic analysis of behaviour has proved numerous correlations with the high possibility of inheritance for depression [14]. Among other factors, temperament [15], behavioral inhibition and timidity [16], neuroticism [17] and sociability [18] may increase vulnerability to depression and be special factors in connection with inheritance. The results of modern temperament studies indicate that a tendency to avoid harm may be considered as the basic factor of biological vulnerability to depression which appears as a characteristic feature as early as in childhood. Harm avoidance refers to an inherited pattern which may appear in the form of passive avoidance and fear of the uncertain [19]. According to studies carried out by Hansen et al. [20], harm avoidance and low self-directedness are in harmony with the degree of depression.

A great number of studies have examined the connection between interpersonal factors and depression. In his studies, Parker [21] noted that those suffering from neurotic depression had received less parental attention, and higher maternal overprotection. In non-clinic groups the signs of depression were also related to less parental attention, and showed a slight correlation with parental overprotection. According to Parker's [22] research results, the correlation between lower parental care and depression was independent of the degree of depression. In his later studies Parker [23] argued that the kind of parental care which is characterised by low attention and high overprotection is linked to the high risk of neurotic disturbance (depressive neurosis, social phobia, anxiety neurosis), while the additional risk for psychotic disturbance is low or completely non-existent. In research carried out by Mackinnon and his colleagues [24] on non-clinic samples, lack of parental care was the number one risk factor of depression, as opposed to overprotection. Narita and his colleagues [25] carried out a study of Japanese samples and found that low parental care was always connected with depression at any age and the connection between depression and overprotection was obvious, also.

Problematic parental care related to cognitive functions and styles may have a negative effect on children's development. Dysfunctional attitudes may have a significant role in the development of depression. The unbalanced gradation of these attitudes with abilities and possibilities may also lead to the development of symptoms of depression. If a person has high expectations of himself and his surroundings in many fields of life, and is not able to meet the expectations of his context, he may then easily have a negative self-evaluation which can directly lead to hopelessness, which in turn can cause the development of symptoms of depression [26]. According to Beck, those characterised with dysfunctional attitudes are more likely to develop depression. These attitudes may not automatically cause illness when they are present separately. Furthermore, some of these insets might be an important drive in society, but their accumulation or high level may create a tendency for pathological development [27].

In Garber's and Hilsman's cognitive diathesis-stress model, in addition to dysfunctional attitudes, another cognitive factor, the negative attributional style, may also play a key role in the appearance of depressive symptoms. It is assumed that copying significant others, parental refusal and uncontrollable stressful events may be responsible for the development of the negative cognitive style. According to Metalsky, Halberstadt and Abramson's studies [29], students with a negative, pessimistic attributive style were more distressed than those who had a more optimistic attributive style. According to Peterson et al. [30], this negative attributional style is connected to physical illnesses; people who can be described with this attributional style do not care about themselves and their negative lifestyle may lead to illness. According to Abramson, Metalsky and Alloy [31], the pessimistic attributional style alone is not an adequate cause of depression. It becomes important when the individual encounters strong or frequent negative events. In their opinion, in the development of depression the extent a person believes his life can be influenced is more important than how he interprets unpleasant events. The belief that he is able to tackle problems increases his resistance to depression.

Those who have suffered from depression are more vulnerable to stressful life events than those who do not have such a history of depression. According to Brown and Harris' vulnerability theory, depression occurs in an interaction between the individual and his environment. The joint appearance and interaction of predispositional factors and external events (provoking factors) are needed for its evolvement. Predispositional factors can be certain personality characteristics (self-evaluation, self-power, conflict solving strategies, degree of distress endurance, relationship ability etc.), traumatic family prehistory, disturbed personality development, and the deficiency of the social criteria system. Life events work as provoking factors, and external events, as stressors, contribute to the manifestation of depression. However, the interpretation of life events is unique, and it depends on the antecedents of personality development. Negative life events do not cause depression, but they may contribute to the development of depression.

The aim of this paper is to find out what role the risk mechanisms, as described in Goodman and Gotlib's [12] model (genetical-biological, interpersonal, social learning related cognitive and stress related factors), have in the development of increased risk for depression in the case of men and women. (Due to methodological difficulties we left out the innate dysfunctional neuroregulatory risk-transfer mechanisms.) The genetical-biological factors were examined with certain temperament characteristics, the interpersonal factors with parental educational purpose, educational attitudes, educational style and parental treatment. In the case of factors related to social learning we looked at dysfunctional attitudes and attribution style. As far as stressors are concerned, we observed the quality of family atmosphere, and the number of positive and negative life events of the preceding six months and their subjective evaluation.

2. Method

Participants

Data was collected among college students at the College of Nyíregyháza, in a county seat in the north-eastern part of Hungary. We collected data randomly at every faculty and participation was voluntary and it was done with their consent. Students filled out the questionnaires individually at lectures with the guidance of the researchers.

700 students took part in the research and 681 of them provided valuable data (465 female and 216 male). According to their majors, the following students participated in the study: 225 undergraduate BA students, 125 undergraduate BSc students, 125 business students, 74 students studying to be infant teachers, 70 studying to be social teachers and 62 students of arts (visual arts and music).

The average age was 19.98 (standard deviation 1.51) the median value was 20 years.

Measures

To study depression we applied an abridged version of the 13 item multiple-choice questionnaire of the Beck Depression Inventory [34, 35]. The inventory studies the following components of depressive syndromes: sadness, pessimism, sense of failure, dissatisfaction, guilt, fear of punishment, self-harm, indecisiveness, social withdrawal, self-image change, work difficulty, fatigability and anorexia.

To study genetical-biological factors we applied the Hungarian version of Cloninger's Temperament and Character Inventory adapted by Rózsa and his colleagues [19]. The temperament dimension measuring scales of the questionnaire were the following: novelty seeking, harm avoidance, reward dependence and persistence.

To study interpersonal factors (effects of family socialisation) we applied the Goch's Family Socialisation Questionnaire [36, 37]. The following scales of the questionnaire were used in the study: maternal educational aims (independence – autonomy, as an educational aim; conformity – conformity as an educational aim), maternal educational attitudes (consistent, manipulative or inconsistent attitude) and maternal educational style (supportive or punitive style).

To study interpersonal factors we applied the Hungarian adaptation of Parker and his colleagues' questionnaire on Parental Treatment [38]. The following dimensions of parental treatment were examined: maternal care, maternal overprotection, maternal control, paternal care, paternal overprotection and paternal control.

The study of cognitive factors related to social learning: We used the Hungarian adaptation of Weismann's Dysfunctional Attitude Scale to examine dysfunctional attitudes [39, 40]. The questionnaire examines the following attitudes: need for external recognition, need to be loved, need for achievement, perfectionism, rightful increased expectations towards context, omnipotence (increased altruism orientation), external control –autonomy.

The attributive style was examined by using Abramson and his colleagues' Attributional Style Questionnaire [41]. The attributive style was valued on the following factors: internal or external attribution, stable or instable attribution, specific or global attribution. The research participants were asked to form judgements about the following situations: judgment of performance (exam failure) and judgment of loss (breaking up a relationship with a close friend).

To study stressors we applied the Goch's Family Socialisation Questionnaire [36, 37]. The following scale of the questionnaire was used in the research: the type of family atmosphere (conflict oriented family atmosphere).

To study stressors we applied the High School Life Experience Questionnaire of Cohen and his colleagues, adapted by Csorba and his colleagues for the Hungarian context [42].The questionnaire focused on the frequent, mainly negative, but sometimes partly positive, life events of the preceding six months. The questionnaire measured the following dimensions: number of positive life events, score of positive life events, number of negative life events, score of negative life events.

3. Results

The Connection between Genetical-Biological Factors and Depression

The presence of biological vulnerability was examined by the use of Cloninger's Temperament and Character Inventory. Linear regression analysis was used in observing the relationship between certain temperament scales (novelty seeking, harm avoidance, reward dependence, persistence) as independent variables, and the values measured by Beck's Depression Inventory, as dependent variables.

Table 1. summarizes the connection between depression and certain temperament scales of the different sexes.

Table 1. The regression of depression on genetical-biological factors

Predictor	β	t	p<
Women: F_{total}=73,670; p<0,000			
Harm avoidance	0.511	12.124	0.000
Novelty seeking	0.165	3.910	0.000
Men: F_{total}=30,994; p<0.000			
Harm avoidance	0.431	7.099	0.000
Reward dependence	-0.158	-2.543	0.012

In both sexes, about the same proportion of depression variance is explained by the genetic-biological factors (24.2% of women, 22.5% of men). In both sexes, we have found a very tight connection between depression and harm avoidance. Harm avoiding people are more likely to be pessimistic, careful, timid, stressed, distressed, afraid of danger, risks, tend to be worried, reserved, hampered and are easily exhausted [19]. Furthermore, in the case of women, novelty seeking had a positive correlation with depression. Novelty seekers are impulsive, and they are open to new things, but lose their patience easily. They are irresolute, they quickly get bored with what they are doing, they are irritable and unstable. Extravagant behaviour, lack of restraint and untidiness may also characterise them [19]. In the case of men, reward dependence had a significant negative correlation with depression. Less reward dependent people are indifferent to social signals, and are more liable to being socially isolated, emotionally cold and pragmatic [19].

The Connection between Interpersonal Factors and Depression

As far as interpersonal factors were concerned, we were primarily interested in the role of parents in the family socialisation process. Among the effects of family socialisation we focused on the parent's educational aims (education for self-sufficiency - autonomy as an educational aim, education for conformity – conformity as an educational aim), educational attitudes (consistent educational attitude, manipulative educational attitude, and inconsistent educational attitude), educational styles (supportive style, punitive style), and parental treatment (care, overprotection and control). With linear regression analysis we examined the connection between the above mentioned variables, as independent variables, and the values measured by Beck's Depression Inventory, as dependent variables.

Table 2 shows the connection between depression and certain interpersonal factors of the sexes.

Table 2. The regression of depression on certain interpersonal factors

Predictor	**β**	**T**	**p<**
Women: $F_{total}=19,944;\ p<0,000$			
Parents' manipulative educational attitude	0.188	3.734	0.000
Paternal care	-0.156	-3.273	0.001
Maternal control	-0.134	-2.974	0.003
Parents' inconsistent educational attitude	0.108	2.020	0.044
Men: $F_{total}=12.615;\ p<0.000$			
Paternal care	-0.204	-2.733	0.007
Parents' inconsistent educational attitude	0.186	2.493	0.013

The interpersonal factors explain nearly the same rate the variance of depression in both sexes. Though in the case of women the rate is somewhat higher (15.3 %) than in the case of men (11.1 %). In both cases depression was closely connected to the parents' inconsistent educational attitude and the lack of paternal care. In the case of women, the parents' manipulative attitude and the lack of maternal care also contributed to the risk of developing depression.

The Connection between Depression and Social Learning Related Cognitive Factors

From the cognitive factors related to depression, we examined dysfunctional attitudes (need for acknowledgement, love, achievement, perfectionism, rightfully increased expectations towards the context, omnipotence, external control – autonomy) and the attributional style (internal or external, stable or unstable, specific or global attribution). With the help of linear regression analysis we examined the connection between the above mentioned variables, as independent variables, and values measured by Beck's Depression Inventory, as dependent variables.

Table 3 shows the connection between depression and certain social learning factors of the sexes.

Table 3. The regression of depression on certain social learning factors

Predictor	**β**	**t**	**p<**
Women: $F_{total}=45.717; p<0.000$			
External control-autonomy	0.289	6.920	0.000
Performance: specific or global	0.256	6.079	0.000
Performance: stable or instable	0.161	3.841	0.001
Men: $F_{total}=11.402; p<0.000$			
External control-autonomy	0.213	3.282	0.000
Loss: specific or global	0.173	2.538	0.012
Performance: specific or global	0.163	2.258	0.019

In the case of women, the cognitive factors related to social learning explained a greater variance of depression than in the case of men (women: 22.5 %, men: 12.8 %). In both sexes, among the dysfunctional attitudes, depression showed a close connection with external control attitude. A person with external control attitudes feels he does not have control over his life, instead things just happen to him. While examining the attributional styles we found that women perceive the causes of losing control over their judgment of performance deficit as stable ("it will always be that way") and global, such that has an effect on every aspect of their life. Men, on the other hand, see the cause of both control loss and performance deficit as global.

The Connection between Depression and Stress Related Factors

When examining the connection between stress and depression we looked at the quality of family atmosphere (its conflict load on the individual's life up to the time of investigation) and the number of positive and negative life events in the preceding six months and their subjective evaluation (the degree of positive or negative effect). With the help of linear regression analysis, we examined the connection between the above mentioned variables as independent variables, and values measured by Beck's Depression Inventory, as dependent variables.

Table 4 shows the connection between depression and certain stress related factors of the sexes.

Table 4. The regression of depression on certain stress related factors

Predictor	**β**	**t**	**p<**
Women: $F_{total}=63.668; p<0.000$			
Evaluation of negative life events	0.374	8.689	0.000
Conflict oriented family atmosphere	0.188	4.358	0.000
Men: $F_{total}=17.658; p<0.000$			
Evaluation of negative life events	0.331	4.772	0.017
Conflict oriented family atmosphere	0.170	2.494	0.013

In the case of women, stress related factors explained a greater variance of depression (women: 21.6%, men: 14.2%). In both sexes depression was closely, significantly connected to both the subjective evaluation of negative life experiences in the preceding six months, and the conflict oriented family atmosphere.

The Role of the Examined Factors in the Development Of Depression

In the following model we included all those variables which showed a strong correlation with depression when examining the different factors (table 5).

The result of regression analysis shows that in the case of women the examined risk mechanisms explained a greater variance of depression than in the case of men (women: 41.4%, men: 36.5%).

The genetic-biological factors of risk mechanisms were stronger in the case of men, since two temperament factors, harm avoidance and reward dependence, proved to be greater risk factors. In the case of women this was only true for harm avoidance.

The interpersonal factors as risk mechanisms did not prove a significant correlation with depression. In the case of women, only the inconsistent parental educational attitude, while in the case of men, the lack of paternal care proved to be risk factors.

Out of the social learning related cognitive factors, one of the negative attributional styles, the experience of control loss as stable ("it will always be that way") proved to be a great risk factor. This acted as a distorting factor for women when judging performance deficit and it had the same effect for men when judging loss. Furthermore, in the case of women we were able to prove the role of another social learning related risk factor, the external control attitude.

Out of the stress related factors, only the subjective evaluation of negative life experiences proved to be a risk factor.

Table 5. The regression of depression on those variables which had a strong correlation with depression during the research

Predictor	β	t	p<
Women: F_{total}=61.561; p<0.000			
Harm avoidance	0.340	8.886	0.000
Evaluation of negative life events	0.244	6.153	0.000
Performance: specific or global	0.166	4.342	
External control-autonomy	0.151	3.831	0.000
Parents' inconsistent educational attitude	0.145	3.806	0.002
Men: F_{total}=25.651; p<0.000			
Harm avoidance	0.365	6.260	0.000+
Evaluation of negative life events	0.267	4.623	0.000
Loss: specific or global	0.158	2.774	
Reward dependence	-0.154	-2.709	0.006
Paternal care	-0.152	-2.602	0.008

4. Discussion

The aim of this present study was to show the differences between the sexes in their predisposition to depression, using a non-clinical sample. We examined what role those factors which are considered increased risk mechanisms (genetic-biological, interpersonal, social learning relater cognitive and stress related factor) play in the development of increased risk for depression in women and men.

The results of the study show that all of the increased risk mechanisms, thus the genetical-biological, the interpersonal, the social learning related cognitive and stress related factors, are connected to the development of predisposition to depression and they explain 41.4% of the depression symptoms' variance in the case of women, and 36.5% in the case of men.

According to the results of our study, harm avoidance, a genetic-biological factor, proved to be the most significant risk mechanism, irrespective of the sexes. Cloninger [43] believes that of the temperament factors, harm avoidance is the most important one as it has a control influence on the other two, and it appears first during ontogenesis. Reward dependence, another temperament factor, was also a risk factor for men. It is in harmony with the results of other studies [19] according to which the ability of emotional reaction is generally not affected by depression, only a specific disturbance of emotional reactions to joyful stimuli can be detected, which may be the result of a malfunctioning reward system. Besides these, the other risk mechanisms – interpersonal, cognitive and stress related factors- also have an important role in the development of increased risk to depression in men and women, though to a different degree, higher for women and lower for men. When examining twins, Kendler et al. [44] found that while the development of clinical, major depression was connected primarily to additive genetic factors, the development of milder, sub-clinical forms of depression was influenced mainly by environmental factors. The results of our research, carried out with a non-clinical sample, prove that although harm avoidance, as a genetic-biological factor, showed the strongest correlation with depression symptoms, it was the environmental factors which were more dominant on the whole.

From among the environmental factors – irrespective of the sexes- one stress related factor, the subjective evaluation of negative life experiences, which implies an increased sensitivity to stress, proved to be the strongest risk mechanism. Nowadays a great number of theorists believe that there are many environmental factors which increase the risk of vulnerability to depression, and that these are inherited. For example, Plomin [45] argues that genetic factors contribute to the difference of variables such as poor parental care or the reaction to stressful life events. In 1978, Brown and Harris [46] already pointed out the fact that sensitivity to stress is genetically transmitted. According to the results of our research, this transmitted factor, which lies behind the harm avoiding behaviour, may be the genetic-biological mechanism. Harm avoidance means the inherited pattern of behavioural inhibition, which may manifest itself in passive avoiding behaviour and in fear of uncertainty. Several studies [19] have pointed out that certain groups of children, even before acquiring social experiences, are more diffident, more uncertain and tense in unknown situations than their peers; they avoid new stimuli, do not adapt easily to changes and their mood is often gloomy and negative. These factors may increase vulnerability to depression by leading children towards choosing or avoiding certain types of environment and making them selectively react to certain aspects of their environment. As a result, the child perceives the world with a bias and reacts more sensitively to environmental stress. This may even be related to the fact that the negative, pessimistic attribution style, a factor related to social learning, also plays a major role in the development of predisposition to depression in both sexes. One of its characteristic marks, the experience of control loss as stable ("it will always be that way"), showed a specific relationship with depression symptoms. This, however, appeared in different areas in the sexes. The relationship was found in the area of achievement in the case of women, while it was detected in the area of loss in the case of men. Joiner and Wagner [47] found moderate proof that the negative attributional style may be a predictor of increasing depressive symptoms in children and adolescents.

While both the genetic-biological and stress related risk mechanisms played an important role in the development of vulnerability to depression in both sexes, the social learning related cognitive and interpersonal risk mechanisms differed in their degree in women and men. Besides the pessimistic attribution style, the external control attitude – another social learning related risk mechanism – had an important role in the development of increased risk for depression. According to Fiske and Taylor [48], when defining a person's self-evaluation and self-image, the extent the individual considers himself effective in a given situation and how much control and influence he believes he may have over it are very important. Therefore, the perception of control is an important aspect of how an individual behaves in a certain situation. A person with external control attitude feels he does not have control over his life, things just happen to him. The resulting passive, inert state, according to Seligman [49], may develop the implicit belief that he has no control over his life and whatever he does has no impact on the course of actions in his life. This might make him passive, his motivation may decrease and he may be liable to depression.

The effect of interpersonal factors seemed to be relatively the weakest in the development of increased risk for depression. The biological and cognitive factors for liability to depression are formed in the interaction of the personality and the environment, primarily within the social context created by the parents. The dissonance between the child's temperament and the expectations and requirements of the social context may act as a predispositional factor for the development of depression [19]. According to our research findings, such a factor for women can be the inconsistent parental educational attitude, and, in the case of men, the lack of paternal care.

5. Conclusion

The mental hygienic interpretation of our research findings is that in the future there should be more emphasis put on the personality development of college and university students, especially on the development of such competencies which aid them in effectively coping in their struggle with the depressive mood. According to Bugán [50], mental hygiene opportunities and methods may be built into the tertiary curricula either in a direct or in a non-direct way. The direct methods mean the incorporation of mental hygiene information in course content, while indirect methods may include the formation of profession socialisation groups - which could act as effective mental hygienic transmitters in the development of the professional personality - and the development of mental hygienic ambulance services at colleges and universities. Bagdy and Bugán [51] found the formation of profession socialisation groups, which functioned as effective mental hygienic transmitters in the development of the professional personality, effective at universities.

References

Kiss, H.G., and Szabó, A., and Rihmer, Z. (1998). A depresszió. Egy népbetegség korszerű megközelítése. [Depression. The modern approach of an endemic.] *Praxis*, 7, 7-13.

Kopp, M., and Szedmák, S., and Lőke, J., and Skrabski, Á. (1997). A depressziós tünetegyüttes gyakorisága és egészségügyi jelentősége a mai magyar lakosság körében. [The frequency and health importance of depression symptoms among the Hungarian population today.] *Lege Artis Medicine*, 7, 136-144.

Kopp, M., and Csoboth, CS., and Purebl, Gy. (1999). Fiatal nők egészségi állapota.]Young women's health status.] In: Pongrácz, T. and Tóth I.,Gy. (Szerk.): *Szerepváltozások* [Role changes.] (pp.239-259). Budapest: TÁRKI.

Margitics F. (2005). A diszfunkcionális attitűdök, megküzdési stratégiák és az attribúciós stílus összefüggése a szubklinikus depressziós tünetegyüttessel főiskolai hallgatóknál. [Interrelations between dysfunctional attitudes, coping strategies and attributional style and subclinical depressive syndrome at college students.] *Mentálhigiéné és Pszichoszomatika*, 6, 95-122.

Angst, J., and Merikangsamm, K. (1997). The depressive spectrum: Diagnostic classification and course. *Journal of Affective Disorders*, 45, 31-39.

Kessler, R.C., and Zhao, S., and Blazer, D.G., and Swartz, M.S. (1997). Prevalence, correlates and course of minor depression and major depression in the NCS. *Journal Affective Disorders*, 45, 19-30.

Kessler, R.C., and Wittchen, H.U., and Abelson, J.M., and McGonagle, K.A., and Schwarz, N., and Kendler, K.S. et al. (1998). Methodological studies of the Composite International Diagnostic Interview (CIDI) in the US National Comorbidity Survey Int. J. Methods. Psychiatr. Res. 7, 33-55.

Goodwin, F.K., and Jamison, K.J. (1990). *Manic-Depressive Illness*. New York : Oxford University Press.

Kessler, R.C., and McGonagle, K.A., and Nelson C.B., and Hughes M., and Swartz, M.S., and Blazer D.G. (1994). Sex and depression in the National Comorbidity Survey II: Cohort effect. *Journal Affective Disorders*, 30, 15-26.

Mirowsky, J., and Ross, C.E. (1989). Social Cases of Psychological Distress. New York: Aldine De Gruyter.

Noel-Hoeksema, S. (1990). Sex differences in unipolar depression: Evidence and theory. *Psychological Bulletin*, 101, 259-282.

Goodman, S. H., and Gotlib, I. H. (1999). Risk for psychopathology in the children of depressed mothers: A developmental model for understanding mechanisms of transmission. *Psychological Review*, 3, 458-490.

Tsuang, M.T., and Faraone, S.V. (1990). *The genetics of mood disorders*. Baltimore: John Hopkins University Press.

Loehlin, J.C. (1992). *Genes and environment in personality development*. Beverly Hills, CA: Sage.

Goldschmith, H.H., and Buss, K.A., and Lemery, K.S. (1997). Toddler and childhood temperament: Expanded content, stronger genetic evidence, new evidence for the importance of environment. *Developmental Psychology*, 33, 891-905.

Cherny, S.S., and Fulker, D.W., and Corley, R.P., and Plomin, R., and DeFries, J.C. (1994). Continuity and change in infant shyness from 14 to 20 months. *Behavior Genetics*, 24, 365-379.

Tellegen, A., and Lykken, D.T., and Bouchard, T.J., and Wilcox, K.J., and Segal, N.L., and Rich, S. (1988). Personality similarity in twins reared apart and together. *Journal of Personality and Social Psychology*, 54, 1031-1039.

Plomin, R., and Emde, R.N., and Braungart, J.M., and Campos, J., and Corley, R., and Fulk, D.W. et al. (1993). Genetic change and continuity from fourteen twenty months: The MacArthur Longitudinal Twin Study. *Child Development*, 64, 1354-1376.

Rózsa S., and Kállai, J., and Osváth, A., and Bánki M. Cs. (2005). *Temperamentum és karakter: Cloninger pszichobiológiai modellje. A Cloninger-féle temperamentum és karakter kérdőív felhasználói kézikönyve*. [Temperament and character. Cloninger's psychobiologycal model. The handbook of the Cloninger Temperament and Character Inventory.] Budapest: Medicina Könyvkiadó Rt.

Hansenne, M., and Reggers, J., and Pinto, M., and Kjiri, K., and Ajamier, A., and Ansseau, M. (1999). Temperament and character inventory and depression. *Journal of Psychiatric Research*, 33, 31-36.

Parker, G. (1979). Parenthal characteristics in relation to depressive disorders. *British Journal of Psychiatry*, 134, 138-147.

Parker, G. (1981). Parental representations of patients with anxiety neurosis. *Acta Psychiatrica Scandinavica,* 63, 33-36.

Parker, G. (1983). Parental „affectionless control" as an antecedent to adult depression. A risk factor delineated. *Archives of General Psychiatry*, 40, 956-960.

Mackinnon, A.J., and Henderson, A.S., and Andrews, G. (1993). Parental „affectionless control" as an antecedent to adult depression: a risk factor refined. *Psychological Medicine*, 23, 135-141.

Narita, T., and Sato, T., and Hirano, S., and Gota, M., and Sakado, K., and Uehara, T. (2000). Parental child-rearing behavior as measured the Parental Bonding Instrument in a Japanese population: factor structure and relationship to a lifetime history of depression. *Journal of Affective Disorders*, 57, 229-234.

Kopp, M., and Skrabski, Á. (1995). *Alkalmazott magatartástudomány*. [Applied science of behavior.] Budapes: Corvinus Kiadó.

Beck, Á.T., and Rush, A.J, and Shaw, B.F., and Emery, G. (2001). *A depresszió kognitív terápiája*. [The cognitive therapy of depression.] Budapest: Animula.

Garber, J., and Hilsram R. (1992). Cognition, stress, and depression in children and adolescents. *Child and Adolescent Psychiatric Clinics of North America*, 1, 129-167.

Metalsky, G.I., and Halberstadt, L.J., and Abramson, L.Y. (1987). Vulnerability to depressive mood reactions. *Journal of Personality and Social Psychology*, 52, 386-393.

Peterson, C., and Semmel, A., and von Baeyer, C., and Abramson, L.Y., and Metalsky, G.I., Seligman, M.E.P. (1982). The Attributional Style Questionnaire. *Cognitive Therapy and Research,* 6, 287-299.

Abramson, L Y., and Metalsky, G.I., and Alloy, L.B. (1989). Hopelessness depression: a theory –based subtype of depression. *Psychological Review*, 96, 358-372.

Brown, G.W., and Harris, T. (1986). Establishing Causal Links, The Bedford College Studies of Depression. In H. Kasching (Ed). *Life Events and Psychiatric Disorders* (pp.125-129) London-Cambridge: University Press.

Kessler, R.C., and Magee, W.J. (1993). Childhood adversities and adult depression: Basic patterns of association in a US National Survey. *Psychological Medicine*, 23, 679-690.

Beck, A.T., and Beck R.W. (1972). Screening depressed patients in family practice. A rapid technique. *Postgraduate Medicine*, 52, 81-85.

Margitics, F. (2005). Prediszponáló tényezők kapcsolata a szubklinikus depressziós tünetegyüttessel főiskolai hallgatóknál. [Interrelation between predisposition factors and sub clinical depression syndrome at college students.] *Psychiatria Hungarica*, 20, 211-223.

Goch, I. (1998). *Entwicklung der Ungewissheitstoleranz. Die Bedeutung der familialen Socialization.* Regensburg: Roderer.

Sallay, H., and Dabert, C. (2002). Women's perception of parenting: a German-Hungarian comparison, *Applied Psychology in Hungary*, 3-4, 55-56.

Tóth, I., and Gervai, J. (1999). Szülői Bánásmód Kérdőív (H-PBI): a Parental Bonding Instrument magyar változata. [Perceived parental styles: the Hungarian version of the Parental Bonding Instrument (H-PBI).] *Magyar Pszichológiai Szemle,* 54, 551-566.

Weismann, A.N., and Beck, A.T. (1979). *The Dysfunctional Attitude Scale*. Thesis, University of Pennsylvania.

Kopp, M. (1994). *Orvosi pszichológia.* [Medical psychology.] Budapest: SOTE Magatartástudományi Intézet.

Atkinson, R.L., and Atkinson C.R., and Smith E.E., and Bem D.J. (1995): *Pszichológia.* [Psychology.] Budapest: Osiris.

Csorba, J., and Dinya, E., and Párt, S., and Solymos, J. (1994). Életesemény kutatás és serdülőkor. A középiskolás életesemény kérdőív bemutatása. [Life event research and adolescence. The Hungarian version of the Junior High Life Experiences Survey.] *Magyar Pszichológiai Szemle*, 50, 67-83.

Cloninger, C.R. (1987). A systematic method for clinical description and classification of personality variants. *Archives of General Psychiatry*, 44, 573-588.

Kendler K.S., and Kessler R.C., and Walters, E.E., and Maclean, C.J., and Sham P.C., and Neale M.C. et al.(1995). Stressful live evens, genetic liability and onset of an episode of major depression in women. *American Journal of Psychiatry*, 152. 833-842.

Plomin R. (1994). *Genetics and experience: The interplay between nature and nurture.* Thousand Oaks, CA: Sage.

Brown, G.W., and Harris, T. (1978). *Social origins of depression*. New York: Free press.

Joiner, T.E., and Wagner, K.D. Attributional style and depression in children and adolescents: A meta-analytic review. *Clinical Psychology Review*, 15, 777-789.

Fiske, S. T., and Taylor S. E. (1984). *Social cognition.* New York: Random House.

Seligman, M.E.P. (1992). Wednesday's children. *Psychology Today*, 25, 61-67.

Bugán, A. (1999). Mentálhigiénés lehetőségek és módszerek a felsőoktatásban. [Facilities and methods in the mental hygienic in the higher education.]: E. Bagdy (Szerk.): *Mentálhigiéné. Elmélet, gyakorlat, képzés, kutatás* [Mental hygienic. Theory, practice, education, research.] (pp.135-140). Budapest: Animula.

Bagdy, E., and Bugán, A. (1997): A pszichológiai csoportmunka, mint a személyiség fejlődésének színtere és eszköze. [The psychological teamwork as the scene and method of the personal development.] In: E. Bagdy (Szerk.) *A pedagógus hivatásszemélyiség.* [Professional personality of pedagogues.] (pp.55-85). Debrecen: KLTE.

Reviewed by Antal Bugán, PhD., Department of Psychology, University of Debrecen

In: Anxiety in College Students
Editor: Benjamin Ayres and Michelle Bristow
ISBN: 978-1-60692-282-8

Chapter VIII

An Intervention Programme for the Improvement of Students' Academic Goals

Antonio Valle, Ramón G. Cabanach, Susana Rodríguez, Isabel Piñeiro, María García and Ingrid Mosquera
University of A Coruña, Spain

Introduction

The question of what lies behind students' motivated behaviour has given rise to a complex network of models and constructs in an attempt to clarify this important issue. A fundamental component of motivation, regardless of the theoretical perspective adopted, is that of value, which includes the goals adopted by students in order to ensure involvement in their tasks, as well as their beliefs regarding the importance, usefulness or interest of the latter (Pintrich, 2003; Pintrich and DeGroot, 1990).

Essentially, the value component of motivation responds to the following question: *"Why am I doing this task?"*, alluding, therefore, to the motives, purposes or reasons for becoming involved in the performance of an activity, these all being aspects closely related to both cognitive and self-regulating activities and choice, effort or persistence (Pintrich, 1999). Despite the existence of a wide range of value conceptualisations, two elements appear as being particularly relevant: academic goals and the value assigned to tasks.

Higgins and Kruglanski (2000) point out that a significant issue in motivational research is to discover how people really manage to achieve what they set out to do. If basic needs give rise to interests, values and goals, how then do people translate these needs, goals and beliefs into action? A fundamental approach to this question implies the use of self-regulation models to describe the planning, supervision and regulation of cognition, motivation and behaviour at the service of a person's goals. The popularity and usefulness of this approach is reflected in the proliferation of self-regulation models that attempt to explain behaviour in different domains that go beyond the field of education (see Boekaerts, Pintrich and Zeidner, 2000).

Models of self-regulated learning currently occupy a central position in educational research, demonstrating that students who set goals and then attempt to control and regulate their own cognition, motivation and behaviour accordingly tend to make adequate progress in academic contexts (Pintrich, 2000a; Zimmerman, 2000).

However, as Rodríguez has pointed out (2000, p.154): *"All too often we restrict use of the term self-regulation of learning to the regulation by students of their cognition and effort through the use of certain strategies. Nevertheless, students should also regulate their beliefs, emotions and attitudes, for which the possession of cognitive and behavioural strategies alone does not suffice, motivational strategies also being needed".*

In fact, research into self-regulated learning has basically looked at the links between a student's conceptual knowledge, his or her use of cognitive and metacognitive strategies and the quality of the learning that has taken place. On the other hand, the relation between students' motivation and self-regulation has generally been limited to exploring how certain motivational variables (self-efficiency, goal orientation, interest, etc.) may explain students' efforts to commit themselves to their learning and their use of cognitive and metacognitive strategies.

This, notwithstanding, an increasing number of studies look at the need to recognise the active role played by students in managing the affective/motivational bases of their learning process. The analysis of self-motivation or motivation-regulating strategies is thus a key factor in obtaining a deeper understanding of self-regulated learning, and has now become one of the most promising domains of motivational research (Dörney, 2000; Pintrich, 2003; Schunk and Zimmerman, 2003; Wolters, 2003; Winne, 2004).

Motivational strategies, unlike cognitive ones, are not directly linked to the codification and processing of the content being studied and learned. They are, instead, procedures adopted by students to seek favourable states of mind and positive results, or at the very least, attempts to avoid undesired events and unfavourable results (Rodríguez, Cabanach and Piñeiro, 2002).

As is the case with cognitive strategies, strategies for managing motivation may be consciously adopted or may come into play in a more automatic way. Thus, for example, some authors (see Bargh, Gollwitzer, Lee-Chai, Brandollar and Trotschel, 2001) have shown that goal achievement can be the result of an nonconscious process, so that the actions taken are of an automated nature and outside a student's conscious control. This implies that motivation and learning models should take into account, in addition to conscious, intentional and self-regulated processes, others of an implicit or unconscious nature (Epstein, 1994). However, students can always actively modify their motivational strategies, in accordance with both personal and contextual factors, and can learn new and/or more adaptive ones.

It is precisely this possibility for students to learn, and therefore to be taught, to manage their motivational resources, in the expectation that this learning will have a positive effect on their academic performance, that has led us to design an intervention programme intended, basically, to enable students to understand and adopt the reasons and motives that lie behind their personal commitment to studying as well as to acquire a repertory of strategies that will allow them to maintain this involvement in an adaptive manner.

The aim of our proposal, in line with the approach adopted by Beltrán (1998) to student motivation, is to ensure that students readily adopt an enthusiastic attitude to the performance of academic learning tasks, persist in their effort to bring them to fruition and, furthermore, direct their actions along the right path towards achieving this goal.

Programme Objectives

The overall objective of the programme is to ensure that students become aware of the personal reasons that lie behind their commitment to studying, as well as of the possible advantages and disadvantages for the affective/motivational, cognitive and academic dimensions of opting exclusively for a specific type of goals or, instead, choosing more flexible options that through the way in which they are combined and matched to contextual requirements and demands become a more valid motivational alternative, and one that is more effective from the point of view of learning.

This overall objective can be broken down into two specific objectives:

- To ensure that participants identify the personal goals that lie behind their commitment to studying and are able to coordinate different goals in accordance with the specific demands of each learning situation.

- To ensure that participants are aware not only of the benefits but also the harm of adopting certain motivation-regulating strategies for their commitment to, and involvement in, learning.

Programme Contents and Intervention Variables

In accordance with the objectives proposed, the intervention programme has been structured in two main blocks (see Table 1). The first block, which occupies nine sessions, focuses on promoting those motives and reasons for learning of greatest effectiveness in study situations.

A second block consisting of sessions focussing on work on motivation regulation strategies, identifying at the outset certain defensive behaviours that the student may be using in order to protect his or her personal self-image within the academic context, and then going on to present and encourage the use of other kinds of motivational strategies that serve to maintain commitment to and involvement in study. This block is made up of sessions ten to eighteen. Session one introduces the programme, whilst session nineteen, the final session, is used for evaluating the programme as a whole.

Block I: The Value Component of Academic Motivation

Task Value

Taking as a reference the proposals put forward by some authors (see Eccles and Wigfield, 2002; Wigfield and Eccles, 2000) regarding the components that determine the value allotted by students to academic tasks, in this part of the programme students will have the opportunity to become aware of the effect of the value allotted to academic tasks, the different subjects they are studying and their studies in general on the goals they set, and consequently on the way in which they approach them.

Table 1: Content blocks and intervention variables in the academic goal management programme

<table>
<tr><th>Content blocks</th><th>Intervention Variables</th><th>Sessions</th></tr>
<tr><td rowspan="3">Block I:
The value component of academic motivation</td><td>Introduction and presentation of the programme</td><td>1</td></tr>
<tr><td>Task value:
• Importance of the task
• Interest of the task
• Usefulness of the task
• Cost of the task</td><td>2 and 3</td></tr>
<tr><td>Academic goals:
• Identifying one's own goals
• Matching goals to the demands of the context.
• Goal formulation.</td><td>4 to 9</td></tr>
<tr><td rowspan="4">Block II: Motivation-regulating strategies in academic contexts</td><td>Motivation-regulating strategies oriented towards defending one's self-image:
• Self-handicapping behaviours
• Defensive pessimism behaviours</td><td>10 to 12</td></tr>
<tr><td>Motivation-regulating strategies oriented towards maintaining commitment and involvement with regard to study:
• Delayed gratification
• Tolerance of frustration
• Strategies for maintaining motivation</td><td>13 to 15</td></tr>
<tr><td>Help-seeking as a strategy at the service of academic goals:
• Help-seeking as a social strategy
• Help-avoidance</td><td>16 to 18</td></tr>
<tr><td>Overall evaluation of the programme</td><td>19</td></tr>
</table>

According to the above-mentioned authors, the value allotted to a task or activity depends on: (a) How *important* it is to do the task well. For example, if a student thinks it is very important to be able to draw well, he or she will assign much more value to drawing classes; (b) the degree of *interest* pertaining to the task. For example, if I find the subject of book interesting, that will be a good reason for me to spend time reading it; (c) the *usefulness* of the task. For example, some subjects may be neither important nor interesting for me, but I have to pass them if I want to get my degree or work in a given profession; and (d) the *cost* that the task represents for us. For example, going to extra-curricular English classes every day may mean that I have no time to be with my friends when we come out of class. Sessions two and three cover all these aspects that have to do with task value.

SESSION 2
• Brainstorming: *Reasons why people study* • Individual activity: *Why am I studying?*
SESSION 3
• Activity on the relationship between value and choices • Presentation on aspects that affect the value allotted to tasks and activities • Activity on the value allotted to subjects • Presentation of an example regarding the relationship between values and goals

Academic Goals

Considering that the different kinds of goal pursued by students are important because they favour qualitatively different motivational patterns and contribute to the deliberate self-regulation of academic tasks, we have decided to centre our action around three basic aspects of academic goals: identification, fit with the context and goal-formulating strategies.

From the traditional distinction made between learning and achievement goals to the latest differentiation between approach and avoidance tendencies within achievement goals (see, for example, Elliot, 1999; Elliot and Church, 1997; Elliot and Harackiewicz, 1996), our aim is that participants identify their own goals and at the same time become aware of the significance and learning implications of the kind of goals they primarily adopt in the academic sphere. The fourth session has been designed to achieve this purpose.

SESSION 4
• Self-evaluation activity: *What are my academic goals?* • Explanation of the main types of academic goal (*learning, approach and avoidance achievement*) • Goal-identifying activity in suppositions put forward by students • Pooling of ideas

In accordance with the findings of previous research (see, for example, Cabanach, Valle, Piñeiro, Rodríguez and Núñez, 1999; Pintrich, 2000b; Rodríguez, Cabanach, Piñeiro, Valle, Núñez and González-Pienda, 2001; Seifert, 1995; Valle, Cabanach, Cuevas and Núñez, 1997; Valle, Cabanach, Núñez, González-Pienda, Rodríguez and Piñeiro, 2003; Wentzel, 2000), we propose the convenience of encouraging participants to develop multiple goals, since this facilitates a better adjustment and adaptation to the diversity of contextual demands that they will come across in the academic context. Sessions five and six are intended to promote this approach to motivation in students.

SESSION 5
• Personal reflection activity: *What do I set out to do in my different subjects?* • Explanation of the concept of multiple goals and the benefits they bring. • Analysis of a case of multiple goals.
SESSION 6
• Initial comment on the importance for academic achievement of knowing how to coordinate and adjust personal interests and reasons with the specific demands of the context. • Activity: analysis of the demands of different academic tasks • Brainstorming: *"What to do when I am not very clear about what is expected of me in my subjects"* • Explanation of some strategies for discovering what lecturers expect from their students.

Taking as our starting point the characteristics of the goals that most favour student motivation (Dembo, 2000; Locke and Latham, 1990), three sessions were designed for the purpose of encouraging the formulation of goals that are *realistic* – in the sense that they should be achievable; *specific* – they should be as concrete as possible; and *time-restricted* – they should have a completion date. Sessions seven to nine are intended to work on these aspects.

SESSION 7
• Activity: establishing realistic goals. Participants have to imagine their lives five years from now supposing that everything that happens is positive, then negative, and finally they imagine what their lives will be like in a year's time from a realistic point of view.
SESSION 8
• Exercise: establishing concrete goals. Participants propose goals to be reached in a year's time and formulate them specifically. • Exercise: establishing short- and long-term goals. Participants divide their goals to be reached in a year into six- and three-month goals.

SESSION 9
• Activity: establishing realistic, specific and time-restricted goals in different areas (academic, social, occupational, personal, etc.).

Block II: Motivation Regulation Strategies in Academic Contexts

Motivation Regulation Strategies Oriented Towards Ego Protection

Considering that behaviours such as self-handicapping and defensive pessimism are disadaptive with regards to commitment to and involvement in study (although defensive pessimism is often associated with higher levels of achievement than initially expected), we decided to include some sessions in which to show how the use of these strategies rarely brings any benefit from a motivational point of view. Sessions ten to twelve are intended to deal with these issues.

SESSION 10
• Activity: individual reflection on the habit of putting things off – *Do I put off starting to study or do my assignments?; Do I hand in my work late?; Do I tend to leave things to the last moment?; Do I usually miscalculate the time I need to do things in?*
• Group discussion on putting things off as an ego-protecting strategy.
• Explanation and analysis of some beliefs that underpin the habit of putting things off.
• Activity: *"Excuses"*. The participants have to select from a list of excuses those that they usually use in order to put off doing their tasks.
SESSION 11
• Explanation of "perfectionism" and group discussion
• Explanation of the strategy of "being very busy"
• Activity: drawing up a schedule in which participants include everything they do in detail. This will serve as a basis for considering: *Do I think I give enough time to studying?; Is my schedule too full with things that interfere with my studies?; Is everything I do really necessary?; Do I use my other occupations as a "one-size-fits-all" excuse when, for example, I fail a subject?*
SESSION 12
• Group discussion on defensive pessimism in the academic sphere.

Motivation-Regulating Strategies Oriented Towards Maintaining Commitment to and Involvement in Studying

These sessions are designed to make students aware of the strategies they make use of to maintain their commitment to and involvement in their studies, valuing their effectiveness and considering the possibility of using new strategies of the same kind. Sessions thirteen to fifteen cover these aspects.

SESSION 13
• Initial commentary on the importance for academic performance of learning to delay gratification in favour of studying. • Discussion in groups of three on the ease/difficulty of delaying gratification in favour of studying and the strategies used to do so. • Production of a *"cost-benefit"* inventory. Participants create a table in which they weigh up the advantages and disadvantages of remaining focused on an academic task or doing something else they find "more attractive"; they conclude by taking a decision that reduces as far as possible the costs of both options.
SESSION 14
• Whole-group discussion on the tolerance of frustration. • Reading of a story on "obstacles" and the importance of persistence in the face of them if one wants to reach one's goals. • Whole-group discussion on the story. • Proposals of "advice" on handling frustrations.
SESSION 15
• Activity on strategies for maintaining effort and motivation in academic tasks: participants select from a list of strategies those they use most often or find most effective. They can contribute their own strategies if they do not appear on the list. • Presentation of a model study plan supported by motivational strategies. • Activity: production of a study plan, supporting it with motivational strategies aimed at ensuring it will be fulfilled.

Assistance-Seeking as a Strategy at the Service of Academic Goals

The purpose of the content and activities of these sessions is to make students aware of the reasons that may lie behind assistance-seeking avoidance behaviours, and of the enormous difference between asking for help to "get out of a tight spot" and for help that will have a positive effect on one's own level of competence. Additionally, students should recognise that the assistance of others is an important resource when it comes to achieving one's own goals.

Indeed, many studies have demonstrated that good students know when to seek assistance and why, and who to turn to for help (see, for example, Karabenick and Sharma, 1994; Newman, 1998; Ryan and Pintrich, 1998). Furthermore, contrary to the beliefs held some years ago, assistance-seeking is considered to be a highly adaptive and beneficial strategy (Butler, 1998; Newman, 2000). Session sixteen to eighteen have been designed to work on these aspects.

SESSION 16
• Game: "Clues". • Discussion on the role of assistance in the game: on the one hand, it is seen as being negative because it results in losing points; however, it is preferable to seek assistance because it may lead to finding a hitherto unknown answer. • Discussion on the viewpoint that assistance is valid in an academic context. • Activity: *Reasons for not seeking assistance.* Participants form groups of four, each group drawing up a list of the reasons that can lead students not to ask for help when they need it.
SESSION 17
• Explanation of the importance of valuing assistance in accordance with the reasons that validate it: "getting out of a tight spot" versus "learning". • Activity: case analysis of students and evaluation of the kind of assistance they need.
SESSION 18
• Presentation of advice on the appropriate ways of asking for assistance. • Role-play: each group has to represent ways of asking for assistance – appropriately, aggressively or uninhibitedly – in different situations in the academic context.

Programme Duration, Structure and Target Population

The proposed intervention programme takes place over a total of *nineteen one-hour sessions*. Although the frequency of the sessions is not fixed, we are of the opinion that two sessions a week would allow students to obtain the most benefit from the programme. Having chosen this option, the programme therefore took approximately two and a half months to complete.

The structure of each session is as follows:

1) Arrival and welcome
2) Review of assignments (if given)
3) Activities planned for the session
4) Evaluation of each activity
5) Setting assignments
6) Evaluation of the session
7) Closure

Every session has the same structure with the exception of the first and final ones. In the first session the instructor and participants introduce themselves, the students comment on their expectations of the programme and the instructor gives the aims of the programme and the norms of behaviour to be observed within the group. The final session is dedicated to an overview of the activities and content of the whole programme and an overall evaluation of the experience of having participated in it.

Although this programme was initially designed and developed thinking that it would be used with university students, we believe that with some adjustments it would be perfectly applicable to other educational levels such as Secondary (12-16) and Sixth Form Colleges (17-18).

The ideal way of applying the programme is through group work. Regarding this, it is important to bear in mind that the groups should not be too large. The best number of participants in each group is between ten and fifteen, the latter being taken as the recommended maximum.

The person responsible for delivering the programme should preferably be a specialist in education (psychologist, educational psychologist, teacher or educator) with experience in working with groups, and with a certain understanding of the theoretical aspects relating to academic motivation that underlie the intervention programme.

Participant Satisfaction

Even when a programme has been correctly designed and is supported by a solid theoretical framework that gives validity to its content, it is also desirable to prove that it is effective in practice, and to this end the opinion of those who have participated in it can be an essential element.

On completion of the programme, those who took part in it were given a series of questions to answer, some structured and closed (Likert scale or similar) and some open, on various aspects: improvement in awareness of their reasons and goals, improvement of behaviour-goal fit, the extent to which the programme met their needs and its usefulness.

The data analysis looked at answer frequency, with the answers to the open questions being seen as a more qualitative form of evaluation. In the quantitative analysis, the percentages of the answers given were calculated, converting them into three values – a lot/quite a lot, to a certain extent, not much/not at all (although initially the answers were given on a scale of 1 to 5, with 1=not at all and 5=a lot).

There can be said to have been considerable improvement in participants' awareness of their own reasons and goals. Thus, 64.6% considered that they had improved a lot or quite a lot in this aspect, with 35.4% considering they had improved to a certain extent, whilst no participant said that he or she had not improved much or at all.

With regard to the fit between academic behaviour and goals set, 30.4% of participants considered they had improved a lot or quite a lot, 64.5% that that they had improved to a certain extent and only 5.1% thought they had hardly improved (not much or not at all).

With regard to the validity of the programme for responding to their needs as students, 79.9% were of the opinion that it did so a lot or quite a lot and 20.1% that it did so to a certain extent, whilst no participant said that the programme did not meet, or only went a little way towards meeting, their needs as students.

With regard to the degree of usefulness of the programme, 88.3% of participants thought that it had been very or quite useful for them, 11.7% that it had been of some use, and no participant considered that the programme had been of little or no use. The specific aspects of the programme considered to be the most useful were: (1) reflection activities with other participants, (2) helping them to become more aware of the importance of goals, (3) learning to set realistic goals and (4) usefulness in their personal and professional lives.

Authors' Note

This work was funded by the Spanish Ministry of Science and Technology (Project: Project BSO2003-00864).

References

Bargh, J., Gollwitzer, P., Lee-Chai, A., et al. (2001). The automated will: Nonconscious activation and the pursuit of behavioral goals. *Journal of Personality and Social Psychology, 81,* 1014-1027.

Beltrán, J. (1998). Claves psicológicas para la motivación y el rendimiento académico. In M. Acosta (Coord.), *Creatividad, motivación y rendimiento académico.* Málaga: Aljibe.

Boekaerts, M. & Niemivirta, M. (2000). Self-regulated learning: Finding a balance between learning goals and ego-protective goals. In M. Boekaerts, P. R. Pintrich and M. Zeidner (Eds.), *Handbook of self- regulation* (pp. 417-450). San Diego, CA: Academic Press.

Boekaerts, M., Pintrich, P. R. & Zeidner, M. (2000). *Handbook of self- regulation.* San Diego, CA: Academic Press.

Butler, R. (1998). Determinants of help-seeking: relations between perceived reasons for classroom help- avoidance and help-seeking behaviors in an experimental context. *Journal of Educational Psychology, 90,* 630-643.

Cabanach, R.G., Valle, A., Piñeiro, I., et al. (1999). El ajuste de los estudiantes con múltiples metas a variables significativas del contexto académico. *Psicothema, 11*, 313-323.

Dembo, M. H. (2000). *Motivation and learning strategies for college success. A self-management approach.* Mahwah, NJ: Erlbaum.

Dörney, Z. (2000). Motivation in action: towards a process-oriented conceptualization of student motivation. *British Journal of Educational Psychology, 70,* 519-538.

Eccles, J. S. & Wigfield, A. (2002). Motivational beliefs, values and goals. *Annual Review of Psychology, 53,* 109-132.

Elliot, A.J. (1999). Approach and avoidance motivation and achievement goals. *Educational Psychologist, 34*, 169-189.

Elliot, A.J. & Church, M.A. (1997). A hierarchical model of approach and avoidance achievement motivation, *Journal of Personality and Social Psychology, 72*, 218-232.

Elliot, A.J. & Harackiewicz, J.M. (1996). Approach and avoidance achievement goals and intrinsic motivation: A mediational analysis. *Journal of Personality and Social Psychology, 70*, 461-475.

Epstein, S. (1994). Integration of the cognitive and psychodynamic unconscious, *American Psychology, 72,* 218-232.

Higgins, E. T. & Kruglanski, A. (2000). Motivational science: The nature and functions of wanting. In E. T. Higgins and A. Kruglanski (Eds.), *Motivational science: Social and personality perspectives*. (pp. 1-20). Philadelphia: Psychology Press.

Karabenick, S. A. & Sharma, R. (1994). Seeking academic assistance as a strategic learning resource. In P. R. Pintrich, D. Brown and C. E. Weinstein (Eds.), *Student motivation, cognition, and learning: Essays in honor of Wilbert J. McKeachie* (pp. 189-211). Hillsdale, NJ: Erlbaum.

Locke, E. A. & Latham, G. P. (1990). *A theory of goal setting and task performance.* Englewood Cliffs, NJ: Prentice-Hall.

Newman, R. (2000). Social influences on the development of children's adaptative help seeking: The role of parents, teachers, and peers. *Developmental Review, 20,* 350-404.

Newman, R. S. (1998). Adaptative help-seeking: A role of social interaction in self-regulated learning. In S. A. Karabenick (Ed.), *Strategic help seeking: Implications for learning and teaching* (pp. 13-37). Mahwah, NJ: Erlbaum.

Pintrich, P. R. (1999). The role of motivation in promoting and sustaining self- regulated learning. *International Journal of Educational Research, 31,* 459- 470.

Pintrich, P. R. (2000a). The role of goal orientation in self-regulated learning. In M. Boekaerts, P. Pintrich and M. Zeidner (Eds.), *Handbook of self- regulation* (pp. 451-502). San Diego: Academic Press.

Pintrich, P. R. (2003). A Motivational Science Perspective on the Role of Student Motivation in Learning and Teaching Contexts, *Journal of Educational Psychology, 95 (4),* 667-686.

Pintrich, P.R. (2000b). Multiple goals, multiple pathways: The role of goal orientation in learning and achievement. *Journal of Educational Psychology, 92*, 544-555.

Pintrich, P.R. & De Groot, E.V. (1990). Motivational and self-regulated learning components of classroom performance, *Journal of Educational Psychology, 82*, 33-40.

Rodríguez, S. (2000). *Autorregulación motivacional del aprendizaje: características diferenciales e implicaciones cognitivo-motivacionales.* Unpublished doctoral thesis. Universidad de La Coruña.

Rodríguez, S., Cabanach, R.G. & Piñeiro, I. (2002). Gestión de recursos y estrategias motivacionales. In J.A. González- Pienda, R.G. Cabanach, J.C. Núñez and A. Valle (Coords.), *Manual de psicología de la educación* (pp. 145-164). Madrid: Pirámide.

Rodríguez, S., Cabanach, R.G., Piñeiro, I., et al. (2001). Metas de aproximación, metas de evitación y múltiples metas académicas. *Psicothema, 13*, 546-550.

Ryan, A. M. & Pintrich, P. R. (1998). Achievement and social motivational influences on help seeking in the classroom. In S. A. Karabenick (Ed.), *Strategic help seeking: Implications for learning and teaching* (pp. 117- 139). Mahwah, NJ: Erlbaum.

Schunk, D. H. & Zimmerman, B. J. (2003). Self- Regulation and Learning. In W. M. Reynolds and G. E. Miller (Eds.), *Handbook of Psychology: Educational Psychology* (Vol. 7, pp. 59-78). Hoboken, NJ: Wiley.

Seifert, T.L. (1995). Characteristics of ego- and task-oriented students: A comparison of two methodologies. *British Journal of Educational Psychology, 65,* 125-138.

Valle, A., Cabanach, R.G., Cuevas, L.M., et al. (1997). Patrones motivacionales en estudiantes universitarios: Características diferenciales. *Revista de Investigación Educativa, 15*, 125-146.

Valle, A., Cabanach, R.G., Núñez, J.C., et al. (2003). Multiple goals, motivation and academic learning. *British Journal of Educational Psychology, 73*, 71-87.

Wentzel, K.R. (2000). What is it that I'm trying to achieve? Classroom goals from a content perspective. *Contemporary Educational Psychology, 25*, 105-115.

Wigfield, A. & Eccles, J. S. (2000). Expectancy-value theory of achievement motivation. *Contemporary Educational Psychology, 25,* 68-81.

Winne, P. H. (2004) Putting volition to work in education. *Teachers College Record, 106(9),* 1879-1887.

Wolters, C. (1998). Self- regulated learning and college students' regulation of motivation. *Journal of Educational Psychology, 90,* 224- 235.

Wolters, C. (2003). Regulation of motivation: Evaluating an underemphasized aspect of self-regulated learning. *Educational Psychologist, 38(4),*189-205.

Zimmerman, B. J. (2000). Attaining self-regulation: A social-cognitive perspective. In M. Boekaerts, P. R. Pintrich and M. Zeidner (Eds.), *Handbook of self-regulation* (pp. 13-39). San Diego, CA: Academic Press.

In: Anxiety in College Students
Editor: Benjamin Ayres and Michelle Bristow

ISBN: 978-1-60692-282-8

Chapter IX

The Impact of a Lecture Series on Alcohol and Tobacco Use in Pharmacy Students

Arjun P. Dutta,* Bisrat Hailemeskel,† Monika N. Daftary,‡ and Anthony Wutoh§

Howard University, College of Pharmacy, Nursing and Allied Health Sciences, School of Pharmacy, Washington, DC USA

Abstract

Studies related to alcohol and drug use in healthcare students, namely nursing, pharmacy, and medicine suggest that drug and alcohol abuse continues to be a growing problem among health profession students. A review of the more recent literature involving pharmacy students, has noted higher levels of alcohol and drug use when compared to the undergraduate student population. Interestingly, the use and/or abuse of tobacco have largely been overlooked in studies involving substance abuse in pharmacy students. This study documented the current alcohol and tobacco use in pharmacy students and conducted a lecture series on the use and abuse of alcohol and tobacco. The lecture series was successful in increasing the awareness of the use and potential abuse of alcohol in the students. Attitudinal changes in students following the lecture series were also assessed.

Keywords: health professions students, abuse, alcohol use, tobacco use

* Office: 503-352-7281; Fax: 202-806-4478; Email: adutta@pacificu.edu; The author is currently the Assistant Dean for Academic Affairs at Pacific University, School of Pharamcy, Forest Grove, OR.

† Office: 202-806-4210; Email: bhailemeskel@howard.edu

‡ Office: 202-806-4206; Email: mdaftary@howard.edu

§ Office: 202-806-4209; Email: awutoh@howard.edu

Introduction

Studies related to alcohol and drug use in healthcare students, namely nursing, pharmacy, and medicine suggest that drug and alcohol abuse continues to be a growing problem among health care professional students [1-11]. A study conducted by Coleman and colleagues found that about ten percent of practicing nurses were chemically dependent, and for many of these nurses the abuse began during nursing school [12]. Some of these studies not only examined trends in use, but have also identified precursors of alcohol abuse that are unique to students in health professions. Causal factors that have been identified include burnout, role strain, peer pressure, socializing, self-medication, and a history of parental alcoholism or drug addiction [11,13-16]. Previous studies (prior to 1990) regarding alcohol and drug abuse in health professions students reported that the level of alcohol and drug use in pharmacy students was similar to the general college population [5-8, 11]. A review of the more recent literature (post 1990) involving pharmacy students, has however noted higher levels of alcohol and drug use when compared to the undergraduate student population [11, 17-19]. Interestingly, the use and/or abuse of tobacco have largely been overlooked in studies involving substance abuse in pharmacy students.

Given the increasing nature of this problem, recent studies have examined the impact of educational intervention programs in the health profession student. One such study assessed substance abuse in health profession students and the efficacy of educational interventions in this group. The investigators found that focusing on drug and alcohol education can influence use [12]. The impact of substance abuse (alcohol/drugs/tobacco) educational programs in pharmacy students has also been documented. [20,21] This is particularly important in light of the fact that healthcare training institutions have recently been among those affected by the Drug Free Schools and Communities Act of 1989. This Act mandates that institutions of higher education that receive federal funds establish drug prevention programs. The US Department of Education's Fund for the Improvement of Post-Secondary Education (FIPSE) annually awards grants to college-level drug prevention programs. Colleges and universities have developed prevention programs that have contributed greatly to the existing knowledge about the impact of educational programs on prevention of substance abuse. Although the vast majority of this existing knowledge has been applicable to undergraduate students, not much has been reported in terms of educational programs or its effect on pharmacy students [11]. In this study we have reported the alcohol and tobacco use patterns in pharmacy students and the impact of a lecture series (3 classes of 1.5 hours each in duration) in changing pharmacy students' attitudes towards the use of alcohol and tobacco. The lecture series was designed to disseminate information on the use and abuse of alcohol and tobacco, the pharmacological action of such substance use, the consequences of alcohol and tobacco use, the related side effects, and results of long-term use.

Methods

The survey population consisted of first year (P-1) professional students (N = 81) at Howard University, School of Pharmacy. We compiled a 20-item survey by an iterative process with input from faculty and the Howard University Student Counseling Center. The survey was pilot-tested by faculty members and students and was approved by the university's Institutional Review Board for the Protection of Human Subjects. The final study sample consisted of 67 students (83% response rate). All students completed an IRB-approved informed consent form prior to completing the survey, and were told that their participation was voluntary and that the survey responses would be kept anonymous. The survey was administered to pharmacy students at our institution prior to the initiation of the lecture series to document the pattern of alcohol and tobacco use. The students were then re-administered a post survey at the conclusion of the lecture series to assess changes in student attitudes regarding alcohol and tobacco use.

Results

Of those surveyed, 67 students responded to the pre-survey, with an overall response rate of 83%. Of those who responded, students were predominantly female (61%), and largely in the 21-26 age group (61%). Most of the students ascribed to the Christian faith (30%) and were predominantly of African origin (70%). Table 1 provides data on the number of participants, gender, race, and their religious belief or practice. Regarding the survey, thirty-nine percent of the respondents reported the use of alcohol at least once during the previous month. Among them, 7% reported using alcohol 10 times or more during the past month. Another 26% reported on having used alcohol at least once during the previous year. Thirty-five percent students however, said that they had never consumed alcohol in their life. In terms of the quantity of alcohol consumed at one sitting, 59% reported having at least two drinks but not more than four. Binge drinking or drinking more than four drinks at one sitting was reported by five percent of the respondents. There was a significant difference ($p<0.004$) in gender in relation to the number of times a respondent drank, with males reported drinking more frequently than females. Moreover, binge drinking was more common among males than females. There was also a positive correlation ($p<0.02$) between socializing with friends and frequency of alcohol use. The longer a respondent spent in terms of socializing with friends the more he/she drank. However, females drank less than males even if they socialized for the same length of time. Such findings are ironic given that 69% of the students believed alcohol consumption to be dangerous to their health. Furthermore, students agreed that peer pressure would often force them to drink more than they intended, as a majority of students felt that participating in parties was important to them socially. The results of this survey seem to be consistence with previous findings in the literature [11, 16-18]. Interestingly, religious belief was correlated to alcohol use as well. Students, who felt that adhering to their religious beliefs and customs was important, drank less often or in fewer quantity than those for whom the practice of one's religion was not as important. This is important in light of the fact that certain religions (e.g. Muslim religion) specifically prohibit the consumption of alcohol. In terms of using tobacco, only 8% students reported smoking during the past month. Among the respondents who smoked (8%), the rate of smoking ranged from 10 cigarettes to about two packs for the entire month. An overwhelming 88% of the students felt that using tobacco was dangerous to their health. This belief seems consistent with the pattern of tobacco use in health profession students. Interestingly, the belief that alcohol is dangerous (69%) was however, not consistent with usage pattern of alcohol (65%). This may be because students drink despite knowing that alcohol may be deleterious to their health in an effort to blend in with their peers. It is also possible that these students do not consider alcohol use to be as detrimental as smoking.

Table 1. Summary of Respondents (Please add numbers)

Category	N*= 67 (%)
Age	
18-20	7 (11)
21-26	39 (61)
27-35	15 (23)
>35	3 (5)
Gender	
Males	26 (39)
Females	41 (61)
Race	
African-American**	47 (70)
Asian	15 (22)
Caucasian	5 (1)
Faith	
Christian	20 (30)
Muslim	11 (15)
Other	36 (55)

* The N for each category/ subcategory represents the number of respondents for that particular category. The total number of responses was 67.

** Includes immigrant students from Africa as well

The post-survey following the lecture series inquired about potential changes student's attitudes towards drinking and tobacco use in the future. A total of 67 students responded to the post survey as well. The results of the post-survey indicated an increased awareness of the use and potential abuse of alcohol. In general, respondents (58%) indicated that they would like to reduce alcohol consumption in parties and social gatherings. Moreover, a majority of students (81%) felt that binge drinking should be avoided and that peer pressure should not compel them to drink more. A significantly higher percentage (95%) of students ($p<0.004$) felt that alcohol consumption was detrimental to them following the lecture series as compared to the previous 69%. Students' attitude towards the use of tobacco was not significantly different following the post-survey. This is probably because there were a very small percentage (8%) of students using tobacco in the first place. Following the lecture series however, only two percent of students indicated that they would probably continue smoking. Thus, the lecture series was at least successful in promoting an awareness of the risks of alcohol and tobacco use together with instilling a desire in the students to reduce their consumption rates.

Although, the post-survey indicated an attitude change towards the use and misuse of alcohol and tobacco products, it is of paramount importance to continue such educational programs throughout the length of the Doctor of Pharmacy curriculum. A constant reminder about the potential dangers of such substance abuse will definitely help students to perform better in pharmacy school.

Implications for Behavioral Health Services

Pharmacists are an integral part of health services delivery and research. Given the proximity and frequency of contact with patients, pharmacists are in a unique position to influence and impact health policy and services delivery as well as research. In this study, the authors have reported the alcohol and tobacco use patterns in pharmacy students at their home institution and the impact of a lecture series (3 classes of 1.5 hours each in duration) in changing pharmacy students' attitudes towards the use/abuse of alcohol and tobacco. The lecture series was also designed to disseminate information on the use and abuse of alcohol and tobacco, the pharmacological action of such substance use, consequences of alcohol use, related side effects, and results of long-term use.

We, the authors believe that an educational program such as the one mentioned above, is important for future pharmacists/ pharmacy residents as they will go on to provide health services to patients. In terms of the journal itself, we feel that our submitted manuscript addresses questions raised in the literature about the lack of mention of alcohol and tobacco use in studies involving substance abuse by pharmacy students. This study assesses alcohol and tobacco use in pharmacy students and also reports potential change in attitude of such use in the study population. This endeavor, in the authors' opinion will definitely go a long way in producing better pharmacists capable of handling the growing need for addressing alcohol and tobacco use in particular, and other substances abuse in general.

References

[1] Kory WP, Crandall LA. Nonmedical drug use patterns among medical students. *International Journal of Addiction*. 1984; 19(8): 871-884.

[2] Conard S, Hughes P, Baldwin DC, Achenbach KE, Sheehan DV. Substance use by fourth-year students at 13 US medical schools. *Journal of Medical Education*. 1988; 63:747-758.

[3] Borkman T, Rosenberg N. What do we know about medical students' use and abuse of alcohol and other drugs? A constructive critique. *Alcohol Health Research World*. 1986; 10: 54-59.

[4] Haack MR, Harford T. Drinking patterns among student nurses. *International Journal of Addiction*. 1984; 19(5): 577-583.

[5] Miller CJ, Banahan BF. A comparison of alcohol and illicit drug use between pharmacy students and the general college population. *American Journal of Pharmaceutical Education*. 1990;54:27-30.

[6] McAuliffe WE, Santangelo SL, Gingras J, Rohman M, Sobol A, Magnuson E. Use and abuse of controlled substances by pharmacists and pharmacy students. *American Journal of Hospital Pharmacy*. 1987; 44:311-317.

[7] Normarck JW, Eckel FM, Pfifferling JH, Cocolas G. Impairment risk in North Carolina pharmacy students. *American Pharmacist*. 1985; 25:60-62.

[8] Tucker DR, Gurnee MC, Sylvestri MF, Baldwin JN, Roche EB. Psychoactive drug use and impairment markers in pharmacy students. *American Journal of Pharmaceutical Education*. 1988;52:42-47.

[9] Haack M. Alcohol use and burnout among student nurses. *Nursing and Health*. 1987;8(4):239-242.

[10] Baldwin DC, Hughes PH, Conard SE, Storr CL, Sheehan DV. Substance use among senior medical students: A survey of 23 medical schools. *Journal of the American Pharmaceutical Association*. 1986; 255(14): 1913-1920.

[11] 11. Kriegler KA, Baldwin JN, Scott DM. A survey of alcohol and other drug use behaviors and risk factors in health profession students. *Journal of American College Health*. 1994: 42(6): 259-66.

[12] Coleman EA, Honeycutt G, Ogden B, McMillan DE et al. Assessing substance abuse among health care students and the efficacy of educational interventions. *Journal of Professional Nursing*. 1997; 13(1):28-37.

[13] Dawson DA, Harford TC, Grant BF. Family history as a predictor of alcohol dependence. *Alcohol Clinical Experience Research*. 1992; 16(3):572-575.

[14] McCaul ME, Turkkan JS, Svikis DS, Bigelow GE, Cromwell CC. Alcohol and drug use by college males as a function of family alcoholism history. *Alcohol Clinical Experience Research*. 1990; 14(3):467-471.

[15] Fillmore KM. Drinking and problem drinking in early adulthood and middle age: An exploratory 20-year follow-up study. *Journal of the Study of Alcohol*. 1974;35:819-840.

[16] Brown SA. Expectancies versus background in the prediction of college drinking patterns. Journal of Consulting Clinical Psychology. 1985;53(l):123-130.

[17] Murawski M., Jeurgens, J. Analysis of longitudinal pharmacy student alcohol and other drug use survey data. *American Journal of Pharmaceutical Education*. 2001:65:20-9.

[18] Noormohammed S., Ferguson K., Baghaie A., and Cohen, L. Alcohol drug use, and sexual activity among pharmacy students at three institutions. *Journal of the American Pharmaceutical Association*. 1998:38(5):609-13.

[19] Miller C., Banahan, B., and Borne R. Comparison of illicit drug use between pharmacy students and the general college population. *American Journal of Pharmaceutical Education*. 1990:54:27-30.

[20] McAuley, J., Akers, A., and Mott, D. Assessing the impact of a substance abuse educational program on pharmacy student's knowledge base. *American Journal of Pharmaceutical Education*. 1999:63:309-14.

[21] Corelli, R., Hudmon, K., Kroon, L. et al., Development of tobacco cessation curriculum for pharmacy students. AACP Annual Meeting, Jul. 2000, vol.101, pg.50. International Pharmaceutical Abstracts, Accession Number: 38-02011

Index

A

B

C

D

F

G

N

O

P

Q

R

S

T

U

V

W

Y